Leaders: Their Stories, Their Words

Conversations with Human-Based Leaders™

Donna Karlin

Dedication

To you, the reader, may the stories in this book resonate with you so you see your greatness within the words and, in turn, touch others, deeply and profoundly.

Contents

Acknowledgments

My deepest gratitude to all of you who generously shared your time in conversation and welcomed me into your worlds through your stories, and to those who have shared their perspectives on what being a human-based leader truly is.

I would also like to acknowledge and thank the following people for their support, contribution and presence in my life.

To John Lazar, my friend and colleague, I appreciate your eye for editing and all the conversations we had to get the manuscript to completion.

To Janette, who took hours and hours of recorded conversations and turned them into documents we could work with. You're a lifesaver!

To Sandra for helping me fine tune the book to the nth degree, thank you for your eye, your insights and your support.

To Ray, who fills my life with joy, laughter, and love, and helps me realise my hopes and dreams. You make everything perfect in my world, even when it clearly isn't. You and the kids constantly remind me about what's truly important in life.

To my family and friends (my family by choice), colleagues, and clients who add a depth and breadth to my life beyond measure and description.

And to my son Michael and his (our) Amy, who bring more pride than any parent could ever expect or hope to have. Michael, you taught me that courage comes at all ages and sizes, and that leadership is an attitude — a way of being. You demonstrate how we can make a difference no matter what our position, title, or age. You never cease to amaze me, always encourage me, teach me, and show me that life is meant to be embraced and never taken for granted. You are a true leader in every way.

Introduction

I would like to introduce you to some amazing people whose perspectives, thoughts, and stories grace the pages of my book. Each of them has a different style of leadership and different professional passions. Even though they represent many disciplines, they all have one thing in common: They lead from what I call a "sense of humanness." They aren't power-based leaders; they're human-based leaders. They lead from a perspective of caring and of stewardship. Even so, they aren't pushovers. They respect others as they do themselves, make difficult decisions when they have to, and set boundaries so as not to compromise their work ethic or values.

This book captures the ebb and flow of an animated discussion. My intention is to hold a conversational mirror in front of them so they may see themselves through fresh eyes. I want them to see the impact of their leadership through what they are doing and how they live.

If you haven't experienced the power of a coach-like conversation, I invite you to eavesdrop and observe, and hopefully be swept along and enlightened. My conversations tend to be edgy and are designed to provoke reflection. I spoke to 28 people and chose 12 of them for my book. This isn't about any particular discipline. It is about what human-based leadership can look like within these professional realms. Just as I asked these leaders to think about their presence and impact on the world, I ask you to notice what might get triggered for you in your world. As I share what I learned in the Reflections section of each chapter, I invite you to ponder what your learning might be as well.

These human-based leaders bear witness for those who are not in positions of leadership: those who are silent, vulnerable, or unrepresented, and whose voices deserve to be heard. They speak for basic human rights, including the dignity, respect, and well-being of all people. Whether these people are students, parents, executives, the homeless, those challenged with illness, or serving in the military, all are individuals who look to leaders to help make this world — their world — better.

I love my work as a Shadow Coach©. I have the privilege of working in "real time" with amazing individuals and teams in complex and chaotic environments. It's situational, observational, and laser-fast coaching. We live in the "I don't knows," where "shadows," behaviours, and "personal operating systems" live. I help clients see what they're not seeing by asking illuminating questions, introducing paradoxes, and co-creating stimulating environments to expand their thinking. My clients hire me to help them think differently more than do differently. It's a meeting of minds, a partnership to generate new ideas. We develop ways of operating to transform and reshape their worlds and those they impact. Our conversations take emergent ideas and the "what ifs" and convert them into reality.

My clients are a diverse group, including political and government leaders, ambassadors, high commissioners, corporate leaders, educators, students, creative designers, and medical professionals. I watch these human-based leaders fly, while their counterparts, power-based leaders, struggle as they "manage" their staff to death, forcing their perspectives and direction onto people they don't care to understand or respect. Such power-based leaders continue to have difficulty leading and engaging others since they live by the philosophy of having power over people, not power with people.

On the other hand, human-based leaders embrace people, recognize their talents, fundamentally desire to see others succeed in their own right, and earn the loyalty and respect of those working with them. People pay attention to what they say, trust in the safe environment they create to share their thoughts and critiques, and choose to engage more fully. They know these leaders have their backs.

When I was teaching a group of masters students, one of them had asked me, "What do you read? What are your favourite books on coaching?" I answered, "I don't have a favourite book on coaching. I read magazines, newspapers, books, and biographies — anything that teaches me something about people and cultures, how they think, and how they live. I need to know about people's stories. Through conversations, I learn more about people than I could any other way."

More recently, I was at INSEAD in Fontainebleau, France, at a conference on the best practices of leadership coaching. I was the only Canadian in the room and an outsider to the organization. A few of us talked about leadership, coaching, global impact, and the myriad of topics that coaches tend to grapple with. We discussed methodologies, measurements, group vs. individual work, corporate vs. government, and every other angle you could imagine. One of the realizations I had, and shared with this group, was that we cannot do our work in the best possible way unless we really know people. We must learn about their drivers, their passions, what got them to where they are now, what keeps them there, and what will move them forward into a future they love. We need to learn about different cultures, organizational structures, and mandates, putting all the puzzle pieces together to best serve our clients.

One of the people I was saying this to turned to me and asked, "How are you going to do that?" I replied, "I'm going to call them up and have the conversations I need to have."

That's when the idea for this book was seeded.

I contacted an equal number of men and women. Most of the men, save one or two, eagerly jumped at the opportunity to have these conversations. Most of the women either declined or didn't respond. Perhaps that's a focus for my next book....

With each conversation, I became more awestruck. Though I was unclear about what form this project would take, I did know I would be sharing it with the public. From that moment on, I haven't looked back. Choosing the right combination of conversations to publish and which pieces to use to illuminate the others became the next challenge. Now that the conversations are captured, and the book is in its beautifully designed frame, I invite you to sit back, get comfortable, and dive into these extraordinary stories. Meet the men and women who — by virtue of who they are, not their role or level in an organization — have inspired and changed the lives of others through their insight and humanity.

They have certainly changed and enriched mine.

Preface

Here you are, at the beginning of a reading adventure. What's important to you? What do you care about? Your answers will guide the investments you make with your time and energy. Do you have business or organizational interests, goals, and aspirations? Are you on a learning path to be a better leader? This book offers a range of views about what it means to be effective as a human-based leader.... Be sure to appropriate what will serve your purposes. Are you interested in people and their "hero's journey"? Do you prefer to make a personal connection, to appreciate someone for who they uniquely are? Through the unfolding narratives, these conversations reveal a leader's history, humanity, and heart. Examples of integrity under fire, courage, and perseverance are apparent. Find and extract your own personal lessons.

This is the work of a dynamic leadership and executive coach published in this non-traditional book format. These stories began as conversations that Donna Karlin held with human-based leaders. Make no mistake — this is not a "how-to" book with recipes, and these aren't interviews. Donna brings her own active sensibility, perspective, and voice to the dialog. Read and "listen" to the conversation, think about its relevance to you, and enjoy the benefits.

Donna Karlin is a force of nature. My hunch is that she has been in "force of nature" mode for a long, long time. We have had a number of years to share experiences and develop a professional relationship (and a friendship) along the way. Throughout, I have been struck by Donna's intelligence, wisdom, and compassion. Though she works primarily in highly political milieus, she takes an even-handed, apolitical stance as a way to serve her clients. She brings her coaching values and care to every conversation. She listens deeply to people — who they are, what's important to them, and what they aspire to achieve. She asks questions that inspire people to explore new directions. She recognizes the implications and consequences of choices well beyond any simple or "obvious" answers. Her knowledge of process enables her to appreciate what works and what requires further work in complex situations.

Buckminster Fuller was right. The velocity of change in our world is accelerating, with its attendant turbulence, uncertainty and ambiguity. Technology is a catalyst that offers both opportunities and challenges. Organizations are pressed to be agile, responsive, cost-effective, and value-adding. If ever there was a time for effective leadership at all levels, this is it. If ever there was a time for us to reconnect with our own, and each other's humanity, this is it. There is a point, already quickly reached, where our typical ways of thinking are insufficient. A shift in paradigm and perspective is called for. How perfect that Donna, not in her role as a Shadow Coach© of leaders, but as a leader in her own right, became the insightful listener/speaker with the human-based leaders she selected for this book.

I recognize that people seem to learn best through stories. Certainly, this has been our learning tradition and heritage for generations. We emotionally connect through another's story, discern relevant patterns, and create our own personal meaning and meaningfulness. Stories feed our soul, enrich our mind, engage our heart, and expand our horizons.

This is an anthology of conversations between two leaders. Each chapter presents a dialog between extraordinary people — and you have the privilege of listening in. A lead quote sets the frame for the conversation that unfolded. Donna provides you with an appreciative introduction to each human-based leader's background. Then, in their conversation, she elicits their stories. Along the way, her questions encourage awareness, reflection, and insight. The discussion reveals the leader's perception of their impact and their vision for the future. Donna offers her own interpretations and personal stories that deepen their shared understanding. At the conclusion of each chapter, she provides her reflections: a view of the conversation, her insight into an aspect of human-based leadership, and how the conversation affected her personally.

I invite you to settle in, read with open-minded curiosity, and be moved by these incredible leaders and their stories.

John B. Lazar

In hard times, the soft stuff often goes away.
But emotional intelligence, it turns out, isn't so soft.
If emotional obliviousness jeopardizes your ability to perform,
fend off aggressors, or be compassionate in a crisis,
no amount of attention to the bottom line will protect your career.
Emotional intelligence isn't a luxury you can dispense with in tough times.
It's a basic tool that, deployed with finesse,
is the key to professional success.

HARVARD BUSINESS REVIEW

CHAPTER 1

JOHN SPENCE
Human CliffsNotes

I first "met" John Spence when we were co-authoring a blog with other leaders from many parts of the world. Even though we had an online dialogue around books and topics relevant to executives, John was one of the few I truly connected with. He is not only insightful, knowledgeable and authentic, but a *human-based* leader in every sense. He looks well beyond the bottom line and works with his clients to lead joyful and fulfilled, not to mention successful, lives.

To give you a bit of background, John's career began right out of college in 1989. He worked for the Rockefellers in one of their international foundations, and was named Executive Director/CEO of that organization at age 26. Just two years later, at age 28, he was nominated as one of the top CEOs in Florida under the age of 40. He left the foundation in 1994 and has been an independent consultant ever since. He was recognized by *Inc.* Magazine as one of the leading young business trendsetters in America in 1995. The Society of Human Resource Managers (SHRM) named him the number one professional trainer in Florida in 1999, and that same year he was nominated as one of the 50 most influential business thinkers in the world in *Fast Company* magazine.

John's dynamic style and rare mix of rigorous scholarship with practical business experience leaves his audiences captivated, inspired, and prepared to achieve new levels of personal and professional success. His energy is tangible, his enthusiasm contagious. Just like he says about a client in our conversation, "He just made it to my top five CEOs I would want to spend my time with." John is someone you should definitely spend your time with if you have the opportunity. It would be a gift beyond measure.

John is affectionately called the "Human CliffsNotes" by many of his clients, a fitting title for someone who is known for reading at least 100 business-focused books a year and listening to 30–50 audio books. He combines their synthesized content with massive amounts of research and personal experience to create customized concepts and solutions for his clients and powerful content for those he teaches.

Just as he has amassed and absorbed an amazing amount of information to draw from in his work, so has he gathered wisdom from global leaders to write his book, *Awesomely Simple: Essential Business Strategies for Turning Ideas Into Action*. John distils the best fundamental business strategies under one literary cover so readers can turn ideas into action.

"Making the very complex … awesomely simple" is no mere catch phrase; it is truly John Spence's mission in life, as is helping people realise and live a life they love.

Come join me in conversation with John…

Donna: I'd love to know what inspired you to go this route to get you where you are now. Tell me more about John.

John: There are two driving forces. One was my first try through college. I failed out with a 1.6 GPA. Not only did I fail out of just a regular school, I failed out of a school where my father was one of the top alumni ever, served on the Board of Directors, and had a wing of the law school named after us. You mess up pretty badly when you flunk out of a college where there's a building named after your family. I realized I wasn't serious about my education and my future, and I probably learned two of the most important lessons I've ever learned in my life: "You become what you focus on" and "You become like the people you surround yourself with." Whatever you think about, whatever you study, whatever your brain is filled with — TV, books, CDs, DVDs, audio books, networking, and those you surround yourself with — are what determines what your life will turn out like.

So in college, my first try, I hung out with a bunch of friends with a 1.3 or 1.2 grade point average. At 1.6, I had the highest GPA of all my friends, so I was focused on the wrong stuff and spent time with the wrong people. Through trials and tribulations, I eventually changed to move beyond that. I applied to the University of Florida, where they literally laughed at me after they looked at my transcripts. Several years later after community college, I got back into a university on probation and ended up doing extremely well. I graduated number one in my major in the Southeastern U.S. and number three in the country.

So driver number one was realizing if I focused on the right things; filled my mind with the right information, with good ideas, uplifting and motivational material, and surrounded myself with bright, sharp, smart, and talented people, it would have a huge impact on the direction my life would take.

I was hired directly out of college by one of the Rockefeller foundations. The gentleman I went to work for was Winthrop P. Rockefeller III. He was an incredibly nice gentleman. A few years later, just a few years out of school at the tender age of 26, I was named CEO of one of his foundations.

That was another lesson. When I was first hired, my first boss at the foundation was not Mr. Rockefeller; it was another gentleman who was evil. He was mean and aggressive and paranoid. I loved my job. I loved the people I worked with. I was absolutely enthralled with the work I was doing. But I would get up every morning, shaking as I put my clothes on, and drive home from work crying every day because my boss, my "leader," was so tyrannical that it was just painful. I learned a huge lesson about the impact leaders have on other people's lives. Whether you lead two people or 20,000 people, you have a huge obligation, responsibility, and incredible impact on the joy, the balance, the love, and the fun in people's lives. You can either make their work exciting and fun or make their lives a living hell. A lot of it comes down to your supervisor or manager. I promised myself if I ever got to be in a position of leadership, I was going to be someone who added value and joy to people's lives, because I can.

Donna: John, I'd like to go back briefly to your college days. You said it was important for you to surround yourself with the right people. Was there anybody in particular who comes to mind?

John: What a great question! A couple come to mind. One person in particular was one of my economics professors by the name of Roger Strickland. He was the first college professor I had in my life. He helped me understand how much fun and how exciting school could be if you understood the rules of the game. He was patient and loving and kind. He sat down with me and said, "Let me explain how school works." He said, "Start a study group … do this, do this, do that, do everything else." Long story short is he made it bearable. I got an A in his class, and A in the next class, and another A, and basically from the time I met him onward, I did nothing but ace all my classes.

Interesting story. It's more than 20 years later and I had dinner with him last night. We're still close friends. We work together. He is an integral part of my family and someone who had such an impact on me that we've been friends ever since.

Another thing was figuring out how I failed out of the University of Miami. I failed out because I didn't ask for help. I didn't study with other people; I didn't go see my professors; I didn't even go to class. My first semester, I literally got the syllabus, bought the books, and went to the beach. I showed up for my midterm exams and had never set foot in class. When I transferred to Santa Fe Community College, the community college I went to before attending the University of Florida, I realized that part of the secret was and still is (and it applies to business as well) to ask for help. Ask everybody you possibly can for help.

So, I started study groups. Anyone who wanted to be in my study group could be, as long as they had a 3.6 GPA or higher. If we needed to, we got a tutor, visited the professor, got a copy of an old test if that was legal and asked everybody in sight for help. By default, we got tons of help. I think college was easier for me than anybody else because I had five friends helping me. I had teachers and professors and teaching aids and everybody else you could think of. It's what I still do today. I'll tell you two quick stories that will underline this.

The first story is a great story I heard about Anne Mulcahy when she became CEO of Xerox. She got on the phone, called Warren Buffet, and asked him for his best advice on what she needed to do to be an effective leader at Xerox. It was my understanding that he talked to her for quite a while, saying, "Here are the names of a couple of people I respect. Give them a holler and see what they have to say." She did that, then called a few more people, and called a few more people, and called a few more people, and she came down with a short list of what all these bright, sharp, smart, talented people told her. There were four points:

1. Surround yourself with a huge network of people who want to see you succeed, who are interested in your success.
2. Ask them for help. You're not supposed to have all the answers. So surround yourself with really bright people, with bright associates, and values-based people, and ask them for help.
3. Learn to be a learner. Treat lifelong learning very seriously. Study, read, get mentors, be a mentor. And,
4. Focus on the people you serve, your employees, and your customers.

I look at that list, "Surround yourself with a huge network of people who want to see you succeed; ask for help; learn to be a learner; and focus on the people you serve, your employees, and your customers," as the best advice I've ever learned. I'll give you the quick version of that from my own background.

About two years ago, I was BBQing (volunteering) at a charity event for people with disabilities. As I was hanging out with them, I got a phone call on my cell from one of my clients. The client said, "John, I need help. I have a corporate espionage problem. A few of my employees are stealing files. They've been downloading computer files and trying to steal my clients and compete directly with me. I don't know what to do. I've never been in that position before. Can you help me?" I said, "Whoa. I'm right in the middle of something else. Let me get back to my office and take a minute to think about this and I'll send you my reply by 2:00 this afternoon. Would that be alright?" And my client said, "Please send it as fast as you can. I need help."

I knew nothing about corporate espionage. I didn't even know how to spell it. So I rushed back to my office, got on my computer, sent out an email to my network of several hundred executives from around the world, and said (without using any names), "I have a client who has this problem. I need to know the appropriate next steps. Any advice, suggestions, or help you can offer would be wonderful." I took out my yellow pad and the next thing I knew the phone rang. It was one of the top key executives at Qualcomm. "You know, John, this has happened to us a bunch of times; we understand what he's experiencing. Let me connect you to our corporate counsel."

I had HR people from Southwest Airlines call me, the head of strategic planning for Royal Dutch Shell call me, and top HR people from Merrill Lynch call me. Within about two hours, I had about a dozen of the top people from around the world sending their best ideas, advice, and suggestions which I put together and sent in a memo to my client. A month later, he told me he showed it to his attorney who said it was absolutely the single finest memo he had ever seen on what to do for a case of corporate espionage. Here's my point. At nine in the morning I had no idea what to do. I could help my client because I had a network of bright leaders who were strong, smart, and knew what to do. They were eager to help. I believe really effective leaders want to help people. They like to be of service. They don't care much about who gets the credit. It's just "What can I do to assist you? How can I help you? What can I do to serve you?"

Donna: About these four points in Anne Mulcahy's list: Do you apply them to your life outside of the workplace?

John: Oh, absolutely. My gosh, yes! In my opinion, our business life isn't a whole lot different than our personal life. Especially if you love what you do, and you're having fun, the two are so intertwined that all of it is just a fun game, whether you're working or at home. Not only do I have a huge network of people who I go to for business, but I have a network of close friends and associates who I ask for help on personal stuff. There's a lot I don't understand at all … so when I get into something I'm not sure about or don't know about, I'm the first one to say, "Let's go speak to someone who's already done this. Let's go find someone who's lived this. Let's go find someone who does this for a living. Let's go find somebody who's an expert in this and ask them for help."

Donna: So you're literally creating an environment with people, experiences, information, and networks that nourish you.

John: Oh, absolutely, absolutely. I realized years ago that if you want to become a doctor, lawyer, or engineer, you go to college for six years to get your MD or PhD. It always surprises me that people don't do that for their own life. What field of study could be more important than studying how to build a great life, be a great person, have clear values, be loving, and make a positive impact on the world?

So I have a list of who I spend time with and what I spend time focused on, what I call my "happiness list" and my "stress list," and I look at it constantly. Am I focused on the right things in my life? Have I surrounded myself with loving, kind, bright, smart, values-based people? Do I have as much stuff on my happiness list as I can possibly think of, whether it's cooking dinner for friends or international travel? On the stress list, have I reduced it to as small as I possibly can, have the wisdom to understand the stuff that I absolutely cannot be in control of, and let go of it? Do I look at the things on my stress list that I do have control over and to try to get control over those things? Are the same processes that I use in planning for businesses or helping clients or coaching clients the exact same process I use in my life every day?

Donna: I love your perspective. A lot of people separate work life from home life, believing they're different people in different contexts. Interestingly enough, the human-based leaders I've been interviewing draw no defining line. They're very humble individuals who are successful — successful being determined in many ways; not only financially. They're happy and lead a joyful life. It's an amazing experience to listen to them tell their stories. It's not only the stories, John. It's the emotion and passion in their voices as they relate their life stories to me. That was one of the things that attracted me to ask you to have this conversation, because you have always been so real. It's evident in everything you write.

John: Thanks, Donna. Years ago, I heard something on super high-achieving self-actualizers. You know Maslow's hierarchy of needs and what it said. As I was driving along in my old jeep, I was listening to it on tape, about the three things that high-achieving self-actualizers do that other people don't do. It totally resonated with me. What I remember about what the tape said was this:

They are not a slave to the good or bad opinions of other people. They've got a deeply held set of values. They have a clear vision of the life they want to lead, the legacy they want to leave, are really clear about the kind of person they want to be. They're open to feedback and input, but not really swayed by what other people think about them.

They're process-oriented, not outcome-oriented. They just enjoy the process of being happy, joyful, balanced, loving, and fun people. Some are rich, famous, and powerful. For others, it doesn't really matter. It's not about where it's going to get me; it's about enjoying the trip along the way.

The last one (and I really love this one) is they take 100% accountability for leading their own life well, and 0% for the control for other people's lives. I always love to think about this because these are people who are high-achieving self-actualizers. They've gotten to the point in their lives where they're dedicated to helping other people. As far as they're concerned, everything's going well, so now "I'm going to help other people get what they want." They know they can't control other people; the only thing they can do is get up every day, day in and day out, and live within the values they hold, live the life they want to lead, because that is the best way they can impact other people's lives.

When I heard that, I remember pulling my car over and listening to it 15 times in a row and thinking, "That is a perfect description of the people I've met in my life that I felt were really, really successful." They just seemed comfortable in their own skin. You can tell they've given their lives very serious thought and were pretty much on track for where they wanted to be. They knew what they thought was important, and they were interested in what other people thought. They weren't trying all the time to make other people happy, impress others, or live up to other people's standards.

They had their own standards, and as long as they could live up to them, they could put their heads on their pillows at night and think, "I'm happy. I live my values every day. I don't have to wear a mask to be able to tell the truth. My life is pretty much what I always hoped it would be. I'm living my dream, whether that's living in a mansion or volunteering all the time and living in a hut. It doesn't matter. What matters is this: Do I live my values? Is my life pretty much where I hoped it would be? I feel successful." Does that make sense?

Donna: It does to me. Two of my mottos are "What somebody else thinks of me is none of my business, as long as I live my life through personal integrity." And "I live my life in direct proportion to the commitments I make and keep, to myself as well as to others."

John: That's beautiful! I love that!

Donna: I believe when you can live your authentic self, you're not proving anything to anyone; you're just giving. That's what I'm deriving from this. One of the people I've interviewed who I highly respect, a retired Senator and broadcaster from Canada, made a comment, "Better human beings make a better world." It sticks out in my mind constantly.

John: That's so true!

Donna: People who live from personal authenticity and integrity do make a better world.

John: I had dinner at a friend's house Saturday night with a busload of folks, and the discussion touched on this a little bit. It's unfortunate, but my take is the vast majority of people are not self-aware an introspective at all. To me, they don't spend a lot of time working on being a better person. There's not a lot of looking in the mirror and saying, "Is my life on track? Do I have clear values? Do I have clear goals? Do I know what I want to be? Do I understand what the meaning of life is? Do I understand what my authentic self is?"

I'll turn the tables on you for a second … you've done this for a living forever. What percent of the average population do you feel is in touch with those four things in their own life? A clear understanding of their core values? A clear, vivid, detailed view of the life they want to lead? A good understanding, at its core, of what happiness is? And what success means to them?

Donna: This is a two-part answer. The first part of my answer is: at least 80%, higher than you might think. As for the second part, my caveat is that I believe most people don't give themselves permission to live in alignment with that.

John: Ahh! OK, great! I never quite thought it through that way before. That's excellent!

Donna: I Shadow Coach people at the highest levels in the corporate and government arenas. I'm there to see every aspect of their character in their environments as their lives unfold. They don't have time to put up a façade. They are who they are. Often I say, "If you want something else, are you giving yourself permission to go after it?" It's not necessarily reaching for your dreams or knowing what your dreams are, because everybody does, even if they don't verbalize them. If you respect and pay attention to your dreams, you give them validity. By not giving yourself permission to go after those dreams which are in alignment with your core values, you're not respecting yourself or your dreams.

But a lot of people don't feel as if they have the permission, that they can. They feel if they do go after their dreams, they're being selfish. There's a difference between self-centeredness and selfishness. Taking care of self is absolutely imperative for a person to thrive and have personal success. To be self-centered means to focus on yourself to the exclusion of the world … everything and everyone. That's the definition I work with.

John: I teach a class on this. I often tell people, "This is not being selfish. For goodness sake, look at your values! Most people have values like family and God and community and contribution. The harder you work on your values, the more you're helping other people, so this is the most selfish way you can possibly be unselfish." For some of them, it finally clicks when they realize, 'It's not just all about me. It's the part of my life I'd like to dedicate to helping other people, serving other people, giving other people joy.' So yeah, that makes sense to me. We could spend a week talking about it.

Donna: I know. The virtual world is great. However one of these days I have to actually meet you in person. How many years have we been talking and writing?

John: I have a feeling that with what our lives are like, we'll end up meeting in an airport somewhere.

Donna: True. So before we continue, this question just came to mind: What is "CliffsNotes®"?

John: CliffsNotes is an American term. They are notes that many use in school — three-minute versions of books. Most colleges have lots and lots of CliffsNotes for all major books.

Donna: OK. Got it! Thanks. Now it makes sense to me why it's your nickname. We both know you have a huge impact on people. Have you been paying attention to how powerful that is?

John: Wow! What a great question!

Let me put it this way. I try not to think too much about the impact and power I have.

When I do what I do, travel and teach, a part of me does recognize that I am making a huge impact. But I believe it's because I care about the classes, care about the people who want their lives to be better … happier … for them to be able to enjoy their work and be better leaders. One big thing that drives me is helping these organizational leaders become more balanced and more aligned with why they're doing this work. It affects their impact right down the line to all of the people they lead.

To go back to your question, I don't think a lot about my impact. I do get an awful lot of notes and cards and emails, even years after we've worked together. Even this morning, I had a small stack of notes from people all across the country, saying things like, "I want to thank you" or "I really appreciate this." I understand my work has an impact on other people, but the other thing is recognizing how I use this information. I see myself as someone who literally spent 15 to 20 years of my life collecting as much information and as many tools as I could to share with and help other people. I'm not a genius; these aren't my ideas. These are ideas from the smartest people in the world. I'm just taking them and putting them together to make them usable and easy to understand. I'm explaining it and making it easier to apply.

Donna: John, you *do* know you're talking to a coach and that I'm going to challenge you on that one, right? Paying attention to your level of impact also means you know you have an impact on the human beings you're interacting with.

John: Oh, I know I do!

Donna: Your impact goes well beyond your understanding, your immediate awareness.

John: Yes, I understand that. When I give a speech to 1,000 people and hundreds end up crying (which has happened many times), I know that I'm touching people. But it's not about me; it's about the information. I always try to separate the two. I love my work, and I know in my work I get to help people make decisions that will make them better people, happier people, and better leaders. But they're the ones who put in the hard work. They're the ones who make the changes. I'm just giving them the ideas that help them see things in a different way. I'm sure you're hearing the discomfort in my voice.

Donna: Yes, I do.

John: I've always avoided being looked at like that. People go, "Oh John! Yeah, he's a famous speaker!" I'm not comfortable with that. I just give people good ideas. OK, I'll stop there.

Donna: John, you absorb all this information, Mr. Human CliffsNotes, and you process it. You do a lot with it.

John: What I do is look at patterns. I found out later in life I have a skill for synthesizing complex ideas and making sense of them, finding a pattern or foundational core. I teach a class on execution now. I bought 21 books on execution, read them all and condensed about 40,000 pages down to one page.

Donna: So you process things, you condense and simplify them, and connect with the people to share that information. Correct?

John: Correct.

Donna: You have a connection because you listen to exactly where they are in their world in order to give them that material. Am I right?

John: Yes, you are.

Donna: So you have the connection, they have your ear, the two of you put your heads together, and you process it in such a way that they can fly with it or move with it. Right?

John: Yep. Exactly.

Donna: OK. So how many people in this world have somebody partnering with them? Someone who is exclusively there for them, helping them remove a roadblock or for whatever purpose they brought you in? Someone who isn't there for their own personal agenda, but is there literally to help others with what they need to do?

John: Very few people. Very few people have someone from the outside to be there for them, who's there 100% for them, offering, "Let me help you. Let me serve you. Let me do whatever it is I can do to assist you." I do a little coaching now. Not a lot, maybe three or four very high-level people in huge companies. One is a CEO who's a great, great guy. When I'm with him, I see the impact he has on thousands of people whose lives, careers, jobs, livelihoods in some way shape this gentleman's ability to run the company well. He's what I call a values-based leader.

To answer your question directly, probably less than 5% have someone who is 100% dedicated to their improvement, their growth, their effectiveness. Very few people are that open, trusting, and willing to ask for help. Some of these people are really high up in their companies. Some of them think they don't need help: "I'm supposed to know this stuff." No, not really. It's really complex; almost nobody knows it.

Donna: Bingo. And that is a huge roadblock to get past when you're working with an individual at that level. It applies to corporate leaders, politicians, and so many other professionals who impact people at a substantial level. In constituents' minds, politicians are supposed to be perfect. They're supposed to have all the answers, right?

Now that you're doing a lot more teaching, how are you growing the next wave of people into their leadership?

John: My work is balanced between teaching high-level executives, groups of 15, 20, 30 executives, and speaking to entire companies, workforces, and associations with a small amount of one-on-one work with high-level executives.

Donna: Are you teaching undergrad- or masters-level classes?

John: I guest lecture at about five to six colleges a year. I'm working at Harvard, Wharton, and a few other schools on strategy and strategic thinking. For the most part, my work is corporate rather than classroom.

Donna: For someone who initially flunked out of college, this is quite the turnaround, don't you think? That's fantastic! So it's professional education, mostly people who are already in their fields of practice.

John: Oh yeah. My current clients are State Farm, Microsoft, GE, Abbott, and Apple, to name a few. I'm flying two to three times a year for each of them to teach strategy, scenario planning, team building, and leadership. I teach leadership for State Farm across the United States, as well as teaching internally at Verizon, Qualcomm, and several other companies.

Donna: Well, that's good! It keeps you out of trouble! You have a gentle strength about you. You really connect with the high potentials. They are craving leaders like you who can help them evolve because you understand how they think. Many soon-to-be retired leaders work with the next wave or their future replacements, based on their ways of thinking, their ways of being, and their ways of operating, which are not necessarily applicable any more.

John: It's actually a huge issue with some of the clients I'm working with right now. I probably have half a dozen clients who are all in the throes of massive succession planning because they realize that "Oh no, 40% of our senior leadership will be leaving the company in three to five years." For the past 20 to 25 years, they have been running the organization and [the companies] don't have enough young leaders coming to fill in those places. "We're in very serious trouble. And with regards to many of the younger ones coming in, we don't understand them. We don't understand what drives them. We don't understand how to interact with them."

You're gonna love this, Donna. In teaching leadership over the last 17 years, my classes are highly interactive, filled with lots of discussion. I approach my courses with a pretty strict structure that works well for me: an hour, hour-and-a-half to two hours' lecture in the morning; some clearly focused reading for about half an hour; introspective self-analysis for about an hour; team workshops for about two hours; then team presentations back together as a whole group.

What I do in a typical class shifts from me teaching them to them teaching themselves to them teaching each other to them then convincing each other what they need to hear to change the organization or change themselves. So, by the end of the day, instead of me telling them what to do, they're all telling each other what they need to do (which is a great place to be).

A lot of recruits I get are high potentials, vice president, or C-level potentials; in other words, the folks who will one day be running the company. Why I'm sharing this with you is because a word has come up in the last three or four years that I've never ever seen before ... ever. The word is *respect*. I have never heard high potential employees say, "The most important thing I need from someone who leads me is to feel respected. I need to have my voice heard. I need to be treated fairly. I want to be seen as important. I want to have a say in things. I want my job to be meaningful and to do meaningful work. At the end of the day, I want to feel like I had an impact and wasn't just doing a job."

I didn't hear this five years ago. I never heard a 60-year-old person say, "I need to feel respected." They just did their job. Now, with this new group that's coming up, three of four say the issues are "I need to feel respected. I need to be treated as an equal."

A lot of people say millennials don't respect their elders. And you'll love this ... here's what it is: they do not respect you because of your title or because of your seniority. It does not matter what it says on your business card; it doesn't matter how old you are. It matters how smart you are and how much you respect them. If you're really good at what you do, highly competent, and you show them sincere and honest respect, treating their ideas as valid, they'll be incredibly loyal to you. But if as leaders you walk around and say, "I've been Vice President for 27 years and you'll do this because I said so," they'll turn around and walk away on you.

They'll quit your company and go someplace else if they don't feel like their job makes a difference in the world. It's about more than just making money. If they're not treated as an individual with a brain and ideas from the day they start, then they are very quick to hop and leave.

Here are two more words I think you're going to get a kick out of and will enjoy. The other words are *courageous* and *communication*.

Donna: Perfect.

John: And what I'm hearing more and more from those I work with is this: "If you want me in this organization, you have to tell me the truth. I need to know that people are being honest with me, they're telling me the good and the bad, and nothing's being hidden from me. I'm a bright person. I can make decisions, I can make judgments, but you have to trust me with information. If you think I'm going to continue working here if you're only going to tell me what you feel like telling me and not give me open, honest, robust, and courageous communication, I'll leave."

And the last one that's come up more and more and more in the last year is *authentic*. I have so many people say to me, "I want my leader to be authentic. I want him or her to be an honest, calm, loving, respectful person." These are the words I hear that I wasn't used to hearing before. I believe the new group of leaders coming up behind us absolutely demands this from their managers. If you're not approachable, authentic, or have a lot of integrity, tell the truth, and treat people with respect and fairness, there is no way that top talent will continue to stay and work for you. These are minimal, non-negotiable standards for the new group of people that are going to be leading organizations.

The question for us is, "What is the power and the authority 40- and 50-year-olds have with that generation?" That's the most important thing. The answer: we have to be living examples of the things they're demanding from their leaders.

Donna: I think the best mix is to take some of the leadership skills of the present leaders who have a different work ethic coming from a different generation and mesh them with what the new leaders or the evolving leaders want. Then have a generative conversation around what would work best so that it's learned and not forgotten.

John: Yes, I agree. One of the ways I do this in one of my client organizations is with a reverse mentoring program. I have a group of 20-something students, just out of college and with MBA degrees, and assign them as mentors to senior executives. Their job is to teach executives what millennials think and what's important to them so senior executives can get a taste of it. Usually the senior executive is the mentor. In this case, the senior executive is the mentee. So the mentors, or the younger generation, can teach them about the generation that's coming.

Donna: That's fantastic!

John: It works incredibly well.

Donna: That brings me back to my earlier question about if you're paying attention to your level of impact. Impact just because of who you are, as much as what you do. Impact on how you live your life, and how you teach the next wave of leaders that you don't have to compromise your life to be successful.

John: Thank you. One of the reasons I love leadership so much, not only being a leader but teaching it, is because you have to live the example you want people to be. I have a workshop I just adopted in the last couple of weeks. I worked with a group of senior executives from a company, gave them a blank piece of paper, and told them to write down in quick bullet points their description of the absolute, ideal team member. We're talking about super high-performing, high-achieving beings. I wanted them to fully describe what that high-performing team member would look like.

I then asked them to give me back the list. You can imagine what was on the list: "highly competent, collaborator, excellent communication, proactive, accountable, unquestioning integrity, honesty, service attitude." I said, "This is great!" When I saw the list, Donna, it made it very easy for me to say, "Wow! I'd love to have someone like that on my team. How many would love to have someone like that on their team?" Every hand went up.

I then said, "Well, here's the deal. If you want to have someone like this on your team, then you have to be like this first." Then I heard a collective "Oh!" Competent, loving, caring, honest, integrity, authentic. And so it went full circle. That's why I love working with leaders so much. In order to be a great leader to others, first you have to be a great leader to yourself. I work hard every day to be an example of the values, the beliefs, the actions, and behaviours that I would expect from the people that I would lead. That means every day I would have to work on myself in being better, more competent, more authentic, telling the truth, and all the things I would expect from a good team member and leader. I can't get mad at somebody else for what I can't do.

I just saw a statistic from a Gallup poll that says 88% of people who leave their jobs do not leave their pay, do not leave the industry, do not leave their workload; they leave their immediate supervisor. They leave because they can't stand the person they work for. Sixty-seven percent of people who lose their jobs are terminated because they can't get along with the people who work with them on their team. It's not about their work products or technical competence. They are told, "The other people can't stand to work with you and I'm sorry but you're going to have to leave."

Donna: It's about chemistry. You can have the most amazingly talented people working for you, but in a group or team context, the chemistry can be so bad, the whole place falls apart. You also can have a team of people who are average but fly because of the energy in the group.

John: I worked with a client just this week, a CEO of a company, who I wouldn't consider a really brilliant guy, or much more creative than anyone else in the organization. He wasn't more advanced than any other person in the company. But his passion, authenticity, and honesty were so amazing, so penetrating, that their company went from a handful of people to over 1,100 people in just a little over a year. He stood up in front of his senior management team of about 100 folks and gave an off-the-cuff, from-the-heart talk about how proud he was of them, how excited he was, and everybody in that room was riveted. I was thinking to myself, "If I had to get a job, I would want to come here to work, not because of what they do, but because I want to be around somebody like that."

Donna: Exactly! That's a huge compliment to that CEO.

John: He just made it to my top five CEOs I would want to spend my time with.

Donna: So what's next for you? What haven't you tackled yet?

John: That's a great, great question. If things didn't change for the rest of my life, I would probably be just as happy as today. I can't believe how fun my job is and how great the people are I work with. This is an interesting step. After 20 plus years of studying this stuff, I now finally feel I have something to say. So I've got a literary agent and I'm working on another book. My first book was self-published and did extremely well. I sold about 25,000 just to my clients. I'm now working on trying to speak to a wider audience, creating some materials, and have some other things in the fire. I'm slightly leaning towards doing more personal development work. I have shied away from it in the past as I felt awkward teaching classes on how to live a happier, balanced, more joyful life. I talked a few of my corporate clients into allowing me to teach a couple of classes in their companies. The feedback has been so phenomenal and the impact has been so strong, I'm feeling more comfortable about it and want to teach that more. So those would be the changes, but frankly, if things didn't change at all, things would still be pretty damn good.

Donna: Great!

John: I get up every day, I'm living my values, and having fun. Business is good, my clients are awesome, and my wife and I are doing great. I think this is the happiest I've been in my life, and I've felt that way for years now. I can't think of too many things that would make life better than what it is right now. It's a nice place to be.

Donna: John, as always, this was great. Thank you! I'm looking forward to many more conversations in the future.

Reflections

Reflections ections

How many people can state what John just did? In his own words, "I get up every day, I'm living my values, and having fun. Business is good, my clients are awesome, and my wife and I are doing great. I think this is the happiest I've been in my life, and I've felt that way for years now. I can't think of too many things that would make life better than what it is right now. It's a nice place to be."

Years ago, I was sitting in my office doing some prep for a client who had just assumed the role of President in a global organization. When the phone rang, I thought he was touching base before our meeting. It was an editor from *Fast Company* magazine (in the early years of the publication when they were still based in Boston). He wanted to talk to me about a piece he was doing on "beware of what you ask for because you just might get it." What perfect timing! My client had assumed a role he had coveted most of his adult life, and had just asked me, "Now what? Now that I'm getting the role I've worked towards what seems to be my whole life, what now?" Other clients had achieved the position of their dreams, had houses around the world, private jets to get there. They had whatever they wanted but were unhappy. They didn't trust that people wanted to be their friends for the sake of who they were. People always seemed to want something from them now.

These successful leaders wanted to continue to make a difference and, because of their success, were stumped at how to attract authentic relationships. They wondered who they could turn to when they weren't happy. If they went to their friends or family, many would respond with, "You have three homes around the world, a jet, a boat, everything anyone could dream of ... a glamorous life, power, and acclaim. And you're telling me you're not happy? You've got to be kidding!"

What now? Now is when this client decided to make a difference in the lives of his future leaders, to mentor them and to create a learning environment so they could discover and strengthen their talents. Another client challenged anyone who came to him for financial support to give a portion of that money to a start-up or non-profit and to help them with a business plan, so two organizations could succeed. Only then would he provide financial support.

What now?

To paraphrase something John said, if you want to be surrounded by amazing people, then you have to be one first. If you want people to be engaged, energized, open to learn, and supportive of each other and the organization, you have to be that first. People will emulate what you do and how you live. If you live from a basis of personal and professional integrity, making that the norm, you will model for others how to live that way as well.

What now when it comes to my world? I realise that all I have available to me for me to do my work, to have a successful business, and to support our profession through my teaching and mentoring, is how I invest my time and energy. If I make poor choices in how I use them, I am limited in how much impact I can have. If I waste my energy, I can't be sufficiently 'present' to be masterful in what I do. I have to be mindful of who I hang out with, what I choose to do in the time I have, and model my values as a coach. For me it's about the boundaries I set, what I accept, and what I stand for.

Alfred Taubman, known as a "Legend in Retailing," put it beautifully when he told me:

> Money hasn't given me happiness and it hasn't made me unhappy. It's given me the opportunity to help other people on a direct basis. Successful businessmen are teachers. You can't do everything yourself. You have to teach people to be self-reliant, learn what they have to learn, and know it better than anyone else. You're investing in people, not in a business. It's the person running the business who will either make it a success or failure. It's going to be on the basis of their knowledge, ability, and energy. That's what will make a difference.

Human-based leaders realise they don't know everything there is to know. They have power *with* people, not *over* people, and they realise that together they can create an environment to succeed.

The key is to offer people opportunities.
What they do with those opportunities is their call.
They all have capacities and dreams.
They are responsible for achieving them.
I am only a facilitator.
The key, therefore, is not managing the people as they do that themselves,
but picking the right people and helping them define their dreams and goals.
Getting there has to be sketched out, but not carved in stone,
as the journey should be lifelong and so much fun.

DENIS KINGSLEY, ASSISTANT DEPUTY MINISTER,
DEPARTMENT OF FOREIGN AFFAIRS AND INTERNATIONAL TRADE, CANADA

CHAPTER 2

RON KITCHENS
Changing a Community

Ron Kitchens, Chief Executive Officer of Southwest Michigan First and the General Partner of the Southwest Michigan Life Science Fund, has been extensively featured in over 100 national and international media outlets, including *The Wall Street Journal*, *Fast Company*, CBS News, NBC News, FOX Business News, USA *TODAY*, *Foreign Direct Investment*, *Forbes*, *Fortune*, *Financial Times*, *The Economist,* and National Public Radio. Southwest Michigan First, nationally recognized for innovation in economic development, is a private, non-profit organization committed to being the catalyst for economic success in the Kalamazoo, Michigan, region.

Since its inception in 2000, Southwest Michigan First has assisted more than 120 organizations with projects in 26 life science company start-ups and funded ten companies through its venture fund. Having announced almost 6,000 jobs in 2008, it continues to be dedicated to creating jobs, company growth, and promoting and strengthening entrepreneurship in Southwest Michigan.

Ron doesn't ignore change. He recognizes it's a fact of life. You can put your life on hold and hide until the crises pass or you can consider the tough economic climate a catalyst for change, innovation, and movement.

He doesn't use a downturn in the economy as an excuse to step back from his commitment to bring business, innovation, and growth to Kalamazoo or an excuse to no longer keep the "Kalamazoo Promise." He uses it as a springboard to do better, do more, and get out there and help create jobs. To Ron, being hungry or not having proper health care isn't an option. His mantra is "It's not about business; it's about people."

He recognizes it's about making choices, no matter what the circumstances. "We're in the people business," he said. "We do this so that human beings who have no jobs or who are underemployed today have opportunities. This is about changing people's lives." Ron's perspective is, "You are in a position to determine your future. So, what is it going to be? What difference are you going to make? Tip the scale in your favor."

Ron's interview came from the heart and spoke to the heart of what matters in life — people. Everything he does impacts those around him in many ways, some measurable and some immeasurable.

The conversation begins.:.

Donna: I can just imagine what you're living these days.

Ron: Apparently, we are experiencing the Chinese proverb, "May you live in interesting times." These certainly are interesting times. It's so wearing and negative on the psyche that people cannot cope. We are so overwhelmed with negativity and bad news that it's hard to define prosperity and positivity for those experiencing a psychological recession.

Donna: That's a beautiful way to put it. I work with my clients to maintain their psychological balance. It's not about how many hours they work and how much time they spend at home. It's not about dividing their day evenly between work and personal hours. It's about doing what they need to be doing and want to be doing, and for how long during the day and night, that keeps them centered. That's what matters. It will change as time passes, depending on a myriad of factors, but as long as they're in psychological balance, they'll be exactly where they need to be in life.

Ron: That's right. I've not heard it said like that, but, as I was telling my team this morning at our daily morning meeting, I strive for an integrated life and a psychologically balanced position.

For example, there are some days when you are tempted to only eat oatmeal. There are other days when only potato chips sound good and other days when you would only eat steak. It's OK. You've got to have the mindset to know that, in the end, it's all going to balance out. You've got to have the total package.

Likewise, I try to get my team to remember that it's OK if some days they only do one thing, as long as they keep the big picture in mind. And I constantly remind them to not let themselves get so overworked that they forget to integrate the rest of their lives. That's a tough thing to teach people; I was probably 40 before I ever gave myself permission to be integrated and aware of my own balanced needs.

Donna: For many of my clients, it took them until they were in their 40s to make the choices necessary to give themselves permission to be a certain way, to act a certain way. Their programming was so strong that they didn't think they could even "go there."

From a coaching perspective, I believe that's one of the gifts we give our clients … to show them that yes, you can give yourself permission to make choices that will give you a more balanced, joyful life, no matter what the intensity of your world is.

Let's go back to what gave you that spark to get you to where you are right now. Was there a defining moment for you? A person so influential in your life that you knew life would never go back to the way you knew it?

I want to hear about you … about Ron … your story. I'll ask some questions along the way, but in truth, I'd like to listen and see what reveals itself. I am always fascinated by how people minimize their level of impact, or ignore how powerful it might be.

Ron: I read your stuff in *Fast Company*. It's actually my favorite magazine because it was the first one that ever quoted me — I'm joking. The way it is written and the topics it chooses to focus on really appeal to me.

Donna: It's the first one that ever quoted me, too. I really loved the original magazine when it was published out of Boston. I read every issue from cover to cover and more than once.

Ron: Polly LaBarre was with them. Polly and I are friends and have been for a few years. As a matter of fact, I have a book that came out in April of 2008 and the title of the book was coined from a *Fast Company* article about my organization [Southwest Michigan First]. It was the first time we ever used the term *community capitalism*. They published it and I got so much feedback about those words, I said, "OK, I think we just discovered something."

Donna: I had been invited to a conference in France which took place at a global business school. In conversation with one of the participants, I said, "We cannot do our jobs properly if we do not know people and what their stories are because we all live and operate through our stories." That's when the seed for this book started taking root. I started calling people at high levels of leadership all over the world, asking if they'd like to have these conversations.

I am fascinated by how those I've spoken to are able to "grow" people, how they approach people, how they live their lives from a perspective of joy and centredness, no matter what they're living. I love being in the middle of a conversation, hearing when people really "get it." It's amazing when I see the "aha" moment happen; that moment where, within our conversation, you see that you have an impact on others and will be able to help shape the next wave of leaders because of it. That's the premise of my book.

Ron: That's fascinating. It's exactly the kind of thing that I really struggle to find to read. When you reach a certain point in your ongoing personal education, there ceases to be many new business books that are dramatically different and from which you will learn something.

There's a reason *Good to Great* is still on the bestseller list every week. It's because it was, and still is, ground-breaking, new, and interesting. Others just come and go.

What I find myself searching out is not just biographies, but biographies about people who changed certain industries. The last four books I've read (and I'm a voracious reader, I probably read close to 100 books a year) have all been about leaders and people who have started large church movements.

What fascinates me are the methodologies they're using and the phenomenal business people who were driven by a single mission. When I go back and I compare them to Henry Ford or to great business leaders of the modern day, it's the same story, the same techniques. I've found it fascinating to study these great people who are pretty honest about their mistakes and their personal missions because it's so much a part of what their faith is.

Donna: Ron, looking back over the span of your career, was there a moment, an occasion, or an experience where you realised that you wanted to do what you're doing now?

Ron: I'll start way back and then you can hurry me up or slow me down. And yes, there was a defining moment. I grew up very poor. My mother was 15 when I was born, my father was 16, and neither attended high school. My father died when I was four.

At that point, my mother was a 19-year-old widow with two children and we were very poor. I can remember, after my dad died, when Christmas came. School was out so there was no school lunch. We'd been eating pinto beans and rice for dinner and lunch for a week, so my mother could save enough money for us to have a little bit of Christmas under the tree.

A box of food showed up on our front porch, including a whole turkey and other food for a Christmas meal. Even now, I can remember our amazement as we took out each can and package and looked at it.

To this day, I've never received a greater gift than that box. But there was something unusual in there — a can of mandarin oranges. I grew up in the Missouri Ozarks. In the 1970s, in my little teeny hometown of Ozark, Missouri, tropical fruit, whether canned or not, was something very rare and to be saved for a special occasion. So here was this can of mandarin oranges.

To be quite honest, we didn't know what you were supposed to do with them — we just knew they were special. That can of mandarin oranges (which probably cost a quarter at the time) went on a shelf in the cupboard, to be saved for an occasion that was special enough to eat it.

It sat there for years, it got bloated, and then the can got thrown away. It didn't just leave a hole in the cupboard; it left a hole in my soul. The can had been a connection to that blessing in my life.

Apparently, I lamented it one too many times to my mother. She came home one day with a grocery sack in which she had a can of mandarin oranges. I was genuinely excited. At this point, I had never even tasted a mandarin orange. I just knew that it was a symbol of the greatest gift I'd ever received in my life.

My mom said, "Here's your can of oranges, but don't put them in a cabinet. Go put them on your desk. I want you to have them there as a reminder of the cost of a lack of education." My father died in an industrial accident. Because he was illiterate, he had to take the worst job in the plant, and he lost his life.

That can of mandarin oranges and its successors have had a place on my desk all the way through high school, college, and graduate school. Even at times when I couldn't get a job and was furiously typing and sending out resumes. In every professional position I have had and even now, I've kept a can of mandarin oranges in my desk.

They've gone on to symbolize more than just the cost of the lack of education. They now represent my responsibility: I have a responsibility to give back, to change people's lives, to make fundamental changes in people's lives and communities.

Donna: You're bringing your roots with you, but you're not letting them hold you back. You're literally letting them fire up the energy within you to make a difference in other people's lives.

Ron: Absolutely.

Donna: Do others get it? Do those who haven't gone through your type of background get it? To them, it would be a conceptual story. Do they realise that everything that everybody does has ramifications that affect the sustainability of our planet?

Ron: I don't think most people do. My whole life, I have been blessed with people who for no reason have done things that have changed my life. I once won a ticket on a radio call-in show.

Like I said, I'm from a very small town in the Missouri Ozarks, with a population then of about 2,700 people. When I grew up there were 100 kids in my high school graduating class. One day, the town 20 miles away had a radio call-in show to win tickets to go see the Kansas City Royals baseball team play.

That's a three-and-a-half-hour drive by bus. I was the fifth caller, won this ticket, and got a ride to the parking lot to leave for a mid-week game. I was 12 years old, had never been to a baseball game in my life, and couldn't have been more excited. When I got on the bus, I was with a whole busload of old people. Who else would be going to a baseball game in the middle of the week?

As soon as the bus stopped, I got off, ran into the stadium, and down to the first-base line to get an autograph from anybody I could find. I was so excited to be there. While waiting for players to come up, this old man walks up on the field and started talking to the kids. He asked each of us, "Where are you from? What are you going to be when you grow up?"

So when he got to me (and I don't know why), I felt compelled to tell this guy my life story. It wasn't like me at all to be so talkative. I told him where I was from and when he asked me what I wanted to be when I grew up, I replied, "I don't know, I'd love to work here. This is the greatest place I've ever seen."

He said, "Work here? Why don't you want to own the place?" I said, "I can't do that. My dad died, and I had to win a ticket on a bus to even get here today. I could never own this place."

He told me to wait right there. He then came up into the stands and took me up a few rows. We sat down and he said, "You know, when I got out of school I started as a salesman. I was the best salesman and at the end of the year, they cut my route in half. The next year, I was the best salesman and they cut my route in half. The following year, I was the best salesman again and they cut my route in half. So, I started my own company. I struggled and built a company. Today, I employ thousands of people. I own this baseball team, and if I can do that, you can do that."

That guy was Ewing Kauffman. There's a quote I'm looking at on my office wall right now from him. He was an incredible leader who had no reason in the world to tell a dirty-faced kid that he could do great things in his life, but he did.

When you grow up poor and without a lot of outside mentors, those times are the ones that have the ability to change your life. I've been blessed over and over with having these kinds of "God just seemed to nudge me in the right direction by putting those people in my path" moments. I'm overwhelmed some days with the blessings.

Donna: Don't you think you are instrumental in attracting that to you, just by virtue of having such an open demeanour and *joie de vivre* that literally makes people want to help you succeed?

Ron: I do believe in the power of attraction and openness. Most people want to be asked to mentor, whether it's officially or unofficially. They're willing to give you a little bit of themselves to help if they believe you're honest and genuinely trying to use that to move forward. I've never had anybody who I asked for help and mentorship who turned me down, and I don't think I've ever turned anybody down either.

Donna: I was going to ask you that. Did you have anybody specific who mentored you through your school days into where you are now?

Ron: Yes, a couple. To pick one, I would say my best friend's mother. My mom is also a great friend and, in a lot of ways, we grew up like siblings rather than a mother and son. My best friend's mother in particular — actually both his parents — made sure I had life experiences and gave me opportunities and standards to help me be what I could be. I owe them a great debt for that.

Donna: I'd love to hear the journey between school and where you are now. What's the chronology? What got you to the next stage and the next?

Ron: When I graduated from high school, I didn't have any money to go to college and have the traditional college experience. A good friend, who was also a business mentor to me, came to me. He owned multiple businesses in my small town, including a little gas station/convenience store.

He said, "I know you don't have the money to go to school. You need to go and you need to graduate, but you can't do that working at a minimum wage job either. I'm going to sell you the convenience store for the cost of the inventory. I'll finance the building, the gasoline, and all the expensive stuff."

I went from being a high school senior to being in business for myself and running a successful store. Then a second successful store, all while going to college part-time nights and weekends and taking day classes when I could slip them in.

It took me seven years to get through school, but I learned a tremendous amount about business and my community. Just before I turned 21, I looked around one day and it dawned on me that all of my friends who'd gone away to school couldn't come home. There weren't any jobs.

I didn't know whose fault it was, but I was angry. There happened to be a City Council election. The announcement showed up in the paper that they were taking candidates for City Council races. I thought, "Well, there's whose fault it is, it must be their fault."

I went in and put my name on the ballot. I then discovered you had to be 21 to be a City Councilman. I happened to turn 21 just before Election Day, so it was decided I could run. I ran, won the race, spent six years as a City Councilman, and ended up being president of the Council. I discovered a real passion for helping communities change. I discovered then it wasn't exclusively the city's responsibility to create jobs. But we did do some great things about bringing jobs into the community. It was then I was convinced that was where I was supposed to serve.

At the same time, I sold my company, because I knew I could sell it for enough to finish school. While in college, I went to work for a United States Senator named Jack Danforth. He later went on to become the U.S. Ambassador to the United Nations. He is one of the two best men I've ever known in my life.

Along with being an attorney and a U.S. Senator, he was also an Episcopal priest. I learned more about how you treat people, how to agree with and, more importantly, how to disagree with people and do so respectfully to build bridges even while disagreeing. He is still one of my favorite people in the world. I was able to work for him for almost two years.

I finally graduated from school and wanted to become a city manager. I wanted to run cities because that's where I thought my heart was. I went to work for a small town as both the Head of Economic Development and their City Manager but soon realized I didn't like the city management part. It wasn't the day-to-day serving on committees and making sure the utilities, police, and fire all worked correctly that excited me. I believed you couldn't change people's lives enough that way.

Today, I don't want to just change somebody's life. I believe if I can help somebody make a fundamental change in their life, then I change their future and I change their grandchildren's future by doing that. We can change four generations of a family and do a lot to ensure they never go back to poverty. That's really where my heart and passion are.

I discovered that it wasn't through city management that I was going to be able to do that. I left that position in Warsaw, Missouri, and went to work for a community called Moberly, Missouri, where I could do the economic development exclusively.

I enjoyed it tremendously. I had great experiences, and after five years, the community of Corpus Christi, Texas, came to me and asked me to consider taking over a program there that had been decimated. They'd had incredible political problems that brought a lot of baggage.

I moved my family there and built a great program that was internationally recognized. My family had tremendous success but found that we liked the change of seasons and family values offered in the Midwest. Also, I wanted to be able to effect more change than I could in Texas.

I believed that the next level of developing community excellence was helping people to be empowered to start their own companies and build their own opportunities. To do that, you had to be in a place that had capital to invest. I came to Kalamazoo five years ago.

Since that time, we've been able to roll out the Kalamazoo Promise, the nation's first program that guarantees every child graduating from a Kalamazoo public school will receive a full college scholarship to any public college or university in the state.

We've established the Southwest Michigan First Life Science Fund, the planet's largest location-based venture fund. The bottom line is we not only make money like a traditional venture, but we attract companies to our region: you have to move here to get our money.

We've seen tremendous job creation done here — almost 15,000 jobs announced in five years. We've built a large college internship program and we're beginning to dramatically change people's lives. That really is what it's all about. My calling is to use the business world and the great things that are found in it and meld that with philanthropy.

We all know the story of the fisherman: "If you give a man a fish, you feed him today. If you teach him to fish, he can feed himself." I want to go to the next level. I want to find the best fisherman, put a business plan around him, and capitalize him. He can then hire 60 other fishermen, and they can feed 600 people in that same capacity and change the entire village's life. That potential of the entrepreneurial fisherman is captured in our model called *Community Capitalism,* in which philanthropy and business work together.

Donna: Got it. You're bringing together the concepts of being the best *in* the world and the best *for* the world.

Ron: Absolutely.

Donna: That is an extraordinary place to be. Are you paying attention to your level of impact? Do you see how what you do profoundly affects people? I know you're putting together all these amazing programs and melding business with philanthropy. Are you seeing the results in individuals who share their stories with you?

Ron: Years ago, my grandfather, who had both a good and bad impact on me, told me, "Don't save all those notes that people write you. You won't save the bad ones so don't save the good ones."

For years I followed that advice. Then a few years ago, I realized that may have been the single worst advice I ever got. There are days when doing all this is hard. There are days when I look around and go, "What am I doing here? Why didn't I go get a job where I could make Wall Street money, set the world on fire, and take care of my family?" It's on those days that I go back and look at those notes from people who tell me how I changed their lives and how amazing things are happening to them because of what we've been able to help them execute.

I remember a story from my career when a children's book company came to town, a company called Scholastic Books. They were putting in a call center. One of the ladies called me and said, "I'd like to get a job there." We don't normally get involved at that level, because you're either going to make somebody happy or you're going to make an enemy.

This lady was married to the guy who was "Mr. Community." Anytime there was a children's sports group, he was the guy to raise the money for the uniforms. He was the one who coached. He was the one who made sure ball fields were always prepared, and he truly dedicated his life to kids. I knew him because of that, so I made the decision I was going to help her and, lo and behold, she got the job. Six months later, she discovered she had breast cancer. It was horrific.

The surgeries were many and the treatments were a year long. Her husband came to me on the day she had gotten her clearance that she was cancer-free, crying in my office. He said, "You don't know what you did for us. We didn't have any insurance at all. She would've died if it hadn't been for you helping us get that job, and we would've bankrupted ourselves to do that. Our children wouldn't have gone to college. We would've lost our home. Everything we have today we owe to you, because you took the time to get her that job." Those are the moments I will never forget.

During your time on earth, you have the ability to change and help other people's lives. A lot of people wouldn't think that was so great. I didn't make any money from that. I didn't get any personal glory or public glory, but that was one of the greatest moments of my life.

Donna: You impacted more than one generation with that.

Ron: Absolutely.

Donna: You gave them a double gift. I know how people struggle to make ends meet, to be able to sleep at night because they know that they're going to be up to their eyeballs in debt just trying to get well.

Health care should never be a bargaining chip. You made it possible for them so they could sleep at night. They could know that their kids would be in school and have the best opportunities available to them, because of what you put in place. If I were you, I would photocopy each and every letter and wallpaper my office with them.

Ron: I've got a thick file and it gets thicker every day. On those blue days, I'll go back and read them. My grandfather was right in this regard: I don't save letters to the editor that don't promote growth. I've been blessed that there have been few negative comments. I'm also burdened with a short memory on those things so I don't remember the negatives.

On those days when it's tough, you go back and you look at those letters of support and you think, "You know what? We are making substantive changes in people's lives, and it isn't stories or numbers on a spreadsheet. It isn't new buildings I can drive by and think that it wouldn't be there but for me. It's people who get up every day, whose children are thriving, and they're thriving because of the little help that we gave them." That's pretty special.

Donna: I firmly believe that just as you were helped growing up, people who you help will pay it forward.

Ron: Absolutely.

Donna: Then you're making a global impact in your world and, hopefully, beyond your understanding or knowledge. What could your peers do more of? How do you light that kind of fire in people around you, so they join you in making such a huge difference?

Ron: I think I'm a great believer in talent, in finding who you are, how you're hardwired, what your talent is, and maximizing that. I see so many people who are industry peers who don't particularly have talent or heart for what they do. They're a lot like golf course groundskeepers who hate golfers. They're people who are supposed to be worried about community growth, but are only worried about tax revenue and traffic patterns.

If you're going to change communities, you have to change people's lives. I mentioned there's a Ewing Kauffman quote on the wall in my office: "The best social program in the world is a well-paying job with health care benefits and a retirement program."

I love people so much that I believe in the need to get them a job where they have the respect for themselves and from their peers for the work that they're doing. If their kids get sick, they can take them to the doctor. They know that if they work hard for 30 to 40 years, at the end, there will be a safety net to retire and live on.

I believe if you do those simple things (those aren't hard things; those are simple things), then people will do amazing things in their lives because they dedicate themselves to their work. If you do those simple things, they'll change the world. They will do great things because of the simple things they've enjoyed. That's what we've got to get more people doing: finding ways to create jobs with safety nets.

I'm not talking about socialism. I'm not talking about anything other than what great employers have known for years. That's why they provide those benefits. They know they get satisfied, high-quality workers who not only do great things at work, but also do great things in their lives.

You go to communities that have those kinds of great employers, like Hewlett-Packard. Carly Fiorina, the former CEO of Hewlett-Packard, is a real hero of mine for a lot of reasons. One of the quotes that I love of hers is this: "Our efforts to make a positive act in the world and in people's lives were not acts of charity, but rather of enlightened self-interest."

If we look at the world that way, look at our community or our state that way, and say, "I'm going to go do the right thing by people and I'm going to help them meet these basic human needs because it's good for me," our children will live in a better world. It means that quality of life will go up and a rising tide will lift all boats.

Too many people out there want to be the street cop of the world by thinking they can grow and do great things by stopping people instead of empowering people.

Donna: Right. I hear a lot from the '50s and late '40s generations. Their perceptions of the millennial generations are that they're very self-centered, not focused, have a very poor work ethic, and have a sense of entitlement. Therefore, they're going to be crummy leaders of the future because they're so self-centered. I believe it's just that they think and act differently than we do. It works for them. What do you think?

Ron: I would argue with those from the late '40s and '50s. I have a team of half a dozen millennials. They're mostly young women who are some of my favorite people in the world. They all volunteer for social causes, spend incredible amounts of time working on community, and are driven to do great things to build their careers.

When you grow up with a single mom, you're very sensitive to the barriers and walls that are put up for women, and these young women are driven to create their own identity, their own careers. In general, I have never been more impressed than with the under-30-year-olds who work with me. They're amazing.

It's my job and my responsibility to mentor and teach. When someone joins our team, it's my job to develop them, to help them be the best they can be. We do a great job using sophisticated science to find people who are incredibly talented.

Because we do such a good job, it's like knowing that every horse in the stable is a direct clone of Secretariat. They're all champions, and now it's about the training and the desire. Some of them may want to be thoroughbreds, but others may want to be polo ponies. It's about helping them find what they want to do and being their absolute best. I have never seen a group of people so driven for an integrated life. It's interesting. We've had to set boundaries on how much volunteer time people can devote because otherwise, they would spend every hour they have out of the workplace volunteering in some way in the community.

I keep going, "Guys, I can't send you off to school for an education and take advantage of opportunities if you're overbooking yourself. Let's talk about how we do that." Those who say they're scared for this generation need to come meet my folks, because they are brilliant.

Donna: I'm so glad you said that! Are you sure you're not a coach deep down?

Ron: I probably am. I think most coaches love people, and they love to help them bring out the best of their strengths to see that, and that's what I love to do.

I gave a speech yesterday to a large group of people, and a guy asked a question. It was a simple question about why I had done something that I had done. I thought for a minute and said, "You know, the greatest part of any day is when I'm inspired by other people."

When a brand new college graduate comes into our organization, we have a process that we use. Everybody who starts here, no matter who you are or what degree you have, starts at the front desk. You have to understand that the first opportunity for us to integrate and sell a customer is on the telephone.

The way somebody moves from there (but we don't tell them this) is triggered when we see them make that first important decision without having to ask. They know how to do it and they do it. That's the most inspiring thing. I shouldn't admit this, but I cry almost every time that happens. When I can bring them in and tell them, "Thank you. You've just received a promotion and here's why. Here's how impressive you are to me because you did that."

These aren't big decisions. They're not deciding whether or not to sign the Constitution; they're deciding how to handle a customer's problem. When you see them do that, you can see where their future is going.

People who don't take the time to be inspired by the people they work with, no matter at what level, are making a huge mistake. I think my own ability comes from the light that others are giving off.

Donna: They're going to remember those conversations for the rest of their lives and that you paid attention. It's all about mindfulness. A lot of people are leaders by virtue of position only, but they don't take on the role.

When people are very self-centered and look to have power *over* others rather than *with* them, that's the disconnect. They can't understand why they can't keep great people. It's because they need to recognize the value in them as human beings, not in their role or responsibilities.

What you're doing is showing them that you're paying attention. I wonder if you have a conversation with them later on, asking, "How could you do what I did with you with those who will follow you?"

Ron: Absolutely. We talk about that. We use a system here. Everybody has a pad on their desk that's diamond-shaped with lined paper that says on it, "Thanks for the best … you're a catalyst for impact."

If you notice somebody in the office doing an act of kindness or of inspiration, whether it's a peer, customer, or supervisor, you write them a note. You then put it on their desk to show them they're acknowledged and valued.

It really makes a difference when you see a senior vice president get one of these from his secretary or his administrative assistant. He did something that he didn't need to do, could have had somebody else do, or showed kindness when he didn't have to, and this was seen and recognized. When he or she receives that note, they are genuinely touched. This isn't about a position of *power*; it's about a position of *influence*. You don't have to have a title, a high salary, or a fancy degree to have a position of influence. We see that in action here every day.

Donna: That's the focus of my book on human-based leaders. It's paying attention, being mindful of those around you, and leading others through impact, inspiration, caring, and recognition of their unique talents and strengths.

Ron: Absolutely. Sometimes that means helping people leave your organization. I have several peers who were shocked about this. We have people who work with me in this organization for whom we have a career plan. It helps them leave to get a different, better job, because I don't have enough upwardly mobile positions for them. I need them to succeed and I don't want to be the one that creates a roadblock.

Does that pay off in the end for me? It does, in ways that I will never know. Some will be obvious but when all's said and done, I'll be sitting in my rocking chair, and it will be those people and the impact they made on other people's lives that will truly be my written epitaph. You can't even attempt this if your mind is set at *selfish* and you only focus on building talent for your own organization.

I would love nothing more than to look around the community or the country and see dozens of people who were formerly on my team, now running great organizations. They are using the tools that I've given them, even improving them to change their own organizations and communities. I think that's where we can truly have a global impact.

Donna: Here's what's interesting to me: many organizations try to hire the best talent and retain the best talent to strengthen their organization. What I'm hearing is that you attract the best talent, not only to strengthen your organization (because you need to be successful to have the impact you want), but to strengthen the individuals within the organization, no matter what that means.

Ron: Exactly. We know that we're going to develop some of them and help them so much that they won't be able to stay with us. Their greatness will eclipse us and they'll need an opportunity. I can think of three people off the top of my head who left us and have gone on to do great things. There's hardly a month that goes by that I don't talk to each of them and have long conversations.

It used to be me continuing to mentor them. Two of them are from South Texas so they'll call and say *El Jefe*, which means boss, they'll call and say, "El Jefe, I've got an idea you never thought of." He might be thinking to himself, "Now it's OK, I want to give back to him, because he gave me things." They bring things to me that I hadn't thought of, different ways or perspectives that nurture me. I think that's the ultimate compliment, when a mentee becomes a mentor.

Donna: Oh yes, that's fantastic. Have you ever thought of holding a *Gymboree*? Do you know what that is?

Ron: No, I don't.

Donna: From a coaching perspective, I do this with specific clients in the same area of expertise. For example, imagine I was coaching dentists and had ten dentists in my clientele who all have similar business-related challenges. While they're great at being dentists, they are horrible when it comes to running their businesses.

I not only coach them individually, but once a month we all get on the phone for an hour and have this cross-mentoring, cross–best-business-practices conversation: "This is what's working for me here. Is it working for you there?" It's literally sharing knowledge, expertise, and insight.

Ron: I've never heard that term before, but I actually do something like that. Six years ago, I discovered that there weren't any professional conferences left where I was learning anything. I was spending all my time out in the hallway trying to find people who were doing unique and different things, because that's not what was being presented in the ballroom.

I and two other acquaintances whom I only knew from the hallway said, "If we were going to do this, who are the 25 people we would invite into the room for two days? Everybody pays their own way. We share what we're doing that are the best ideas, our frustrations, our insights, and we engage."

We have now run that for six years, the three of us, completely volunteering. Nobody makes any money on it. Everybody pays their own way. We have a list now of probably 50 people. Some come some years, and some come others, where we do that exact same thing.

We look for innovation, insight, and talent. When you're a CEO of an organization where you don't really have an HR department, there's nobody to help you plan your career or to let you know what's important and what's not.

We talk about those kinds of things and it's been a godsend to me. We do it at the same time, the week after Thanksgiving, in a different city. I like the idea of trying to get a smaller group and doing it on a monthly basis. I think we'd see great insights.

Donna: You would not believe how people leave that call pumped, inspired, and armed with some new information that they can tackle something with.

Ron: Do you set the topic before the call?

Donna: You can. You could ask the people who would be on the call, "What are you living right now that you would like to discuss?" Often, about half the people have the same or a similar situation they'd like to discuss, so you just amalgamate them into one and have that conversation. It could just be an *ad hoc* thing, depending on the environment.

Ron: I'd do that. I think that could be a fascinating way to get a lot of minds thinking through a specific problem or issue. We lie awake at night worrying about things and believe we're the only ones worrying about it. Then you mention it to two or three people and they have all had that problem or are having the problem. When you shine the light of day on it, along with some good thoughts and minds, it disappears.

Donna: That's right. Every month, you're setting up your own community where you have the conversations you all need to move forward individually, within your organizations and within a profession or field of practice.

Ron: That's a great idea!

Donna: What else would you like to share with me that we haven't touched upon, if anything?

Ron: I don't know. When I look at where I'm at, one of the struggles I have is this: when your life has exceeded your dreams, how do you then evaluate and continue to move forward? It's easy to get materialistic and say, "OK, I've exceeded my dreams; I'm having this great impact. Where do I go?"

You look around at other people who are successful, and they have lots of stuff that is easy to model, but that isn't what "significance" is. One of the things I struggle with every day is how to define those levels of significance to begin working towards, because I believe you have to work with intention.

I get up every day and when I look in the mirror, I don't focus on a wrinkle or two. Instead, I repeat my goals about 12 times. My personal life's goals folder is lying on my desk. I review it every Tuesday morning; I go over it and reaffirm my goals in my mind.

When you've achieved those great things, when you've achieved more than you ever thought possible, you need to set goals that aren't monetary or materialistic for that next level of impact. And frankly, I think if you do all the other things well, you get those, too.

I would love someday to be a U.S. Ambassador. I love this country so much. When I see the misrepresentation of the American way around the world, I would love to be able to impact other people's perceptions of the United States and of Americans.

There are some things about the U.S. that I don't like, but there's very little about Americans I don't like. I love these people; they're diverse and they're different. Some of them I wouldn't want to have in my house for dinner, but there's still uniqueness and great things about them, and I love that.

I don't know how I'm going to get there someday but it's on my life goals list. I think the other thing I struggle with is a real sense of urgency and burden. I feel the need to share what we know and have created with as many people as possible. I think that the models we've created in Kalamazoo and the things we've done here absolutely can change people's lives, if we can enlighten them (I call it "burden them") with knowledge, skills and ambition. If we can burden them with this knowledge, that's the opportunity. Not everyone will be able to see it, but if I don't find ways to show them a path with hope and possibility, shame on me.

Donna: *Who* do you need to know that you don't know, in order to expand your knowledge and your circle of influence?

Ron: The "who" question is one I haven't conquered yet. My "who" is everyone. "Everyone" can make me a better person. I do the "what?" and sometimes the "how can I?" but I wasn't doing the "who." That's a good place to start looking for those people that I can interact with, people who can both give and take.

Donna: Yes, and then connect the dots. How are you impacting people? What are you doing that is changing the world to make it sustainable for all the right reasons? That's the question, right?

Ron: That's right, yes. That is the question. The industry sector isn't as important as the results. Here are two important questions for me: "How are you creating and leaving the world a better place? How are you changing a person's past and future?" And by that, I mean, what programs can you put in place, and what opportunities can you offer that will enable a person to transcend the cement-like hold on their current socio-economic status and give them and their future generations a better quality of life?

Donna: How could you translate what you just told me into advice for the younger generation that will replace us as the leaders of the future?

Ron:	Open yourself up to both people and change. Commit to changing people for the better and letting them change you for the better. And remember to speak to everyone in their own language when you are doing it.

Donna:	That's right, because otherwise, you're talking *at* them, not *to* them.

Ron:	And they won't hear you.

Donna:	Exactly. That's a question I will leave you with to think about. Let me know when you have the answer. I'll leave it with "To be continued…" The conversations, along with our insights and awareness, shall continue to take shape and unfold. Looking forward….

Thanks Ron … this was amazing. One last question: If I asked you to open your desk drawer right now, would I see a tin of mandarin oranges in there?

Ron:	Uh huh. It's right here.

Reflections

Reflections Reflections ections

I had the great opportunity to carve out some quiet one-on-one face time with Ron within his crammed schedule. We touched upon everything we could fit into the time available before he flew out of Kalamazoo to honour an old friend who was retiring. We discussed what's next for Ron. He looks at his world from a perspective of "How can I continue to have a positive impact on our community? What can I be doing that I haven't thought of yet? What or who do I have to pay more attention to?"

We bantered and explored, and looked at how he supports people and organizations to be and do their best without relying on him. There's a fine, although definitive, line between helping someone evolve a new organization into something viable, sustainable, and successful, and being responsible for that continuing success.

He's one person. How much can one person do, even with an organization to back him up? How many places can one person travel to? To how many meetings can one person travel to be a speaker in order to reach more people? How many people can he, as one individual, mentor and grow? He asked questions many of us ask every day: "How can I do more when I don't have the time to do more? How can I take what I'm already doing and do it in some other way to have a bigger impact or reach more people?" I'm not sure there are ever right answers to those questions. The fact that he's asking opens the space where solutions will reveal themselves.

Human-based leaders continually expand their staff's best efforts. Leaders act as catalysts and accelerants to success. Staff know their leader is there for them, enabling them to be better, to grow, learn, and become leaders in their own right, regardless of level.

"'If you give a man a fish, you feed him today. If you teach him to fish, he can feed himself.' I want to go to the next level. I want to find the best fisherman, put a business plan around him, and capitalize him. He can then hire 60 other fishermen, and they can feed 600 people in that same capacity and change the entire village's life."

This is a reality check for me as well. What do I need to do so my clients don't come to rely on

How can I shift the balance in our relationship so clients begin to shadow themselves? How can they become mindful of who they are and how they interact with people and their environment? For a coach, "teach him to fish" means to teach him to be mindful of whether or not his choices and actions serve him. The coach also models how to create a safe environment so he can make the changes necessary to learn, grow, and evolve.

For Ron, in every conversation, he continues to be open to possibilities, both for himself and all those he touches. He has a deep commitment to helping people change for the better so they can create better lives for themselves and their families. He speaks *with* them, not *at* them, connecting from the heart. Those he's touched know there's nothing mechanical or superficial about what he does or his desire to create positive change. The ripple effect is huge and its impact enduring.

You are the centre of a circle, the diameter of which is determined by your circle of influence. You won't always know how wide that circle is, as what you do impacts people well beyond your knowing. Ron continues to find that out. Teach a person to fish and…

> *"I am personally convinced that one person can be a change catalyst, a "transformer" in any situation, any organization. Such an individual is yeast that can leaven an entire loaf. It requires vision, initiative, patience, respect, persistence, courage, and faith to be a transforming leader." – Stephen R. Covey*

Life is made up of small pleasures.
Happiness is made up of those tiny successes.
The big ones come too infrequently.
And if you don't collect all these tiny successes,
the big ones don't really mean anything.

NORMAN LEAR

CHAPTER 3

JOE SALTZMAN
Influencing Thousands

Once I decided to dive in and write this book, I immediately emailed Joe Saltzman and asked if he would agree to be interviewed, and he accepted. When we first met, one of the things I noticed about Joe was how humble he is. Ironically, our first in-person meeting happened when he came to Toronto to receive one of his many awards.

Joe Saltzman, the director of the *Image of the Journalist in Popular Culture* (IJPC) Project at the University of Southern California (USC) and the author of *Frank Capra and The Image of the Journalist in American Film*, is an award-winning journalist. He is Professor of Journalism and former Associate Dean at the Annenberg School for Communication & Journalism at USC. His chief professional passion is the exploration of the conflicting images of journalists in the media and how those images have affected the American public's perception.

After working for several years as a newspaper reporter and editor, he joined CBS television in Los Angeles in 1964 and for the next ten years, produced documentaries, news magazine shows, and daily news shows. He won more than fifty awards, including the Columbia University-duPont broadcast journalism award (the broadcasting equivalent of the Pulitzer Prize), four Emmys, four Golden Mikes, two Edward R. Murrow Awards, a Silver Gavel, and one of the first NAACP Image awards. He was among the first broadcast documentarians to produce, write, and report on important social issues, including *Black on Black*, a 90-minute program with no written narration on what it is like to be black in urban America in 1967; *Rape*, a 30-minute 1970 program on the crime that resulted in changes in California law; *The Junior High School*, a two-hour program on education in America in 1970; and *Why Me?*, a one-hour program on breast cancer in 1974 that advocated changes in the treatment of breast cancer in America and resulted in thousands of lives being saved.

In 1974, he created the broadcasting curriculum in the USC School of Journalism. During his tenure at USC, Saltzman won three teaching awards and remained an active journalist. He produced medical documentaries, wrote articles, reviews, columns, and opinion pieces for hundreds of magazines and newspapers, and functions as a senior investigative producer for *Entertainment Tonight*. He has been researching the image of the journalist in popular culture for over 12 years and is considered an expert in the field.

He spent 15 years researching and meticulously cataloguing such images in films, television and radio shows, commercials, cartoons and popular literature. His vast collection includes thousands of hours of TV shows and old radio programs. He brings this passion to both his research and the classroom.

Join us in conversation...

Donna: What or who was the driving force to inspire you to get to where you are? Was there a person in your life who mentored you or encouraged you to reach for your dreams? Was there a passion, cause, focus, occasion, or experience when you realised you shouldn't be doing anything else?

Joe: I came from a poor family. No one before me had gone to college. I loved to write, and I worked on the Alhambra High School newspaper, *The Moor*, in Alhambra, California. The journalism adviser was my English teacher, Ted Tajima, and he named me editor in my junior year. I also freelanced for the community newspaper, the *Alhambra Post Advocate*, and made money by being a photographer. I had always admired Clark Kent and Hildy Johnson (of *The Front Page*) and loved the idea of being a newspaper reporter. With Ted's encouragement, I was convinced I was going to go into journalism.

The high school counselors were talking to students about college, but were ignoring me. So I went into the counselor's office and asked why. He told me I was not college material and would be better off working with my father as a window cleaner and janitor. I left the counselor's office very angry and nearly in tears. I was standing in the hallway when Ted came over and asked me what was wrong.

I told him, and he became furious. He said that was baloney. The counselor was wrong. He told me he would make sure that I would go to college. In fact, he said I would go to USC, because it was one of the best journalism schools in the country.

He excused himself and went into the counselor's office to tell him he was way out of line. During the next two years, Ted worked with me to apply to USC. When I was accepted into USC, it broke my father's heart — he had planned for years that he and his son would own a window cleaning company. But he could see that my future was somewhere else and didn't stand in my way. In fact, he borrowed money on our house to pay tuition.

Once at USC in 1957, I spent day and night on the student newspaper, the *Daily Trojan*, becoming city editor, and in my senior year, editor. From there, it was Columbia University's Graduate School of Journalism. In the late 1950s, once graduated, I got a job, got married, and had children. I married another USC student, Barbara Epstein, who became one of the first female editors of the *Daily Trojan* in 1961. I got a job on a local newspaper for $75 a week and in 1964, we had our first child. I didn't think life could be any better than the life I had — all thanks to Ted Tajima.

Donna: What was the transition between the thinking of what you wanted to do, knowing you should be doing it, and doing it? Many dream of doing something or put it on a list, but few actually dive in and do it.

Joe: There was never any doubt. In the late 1950s, the choices were fairly simple – good people got a job, got married, had children, and led a responsible life helping people. There weren't as many options as there are today for young people. I never doubted that I would be a journalist, get married, have children, and do everything I could to help people. As I tell my students, there is no reason to go into journalism except to help people and be of service. There are many other occupations where you can work less, for more money, and have a better social life. The only reason to be a journalist is because you want to help people whom no one else cares about. Often, the journalist is a "court of last resort," after government, the courts, business, and everyone else have ignored the individual.

Journalism has given me a life I never imagined. In what other occupation could a window cleaner's son and a postman's daughter grow up to meet presidents and celebrities, to have the opportunity to be in someone else's shoes, and to experience what it is like to be a fireman, a governor, a breast cancer victim, a welfare mother, or one of the richest persons in the world? Journalism has given me the opportunity to influence thousands, to change lives, to serve my community, and, in the end, to have a good life surrounded by wonderful family and friends.

Donna: What was the journey like getting there?

Joe: The journey is all the fun. I tell my students that if you get into journalism to win awards, personal fame, and money, you will be disappointed. Those rewards will only come if your primary objective is to help people and do the best job you can on every story you cover. The great joy, for example, in producing a documentary is the reporting and the editing of the final product. Once the final product is finished, the rest is tiresome: publicity, screenings, reviews. The joy of the journey is getting there.

Donna: What attribute contributed most to your success?

Joe: I think I have been successful because I do everything with passion and total commitment. It doesn't matter what the assignment or the job is, no matter how trivial or unimportant it may seem. I put the same effort into everything – to do the best job I can under the circumstances.

Donna: What are the best lessons you've learned along the way?

Joe: The best lessons I've learned along the way are these: always put others ahead of yourself, and never do anything solely for personal gain. By helping others, by doing the best job you can on everything you do, true joy will be yours. The unhappiest people I know are the ones whose goals are trivial and unimportant, and who put what they do second to what they want to get out of it. I believe that if you care about what you do and put all your talent and time into it, the rewards will come. But to do something simply because of those rewards is to fail. In journalism, the story is the most important thing and everything must be sacrificed, including personal comfort, in the service of that program or story. To do anything less is to not live up to your true potential, and to the true potential of the project at hand.

Donna: There is a difference between being the best *in* the world or being the best *for* the world. Some can achieve both, though defining "best" is a conversation in itself. Where are you in that? What is your impact?

Joe: I never do anything thinking of the "impact" of what I am doing or what is best for the world. I do the best I can — whether it is producing a documentary, writing a story, or teaching a class — because that is what I believe everyone should do: the best they can on everything they attempt. If the end product — the program, the story, the graduating student — turns out to have an impact on the world, then that is a bonus. That is not the goal. The goal in journalism is to inform and help as many people as you can. The goal in education, in being a college professor, is to help each student reach their potential and hope that they will have an impact on the world upon graduation. I get as much pleasure out of turning an average student into an above-average journalist as I do taking a talented student and making him or her even better.

Donna: How are you positively impacting others? Growing others? What more can be done by your peers?

Joe: I never think of how I impact my peers or the students I teach. I think that's a waste of time. I give them everything I have to give and hope something I say during the class will be of value to them. If they go on to be successful and to have an impact on others, that is a bonus, but not my personal goal. I don't believe in taking credit for a former student's success (although it makes me happy to see it). I believe it is the student, the individual, who is responsible for these achievements, and if I can help a student to get to where he or she wants to be, I feel I have done something important.

It is very satisfying to see many of the students I have taught become teachers themselves, influencing new generations of students. It means, in a small way, that I have given back something to Ted Tajima for everything he has meant in my life. And if I can have one-tenth of the influence on my students that Ted had on me, I will die a happy man.

Donna: What are your perceptions about the differences between the millennial generation and ours? Do you feel present leadership (teachers and others) speaks to the differences? Or do they try to lead or teach based on their own ways of being?

Joe: I don't believe anything changes. Human beings are human beings, and the underlying values of living a good life have not changed from the dawn of history to the 21ˢᵗ century. Every human being has the right to fulfill his or her potential without prejudice or interference. As long as we cherish the old-fashioned values that lead to this, the country and the world will be in good shape. Alas, that is not what we are seeing in many parts of the world. Women are still considered property; different tribes continue to engage in old-fashioned warfare; and the value of the individual is not cherished.

There are thousands of elementary and high school teachers, for example, who, against great odds and with little support, are still trying to teach young people the basic values of a good life. Those are America's true heroes.

Donna: What would inspire others to follow you? What thoughts and words of wisdom would you pass on to them?

Joe: I tell my students, "We can teach you how to do things. We can give you the techniques and the knowledge to create good journalism, but it is up to you to bring the passion, the concern, the caring to the job. We can't teach you that."

I would tell anyone, "If you want to have a good life, do everything you do with passion, with caring, with the goal of making your life an inspiration to others.

"Never do anything just to do it. Always enjoy everything you do and do it because it is important to do, not because it will bring you personal wealth or power. Help others because by helping others, you make your own life so much more satisfying, interesting, and important. All the awards, all the money, all the power in the world only makes life easier, not better. What makes life truly fun and exciting is knowing what you have done has had a positive impact on others."

When I produced the first documentary on television on breast cancer and it was credited with saving thousands of lives throughout the country, I was more thrilled with that experience than any of the awards I have won, any of the paychecks I have cashed. It was a rare experience, a rare gift to be able to do something in journalism that had such an incredible impact on the public. It was, to me, what journalism is all about. I was lucky to have had the opportunity and smart enough to take advantage of it.

A rich man once told Barbara and me something that I will remember for the rest of my life. He said, "You and your wife have created projects that could take you 24 hours a day, seven days a week to do, and you don't make one red cent out of those projects. You are the dumbest people I have ever met in my life. If you put that effort into money-making projects, you would be rich today beyond your wildest dreams. I just don't understand people like you."

What he didn't understand is the tremendous pleasure and satisfaction we get from these projects. Barbara runs The Jester & Pharley Phund, a nationwide charity that was built on our son David's book, *The Jester Has Lost His Jingle.* In addition to teaching, I run *The Image of the Journalist in Popular Culture* project.

The joy of creating something out of nothing and seeing it have an impact on so many lives is something our wealthy friend may never understand. And yet, I wouldn't trade any part of our life for all of his money, world travels, and success as a businessman.

The story of the Saltzmans continues...

When I called Joe and asked him to be a part of this project, his response was, "OK, although you should be doing this with Barbara, not me." I had fully intended to have both of them represented in this piece, as they are both extraordinary people in my book (excuse the pun), as you'll soon see.

Their story contains history and a narrative with some twists and turns, so bear with me. It's about a family who individually and collectively blow me away and, I hope, you as well.

In the Fall of 1998, I was introduced to David Saltzman's book. I was co-leading a retreat with a colleague from Illinois. While sitting outside on one of our very rare breaks, my co-leader, Ross, told me about this book called *The Jester Has Lost His Jingle*. He insisted I buy it as soon as I returned home.

Knowing better than to argue with Ross (although I often try), I came home, called our local bookstore and ordered it. About a month later, I received a call from the store telling me the book was in. Off I went to pick it up, forgetting it was two days before Christmas. I stood in line at the cash for almost an hour waiting to be served. The cashier handed over the book and as I glanced at it, was taken aback to see it was a children's book. I thought they had made a mistake, but after being assured there were no other books by that name or author, I paid for it and went on my merry way. I was puzzled but intrigued at the same time, as the book was exquisitely beautiful in look, in touch, and, soon to be discovered, in content. Of even more impact for me was that through this book, I met the Saltzmans.

As soon as I got home, I opened the book. There was David Saltzman's picture smiling back at me. I began to read his story.

> *David Saltzman graduated* magna cum laude *as an English and art major from Yale University in 1989, receiving the David Everett Chantler Award as "the senior who throughout his college career best exemplified the qualities of courage, strength of character, and high moral purpose."*

> *During his senior year at Yale, David was diagnosed with Hodgkin's Disease. For the next year and a half, he kept a comprehensive journal of his thoughts and drawings while completing* The Jester Has Lost His Jingle *and other stories.*

> *In his journal, David wrote, "The best we can do is live life, enjoy it and know it is meant to be enjoyed — know how important and special every time ... moment ... person is. And at the end of the day say, 'I have enjoyed it. I have really lived the moment.' That is all. All is that. Is. 'Is' is such a powerful word. It's not was or will be. It is IS: It is alive."*

> *David died on March 2, 1990, 11 days before his 23rd birthday.*

When I read that last statement, I felt as if I was hit by a truck. Here was a young man who, through what must have been a living hell, finished a book about humour and laughter, with a message to enjoy the now, enjoy life, and remember to never lose your sense of humour.

I won't go into the book, as I really do believe you should all have a copy, and if you do buy it, you will learn its magic for yourselves. I will say, however, that because of it, I called the Jester & Pharley Phund and my journey towards meeting the Saltzmans began.

We corresponded for a while, and after learning the story of my son's own health battles, Barbara Saltzman wove her magic by sending us a Jester doll with a message that included *"…through your thoughtful words and in sharing your circumstances, you make us believe more than ever that it has been worthwhile to publish David's book. it would have made David especially happy to know the wonderful ways his Jester & Pharley are affecting you … I'd like you to have a Jester & Pharley doll to help remind you where laughter is hiding and to never lose your jingle."*

Over time and distance, our friendship blossomed, and, even though it would be years until we'd meet in person, that connection remains. Barbara inspired me and grounded me, if you will, as I was helping my son, Michael, through surgery after surgery. The Jester doll remains perched on my bookcase in our den as a constant reminder to always keep our sense of humour. It was a no-brainer for me to choose this family to include in my book, and that was before I knew how accomplished they were in so many other ways.

Not only did this experience lead me to this wonderful family, but it taught me to never hesitate to reach out, connect people and connect with people, even those I had never met before. By connecting The Jester with the Ronald McDonald House Charities, not only did the Houses receive books and dolls from The Jester's donor program, but I connected with a family that has become near and dear to me. They might be accomplished, recognized, award-winning leaders; however, in my book, their first-prize recognition really comes for being warm, giving, very "human" people.

Reflections

Reflections ctions

I was thinking about how revolutionary television has been in our lives. I can't imagine how enormous a project archiving TV, film, radio, and commercials would be, so it could be accessed and studied. The scope is beyond belief. The movie *Pleasantville* comes to mind, seeing the different family dynamics of the '50s compared to present day. I remember growing up and sitting around the TV with my family, watching our favourite shows, such as *Ed Sullivan*, *Mission Impossible*, or *The Twilight Zone*. It was a "whole family" activity. We only had one TV and definitely no computers. We planned parts of our evenings to share the experience of TV, then discussed it at family dinners throughout the week, of course, sharing what we thought might happen in the next show.

In the late '90s, I was quoted in *Fast Company* magazine. It was an issue that featured someone I greatly respected, Paul Wieand, the Chairman and Founder of the Center for Advanced Emotional Intelligence. In his piece, he spoke about using film in his work with high-level corporate executives. "With a film," he said, "you can show people a vision about emotional identity that they'll never forget." That really resonated with me. I emailed him to let him know that I used music with my clients in a similar way that he used film. Within an hour my phone rang, and there was Paul on the phone. The conversation was rich and enlightening for us both. Long story short, he then considered using music in his work and I was looking at what films I might match with some of my clients.

Near the end of our conversation and as an aside for him (and life-altering moment for me), he asked, "Why are you working with another company?" (I was a consultant with another firm back then.) "What are they doing for you? You need to start your own company and make a name for yourself, not them." The next day, A Better Perspective© was born, the company name registered, and I have never looked back.

For those clients going through difficult times, I match a "hug song" with them, and for those needing to stretch beyond their comfortable world, I match a "stretch song" with them. For those who really relate to films, we go into what movies really resonated with them and then discuss further. Film, TV, music, commercials — all these media have a way of getting into our psyche and sticking.

I can teach models and concepts, but there's nothing as powerful as putting scenarios and metaphors to those models, sharing real-life situations that connect with people to create meaning for them. Discussing movies and music gives added dimension. Sharing them brings tears, laughter, and unleashes our imagination, as we create dreams around the possibilities these conversations evoke.

I can teach a methodology using clinical data and behavioural response examples. On the other hand (and as I often do), I can take powerful, real-life cases and use them as illustrations of how my methodology works. Through these cases, the class sees people's lives, not just clinical responses. Participants literally lean in as the cases unfold. They start identifying with the people in these cases. They feel for them, anticipate how they'll react, bring in pieces of their own stories as they share examples of when that happened in their worlds. Before I know it, they're percolating on the "What if I…?", "What can I do?", "What could I have done?", and "What didn't I think of?" questions. We learn as we teach and teach from what we have learned. And through the sharing, we connect with others and evolve beyond just our own stories.

As Joe says, "The goal in education, in being a college professor, is to help each student reach their potential and hope that they will have an impact on the world."

For me, this conversation brought to light two of the hats that I wear in my work: executive coaching and teaching. What I learn as I coach I can integrate in my teaching. What I learn while working with students I can integrate into my Shadow Coaching. Where do they connect? How can I, through my coaching, teach my clients to shadow themselves and use an appreciative approach in their leadership? How can I teach students to be masterful Shadow Coaches as they support leaders to strengthen their human-based leadership?

Human-based leaders know that the more aware everyone is, the better choices they can make for themselves. They help others discover their values, talents, desires, and dreams, as well as understand what motivates and inspires them. They light a fire beneath those discoveries, leading people on a path that will help them evolve, perhaps even with a few "accidental" discoveries along the way.

Thought flows in terms of stories — stories about events,
stories about people, and stories about intentions and achievements.
The best teachers are the best storytellers.
We learn in the form of stories.

FRANK SMITH

CHAPTER 4

LAURIER LAPIERRE
It's No Accident

In putting this book together, I've had many conversations about what leaders think *human-based* leadership is. Laurier L. LaPierre is a Canadian icon. He isn't afraid to speak his mind. Even though he sometimes causes quite the stir (as you never know what will come out of his mouth), you do know it will be impactful, from his heart, and with passion that overflows in his every word. My short conversation with another Canadian leader is a perfect *entré* into Laurier's conversation, because it's about legacy and living your word. Denise Amyot is someone who "grows" people for a passion and a living in the Public Service of Canada. She shared the following:

> "Human-based leadership calls to the individual … calls to the head, heart, and gut. It touches all aspects of the person, brings the humanity of the person, and calls to the humanity of people. Human-based leadership puts humanity into the workplace. People live by it. I look for it when I recruit. I talk about humanity in the workplace.

> "For the last six years, I've been reflecting on legacy. I declare my legacy to the groups I speak to. They must think, 'What kind of yahoo is this person?' I declare it whenever I speak. If I do a talk about leadership, the more I say it, the easier it becomes. Then people look for it. I live my word. Then people expect to see it. People help realise it after I declared it. And it inspires others to declare their legacies. It's helped me be my beacon and become my lens. My own behaviours need to reflect that, and I think about it daily.

"When I left my previous job, I was given a certificate that thanked me for that. The certificate reads: 'In recognition of your leadership and for bringing humanity to our workplace through your honesty, positive attitude, and support for every one of us.'

"Human-based leadership is about being seen, recognized, and appreciated for inspiring others. It's not something I talk about every week, but I live it. The more people who do it, the more will do it. It starts at the top. It's not linked with hierarchy, not linked by level, but by way of being. It has extraordinary impact. It's not only present in the workplace; it's where you go, how you treat the cab driver, the person knocking at your door at dinner time. It's part of your DNA.

"Some are born with it. Some discover it. It's a part of personal development. Some discovered there was a better way to lead. Others don't get it or see it. In those cases, they can't retain staff. Staff don't perform 150%; they feel disempowered. The more people who know the potential of emotional intelligence (which is a huge part of human-based leadership), the more people will aspire to it. It unleashes the energy, potential, power, and success of everyone."

Unleashing power and potential. That's also a by-product of what happens in conversations with Laurier.

I first met Laurier at a social event. To say I was captivated by him is an understatement. I would mingle, talk to friends, but ultimately would be drawn back to Laurier and his partner to continue the conversation. There's something about Laurier, an energy and a directness that attracts people like a magnet. And it's more than that. It's sensing his passion about life, people, his country, and its future; a passion that is so fierce and all encompassing that you can almost reach out and touch it.

First, some background. Laurier is a retired Canadian Senator, a former broadcaster, a journalist, and an author. He is a member of the Liberal Party of Canada. He is best known for having been co-host with Patrick Watson of the notorious public affairs show, *This Hour Has Seven Days*, in the 1960s. To him, being literate "is an essential part of life."

After the show's cancellation, Laurier moved to politics as a "star candidate" for the New Democratic Party of Canada in the 1968 Canadian federal election. The party was hoping he would help achieve an electoral breakthrough in Quebec, but he only managed to come in a distant second place.

He returned to broadcasting for the next several decades until his appointment to the Senate in June 2001. As a member of the Liberal caucus, he was an outspoken supporter of Jean Chrétien against supporters of Chrétien's rival, Paul Martin. He has a PhD in history from the University of Toronto. He is an author of many books, has been published in the *Financial Post* and *Encyclopædia Britannica*, and was one of the few openly gay senators.

He has been an activist with EGALE, a lobby group for gay and lesbian rights, since coming out as a homosexual in the late 1980s. He retired from the Upper House upon reaching mandatory retirement age of 75 on November 21, 2004.

"If you are a homophobe, get out! If you're anti-Islam, get out! If you think all native people are drunk and stupid, get out! Get out, get out!" Senator Laurier LaPierre gripped journalism students on November 25, 2003, with a speech that touched on or rather, hit a slew of issues from hate and media concentration to life and the death penalty, and continues to this day to maintain his stance on human rights issues. "Only barbarians kill their people," he said. "It is profoundly disgusting." Along with other famous Canadians, including Pierre Berton, he was involved in a campaign in the '70s to save 13-year-old Stephen Truscott, sentenced to death for rape. The sentence was eventually lifted when forensic testing found the boy was, in fact, innocent.

Laurier also spoke about the concentration of media ownership. "[It] limits the possibility of a marketplace of ideas," he said, and added, "In the marketplace of ideas, the citizen must have access to the means of production." He pointed to the statistics. "Seventy-four per cent of people in B.C. [British Columbia] receive their information from CanWest…. This is unconscionable."

Laurier worked for the Historica Heritage Fairs and for Youthlinks. During that time, over 200,000 young people from grades four to nine participated in an exercise: remembering Canada's history and heritage, and our individual place in that history and heritage.

Laurier LaPierre is an Officer of the Order of Canada. When he received the award, he was introduced this way: "A well-known television journalist, former McGill University professor, and authority on Canadian constitutional history, he is one of the country's most valuable political commentators and respected champions of social justice. He has introduced the Canadian public to world leaders, philosophers, and artists, as well as to some of the most important and sometimes controversial social and political issues of the day."

It is my honour and privilege to know him. Come and meet Laurier…

Donna: Tell us your story: where your career began, why you chose this career path…

Laurier: Everything's an accident. It's all about stories. We tell stories. We don't plan our lives from the beginning. Accidents happen. We don't make choices at the beginning; we make them through accidents.

I decided in grade four or five that there weren't enough books to read and not enough time to read them. I packed my mind with knowledge, with stories. I was fascinated by history. Fascinated by the stories that were being told, fascinated by my capacity to amplify them, to enlarge them into mythical dramas in my mind. I came to the conclusion that all that really matters in life are the people around you, people you're in contact with, and the people on the planet — humanity.

My grandfather would tell wonderful stories. He was completely and totally illiterate. My father was, too. My father only learned to read later in his life. My sister taught him when he was in his 60s, primarily so he could read the newspaper. They could tell stories. It dawned on me the joy my father experienced without recognizing it as a gift or a right.

I loved scouting. I was a boy scout, a king scout. It taught me things about survival, about ingenuity, and my capacity to learn. I wasn't great at sports. As a matter of fact, I was lousy at sports. The only thing I could do well was kick the ball, so when I wasn't called upon to kick for the team, I was sitting on the bleachers, reading. My sport was reading. It made me more aware of what my parents missed and how it affected their intellectual development. The greatest gift to illiterate people ever was TV. It taught them what they couldn't read about. I remember when my mother heard about the country Tanzania — she had discovered Africa! It brought to them a world they didn't know existed.

Grade nine was the end of the obligatory school system. I couldn't go on so I went to Baltimore, took a commercial course, and learned how to type. I worked for Ingersoll Rand and Dominion Burlington clothing. At 19 or 20, I realized that was not for me. I asked myself, "What avenue do you have?"

The idea came to me that I wanted to be a priest. I applied, went off to New York, and was interviewed by the head priest. I went back to school. I did two years to finish high school and then went on to do the first two years of college in Baltimore. I studied with the St. Charles Sulpician Order of Priests who came from France. They were greater teachers than the Jesuits. They were astonishing.

Donna: What made them so amazing for you?

Laurier: They talked to me as if I was human. They did not pity my ignorance. They taught more than facts; they taught us that we learn facts through emotion.

Donna: When you say, "We learn facts through emotion," are you saying that there is an emotional attachment to what we learn? Something that triggers our memories beyond mere data that cements that learning for a long time to come?

Laurier: Yes. We learn all sorts of things in school. When we learn something we're interested in or passionate about, we become emotional about it. We'll remember what we learned because of that emotion.

It was a four-year period, two years high school and two years college at the novitiate in New Jersey. I was sent away because I had a sexual affair with another novice. I didn't know what a sexual encounter meant in those days. I had felt I had done something wrong and felt honour bound to tell the priest.

From there I went to Sherbrooke, Quebec, for half a year and then to University of Toronto to finish my BA in History. I finished a Masters in History and then a PhD. When I graduated, I taught history at Western [University of Western Ontario], then taught at Laval University [Université Laval] and moved back to Toronto.

Then, remarkably, I was doing television with Patrick Watson and Douglas Lighterman. We did *Seven Days* until finally the CBC fired us. I had used the word "damn." That wasn't acceptable. CBC management was tired of having to answer to Parliament for what I had said on air.

After teaching, I joined the New Democratic Party [NDP] because of Tommy Douglas. He was the leader of the party then. He wasn't easy, I suppose, but he was kind and generous. I ran but didn't win, so I moved back to Montreal.

Donna: I didn't know much about the NDP party in those days. I was a Liberal, born and brought up in Montreal. Trudeau was my MP [Member of Parliament]. I had met Ed Broadbent when he was leading the NDP party at a reception at the American Ambassador's residence. He was fascinating.

It was a really hot and muggy evening. There was no air conditioning in the house so we both ended up outside to get some air. We started talking, and in conversation I remember telling him he was a member of the wrong party. He laughed and said he had been told that often.

Laurier: He got that 17,000 times a day!

I came back to Montreal to teach, first at Loyola and then at McGill for 15 years. I did freelance, worked, and travelled. I went into politics, wrote two or three books, and was asked to speak all over the world. That's nothing to sneeze about. The only thing that mattered was Canada. It wasn't whether I was French or English. I am a Canadian. That is my destiny. I want nothing other than to be a Canadian. There are 200 ethnic groups in our country. It is the most diverse country in the world, both for its people and the environment. What fascinated me was they wanted to learn. If you don't know people, you can't be a leader.

Donna: That's exactly right. It's one of the reasons why I was compelled to write this book.

What enticed you to change parties?

Laurier: I was a Liberal before. Loving this country and loving the people. A father of one of my students came to me and said, "You ruined my life!" "Why?" I asked. He said, "My son and daughter came to me. We were talking at the dinner table about the Christmas holidays. They did very well in school so I asked them, 'Where would you like to go on holidays in the United States?' My son, backed by my daughter, said, 'Dad, we don't want to go to the United States. We want to go to Nunavut.' 'Where the hell is Nunavut?' the father asked his kids. He continued, 'My son took me by the hand to a map and showed me where it was. I looked at my son and asked, 'Is this one of LaPierre's crazy ideas?' It was the greatest trip we ever took. Within an hour, my children made friends."

Canada is the second largest country on the planet! I used to think we were [the largest], but Russia is, and we are second. We never annexed anybody. Kids don't know our history … they don't know our geography, and their parents don't, either. However, these are basic issues. There are basics that have to be learned first. I don't fight these battles, because I know inevitably they will be changed, and as a historian, I know that.

You learn things that you can access easily. I'm teaching what they can't access easily. I don't mind that they teach them how to read, write, and all of that stuff…. I don't want to be teaching them that Jacques Cartier discovered Canada in 1534. It's not about facts and dates, because they can access that on the internet; it's all the rest. I want them to find out their stories.

Donna: I was just saying to my clients, "I don't care if you're 26 or 56. I want you to share your story."

Laurier: Or like me, for instance. You would say to me, "Laurier, I know you are 99,000 years old."

Donna: Laurier, I know you're *not* 99,000 years old! I love what you share with me and the readers would love it as well. You would have a readership well beyond your immediate circle and far beyond your imagination.

When I was in school what we learned about Canada was next to nothing.

Laurier: And girls had no intelligence, of course; no instincts [said tongue in cheek].

Donna: When I did my field work for my practicum, I did it in Whitehorse, Yukon. When family and friends asked me why the hell I chose to do it there, my answer was, "I'll be working with the next wave of 14 First Nation [Aboriginal or original peoples of North America] leaders. How much better does it get than that?"

In I walked, and trust me, they had never met anyone quite like me before. We'd talk on breaks and after class. They started telling me their stories. Some of them are being revealed to the public through court cases and residential schools history. Many wrote books on it, not for the public, but for their people. Two from the class gave me story books … stories of their people and what happened when they were to be assimilated. I was in tears. I was angry. I wanted to know why I was just finding out about this now! It gave me insight into the lives of Native Canadians. Their treatment was unacceptable.

Laurier, what message do you want to give to the next wave of leaders in Canada? What spark do you want to light in them?

Laurier: Be more conscious of our freedom in this country. Get to know people. Travel, first in our country, then through the world. Get to know Canadians. We may not have fought as many wars as other countries, but in the ones we did fight, no one has ever denied our courage. We are great conciliators. A fundamental flaw is our own people don't know this country. They only know their region. They go to the U.S. and travel before they'll travel in Canada. Go to Nunavut. Get to know the people who live in the snow. Watch Canadian programs! Write more.

We are the first country to believe in diversity. The question of language is no longer necessary. Get to know people's souls. It's in their art and literature. Learn languages. Travel. I want the people of my country to know the stories of my country. Look at human courage. Education is more than knowledge … it's an instrument of discussion. Know what makes our country *be* right now. Connect with people. We used to have pen pals. Now, through technology, it's even easier. Use technology that is available to you to be better human beings. Better human beings make a better world. Ultimately, if you fail, you will be the generation of the greatest failure in the history of mankind.

Reflections

Reflections ections

Nobel Peace Prize winner Wangari Maathai said, *"In the course of history, there comes a time when humanity is called to shift to a new level of consciousness, to reach a higher moral ground. A time when we have to shed our fear and give hope to each other. That time is now."*

What Laurier said, "Ultimately, if you fail, you will be the generation of the greatest failure in the history of mankind," sticks in my mind. Most of our conversations continue to play back in my memory. As I make choices in my work and life, I recognize there is no better time than *now* to make those necessary shifts. How does that translate in my work? What am I not yet doing to support leaders in the work they do? To what dimensions of stewardship must I pay attention to ensure I don't negatively impact the great work they are already doing? Any change brings with it implications upon implications upon implications. I need to anticipate at least three levels of possible implications and their consequences.

We meet people by chance or design; so many of them have an impact on us. Some stay in our lives for a time and shift the direction and choices we might take. Others, no longer a part of our present world, still profoundly impact how we live, what we do, who we are, and how we hold ourselves.

Two people who left deep footprints in my life come to mind. The first is someone I met many years ago, when I was a little girl travelling in New York City with my parents and older brother. We were parked outside a department store in Manhattan. When we came out of the store, our car was blocked by a cavalcade moving down the street; throngs of people lined the streets waiting for its approach. I stood with my family by the car (with Canadian plates) and watched as the cavalcade moved at a snail's pace. People were walking alongside the cars. A smiling man came over to me and knelt down to eye level. He took a large button off his lapel that had his picture on it and said "Do you know what it means to be the President of the United States?" As he put the button in my hand he continued, "You hold onto this button, because if I win and become President, it will be worth a lot some day."

It was JFK.

It was a moment I will never forget. I've thought a lot about it over the years. He didn't have to stop to talk to me. Our family couldn't vote; we were Canadian. As young as I was at the time, I felt deep down that he spoke to us because he wanted to, not because of any hidden agenda. I remember everything about that exchange. As I now work with political leaders, I know they have moments to connect and either be loved or hated by the public and the media. They will be painted by the same brush with the colour of that initial impression, over and over again. We have no idea how much good or harm President Kennedy could have done, but for one Canadian, who followed his every move from that moment on, the impact of that meeting will remain.

The second person who touched me at such a profound level is Laurier. I recently brought together my personal and professional worlds for the first time — I invited Laurier and his partner to join my family and friend for dinner. I watched the interactions as they all shared stories, bantered, and took the conversations in many directions. Laurier wove his spell around everyone at the table, leaving them in awe, impressing us as he shared stories from the spirit of his convictions. It was amazing. As a human-based leader, Laurier helps people navigate, through curiosity and learning, to expand the realm of what they don't know into what we now do know, by living in a world of constant discovery.

As we let our light shine,
we unconsciously give other people permission to do the same.
As we are liberated from our own fear,
our presence actually liberates others.

MARIANNE WILLIAMSON

CHAPTER 5

RUTH ANN HARNISCH
Charge Neutral

Ruth Ann Harnisch, president of the Harnisch Foundation, has given grants to hundreds of non-profit organizations since its founding in 1998. She is an advocate of creative philanthropy and these out-of-the-ordinary charitable investments landed her on *Oprah* and the *Today* show. Not only does Ruth Ann support non-profits that make a difference globally, she encourages others to get involved, to donate, support, coach, listen to, and light a fire under others to do the same.

She wears many hats, brilliantly and authentically.

After retiring from her journalism career, she chaired the board of the international non-profit More Than Money, creating peer communities and producing educational materials to help top wealth holders put their money where their values are. That organization's coaching program inspired Ruth Ann to learn about the emerging field of professional coaching. She joined the International Coach Federation (ICF) and the International Association of Coaching (IAC), serving as a Director of the ICF Foundation Board of Trustees and on the IAC Board of Governors as Treasurer. Ruth Ann is an IAC certified professional coach. She has been a thought partner to scientists, authors, executives, performers, and other dynamic individuals. In her words, "I work every day to apply my money and my moxie to the biggest problem in the world — untapped capacity. In my coaching, my grant making, my donor activities, and my involvement in non-profit organizations, I want to help people discover the extent of their resources, and how to make the most of what they have for themselves and for others."

I love our conversations. Of course, there are never enough of them for my liking. I know whatever topic we start on, we'll veer off of it many times over, all paths fascinating in their own right. Each subject or question we tackle might reveal ten others to touch upon or park for another time, but I know I'll leave the conversation wondering, thinking, creating, and percolating on the "What more can I do with what I'm already doing that will make a difference?" and "What more can I be doing that I haven't thought of?" questions. She will challenge you to give of yourself but not leave you hanging. She always asks, "How can I support you in this?" She doesn't offer it lightly and expects commitment; she will never ask more of you than she would ask of herself. I know that no matter how busy she might be, if I shine the "bat signal" and call out for help, she's there in a New York minute.

Ruth Ann is a presence, a powerful force in who she is and in all she is.

Join me in meeting and getting to know Ruth Ann…

Donna: Hi Ruth Ann. What's happening according to Ruth Ann?

Ruth Ann: The world as we know it has changed considerably in recent times. Since the economic crisis began, it's a much different world financially, and not one of us is unaffected. It's been an interesting time to exercise my own leadership during these challenging times, especially at the outset when people were panicking.

It's important for me — for any leader — to model equipoise in the midst of the storm, whether that's a literal or figurative disaster. Financially, as in every other aspect of life, nothing stays the same. One day up, one day not, and that's the way the world works.

What I've learned through years of those ups and downs is the beauty of remaining the strong, calm center. That means not being too excited when you're up or depressed when you're down, and never failing to be grateful for what you have now, without regret for what you either no longer have or will never have.

This is part of the leadership curriculum of developing one's coaching personality. Do you remember Thomas Leonard's admonition to us to become *charge neutral*?

Donna: Yes.

Ruth Ann: That was a very difficult concept for me, because in my prior life I was rewarded for being charged. The rewards came from being very definitive about standing in a place and doing so with color, sparkle, and noise. It's kind of interesting. It seems to me that Thomas did that.

Donna: He did in certain ways. I think sometimes he almost scared himself and then backed off a little bit.

Ruth Ann: When I showed a more passionate personality, I got paid for it. I was an op-ed writer, a radio talk show host, and television newscaster. My value was in the peaks of personality, the appeal, the charisma of creating something that others would be drawn to, not by its safety, but by its danger, its boldness.

I found a way to bring the boldness into coaching and leadership. I've found a way to be safer, to be a better custodian of the energy.

Donna: It's part of a stewardship role.

Ruth Ann: It is. Have you ever seen an old dog and a puppy together? The puppy is bouncing all over the place. Bounce, bounce, bounce, dash, bounce, bounce, dash, bounce, bounce, and the old dog is just lying there. The puppy is bouncing all over him, biting and tugging, but the old dog is passive and peaceable. I used to be the puppy; now I'm the old dog.

Donna: I'm not so sure about the old part, Ruth Ann, but I know what you mean.

Ruth Ann: I cannot bounce with the highs of the past nor sink to the lows of the past, nor do I have judgments, evaluations and opinions as I used to have. I used to get paid for my opinion. Now, I see part of my leadership role as being. Being is the only opinion I have. My foundation is "All is well and all shall be well."

The only opinion I have is we're all here for something more. And we're all in this thing together. Those are the only opinions I have. I no longer want to pass judgment or say that what I think is the way anyone else should approach life, because all I know is what I know. I don't know what you know.

Donna: What was the driving force or key point that transitioned you between what you used to do and what you're doing right now?

Ruth Ann: As an ardent feminist, this is a very interesting thing to admit. It is the process of having spent the last 23 years in the company of the man who has been my husband for the last 20, because he and I saw life through such vastly different lenses.

He is so intelligent, experienced, and successful in so many ways that I could not dismiss his opinion solely because we didn't agree. I used to be able to dismiss people whose opinions I did not share, and it was easy for me to judge them.

However, because I lived with this person in an intimate situation, because I love him so deeply and respect so much about him, I was forced to recognize a terrible thing: I'm not always right. Not only am I not always right; somebody else, just because they disagree with me, is not necessarily wrong. Every point they make, even if I disagree with their conclusion, might be a fact that I need to know and consider as I make my own evaluation.

Being with someone so smart and different has been a multi-year, in-depth course in how to find the value in the argument of the other, how to value that contribution, how to integrate it into my own world view, abandon what does not make sense, adapt and adopt where possible, and evangelize where necessary.

Donna: How did that impact the coaching world? In my mind, there is a direct connection, but I'd like to hear that from you.

Ruth Ann: Nobody can yet agree on "What is a coach?" The definitions are probably going to be argued as long as there is human interaction we call coaching. If coaching is anything, it appears to be a relationship and process by which both coach and coachee exchange information and experience transformation.

Donna: It's different then than your previous world, because it wasn't a generative dialogue *per se*, was it?

Ruth Ann: It was more debate where one makes one's point and hopes to win. But it seems to me we have come to a place in human history where that game is no longer serving us. Recent years have exposed a crisis of leadership. When disasters, both natural and manmade, began piling up, the myth of effective and ethical leadership was shown to be a dirty little secret.

I think we've been made painfully aware that we can't save people from natural disasters. We can't save the financial system. We can't give people appropriate health care. We can't educate people effectively and joyfully.

There are so many systems that are so far from effective, where leadership is a fantasy. Now is the time when genuine leaders, mature, charge-neutral people without a partisan political agenda, can say, "Times have changed, and we must change."

I've been greatly saddened by the polarizing politics that prevent us from finding common ground to create solutions. We can no longer afford the luxury of denigrating our fellow citizens with whom we stand shoulder to shoulder. Every one of us is needed to work together for a prosperous and peaceful future.

For me, true leadership is the ability to be calm and at ease, to be of comfort and of encouragement, and to elicit the greatness that exists in all of us by being realistic, now and future focused, and taking logical steps to heal our communities.

Donna: You're defining coaching … as I see it, certainly. I had this conversation just yesterday with a Fortune 100 organization where I said, "Coaches do not fix people. We don't fix. We help remove road blocks, help people become aware of their magnificence, and help them evolve into their excellence."

The minute we get into a fixing mode, we're dealing with what was and should be and not with what can be. In my opinion, many coaches live in a world of going into interventions to fix what's not working rather than creating something magical. There is a huge difference.

To be at ease, be comfortable, encourage people to be their best, and elicit the greatest in all of us: that is what a coach does.

Ruth Ann: I think you can say with accuracy, this is what the great coaches do. I think you have to say *great* coaches.

Donna: And great political leaders, great leaders, period, help people see how extraordinary they can be.

Ruth Ann: Indeed! In my *pro bono* coaching work, I'm constantly encouraging people to recognize that they've created artificial distinctions between themselves and other people they've put on a pedestal for one reason or another.

For instance, people often say to me, "I would love to be a philanthropist one day. I love what you do and I think that would be so wonderful to be a philanthropist."

I hear that at least a hundred times a year. I've heard it from someone who's become a new client of mine just two days ago. I said, "Stop right there. Tell me the last few things you can think of where you gave money, or invested your resources in that something that wasn't merely for you and your selfish needs? What have you done for someone else with your money, time or ideas?"

Before she knew it, she had a whole list. I said, "Would you call that philanthropy?" She said, "Yes, but I'm not like you." And I responded, "Would you like me to feel unworthy as a philanthropist because I can't give at the same level Melinda Gates can give? Should I feel bad and diminish what I do because it's not as big as what she does? Well, of course not."

I told her, "How dare you diminish the richness you've contributed to the world!" She now sees herself as a philanthropist and she understands how unproductive it is to measure one's gifts against another's gifts.

Donna: That's one of the questions that I've been asking when I interview people. I'm asking you now, do you pay attention to your level of impact?

Ruth Ann: I pay attention. I have paid attention, and it's been part of my professional life to pay attention. I used to be a media celebrity, so I had all kinds of input from the public all the time, and not all of it, by the way, was encouraging. Some of it was actually life-threatening. Much of it was ego-bruising and some of it was soul-killing.

In order to survive emotionally, I used to have a little file called "Reasons Not to Kill Myself." The file contained evidence that my presence in the world was making a measurable difference. I have boxes of "Reasons Not to Kill Myself" now. In fact, I added to the file today. At a meeting I attended, I met a woman who told me, "You don't know this, but you inspired my philanthropy years ago."

I'm a book evangelist. When I find a book worth sharing, I buy in bulk and give them away. The most I ever bought of a single book was 20,000. With that one, I was trying to jumpstart a political movement. I still love dead-tree-edition books, even though they'll soon be relegated to the print museum, and I think book evangelism is creative philanthropy.

Anyway, this woman said, "Do you know that book you gave away?" I said, "Of course! I've given over 10,000 copies of that book." She said, "You gave me a copy, and you didn't know it. You sent copies to an organization I belong to and that's how I got one. I read it and I thought it was so good that I bought copies for my friends and now I've started doing that with other books too." She said, "When I see a book I like and I think it's an idea that other people should know about I just go ahead and buy ten or 20 of them and start giving them away."

That's another one of my "Reasons to Not Kill Myself." I have inspired others to be book philanthropists. One day, somebody I met while I was doing the most random of things, like standing in line at a bank, said to me, "You don't know this, but you changed my life." "Huh? How did I change your life?" I asked, bracing myself to hear what terrible thing I had done.

She said, "On one of your radio shows you were talking about…" You know how people say, "Oh, I couldn't possibly do that because it would take five years." And the coach says, "So what? You'll be five years older whether you do this thing or not. So why not?"

She heard that, took it quite literally, and decided to do what she dreamed of doing. She went from being a housewife listening to my radio show to a major corporate executive. When she was listening to that radio show, she didn't even have a college degree. But she said, "Why shouldn't I go back to school? I'm going to be four years older anyway!" She went back to college, then got a graduate degree, and then landed a major executive position.

I thought, "If I hadn't run into this woman in this random place, I never would have known that a few words I said on the radio inspired her to completely transform her life." This means there are probably dozens of stories of lives that are in some way made better because of something I said or did.

Donna: The difference between being the best in the world and being the best for the world … or both.

Ruth Ann: I'm both. Do you know Seth Godin's book, *The Dip*?

Donna: Yes.

Ruth Ann: He says, "Find out the stuff you're best at and do that and forget about everything else, because it gets too discouraging."

Seth says, "Only do those things at which you stand the chance of being the best in the world." So that's how I've tried to arrange what I do and how I triage where I go and how I spend my time. It's one of the reasons I chose to spend this time with you, Donna. You've said to me, "It's very difficult to get somebody whose time is worth $100,000 an hour to just go ahead and give me an hour."

You're in a unique position. The time I invest with you might turn into something like that lady saying, "You don't know this, but…" Whatever you're doing with these interviews, Donna, I'm betting it has great potential to produce "You don't know this, but…" stories about changed lives.

Donna: I thank you. I remember talking with you about this at CAM [Conversation Among Masters] a couple of years ago when I said we have to start having these conversations. We need to know people, to "get" people so we can do our best work with people.

I was getting tired of so many coaches directing clients or clients-to-be, saying, "This is what you should be doing" rather than getting to know people through their stories, what sparks them, and gives them that passion. We can help them discover more of it and make a global impact, even one person at a time.

Ruth Ann: Can I tell you what I did at lunch today?

Donna: Of course. I'd love to hear!

Ruth Ann: It scared even me. The man introduced himself to me as Patrick. I said "Hi, Pat," and before I even sat down I said, "I'm sorry, Patrick." I said, "I heard you say Patrick, but I instantly said Pat, because one of my favorite old boyfriends was Pat." So I automatically defaulted to that. He wound up telling me a long and interesting story about why he's "Patrick" now and not "Pat," the name by which he had been known his whole life.

Later, when it was time for dessert, the waiter ran through the list of about seven desserts. I said, "Patrick, *crème brûlée*?" He asked, "How did you know?" I said, "I was just checking to see if I could tell by the *tell*." You know what a tell is? It's some little tic or twitch or change in expression, however fleeting, that a poker player will search out in the opponent's face.

He said later, "I must have given you a tell about Pat, because I didn't say anything but you instantly corrected yourself." I realized that that's how fine-tuned my antenna is now on "What is your story?" Not "What's my story to impose on you?" but "What's *your* story?"

I have developed my animal instincts for sensing a change in your literal figurative scent. When the waiter got to the *crème brûlée* on the dessert menu, I detected a twitch of an eye muscle, combined with one twitch of a mouth muscle. I checked it out because I wanted to know if I really saw what I thought I saw.

Donna: So you not only took the time to find out his story, but to validate your intuition and what it was telling you about him.

Ruth Ann: Exactly. That's why I'm reporting this to you, because one of the things you're doing is dissecting the skills of a great one.

Donna: Say more.

Ruth Ann: These conversations are helping you to dissect what makes the great interacters truly great. What makes a real leader? Part of it is the ability to pay highly focused attention, to sharpen their native skills, their intuition and their lifetime of learning, and to test their assumptions so they can sharpen those extra-sensory and intelligent assumptions and conclusions. That way, they have confidence when they have a sense that they might be on to something.

Have you interviewed Bob Lee of Lee Hecht Harrison yet?

Donna: No.

Ruth Ann: Bob told me that he has learned that a lot of reporters go into coaching. Reporting skills are very important to coaching and, of course, I'm a former journalist. One of the skills of a journalist is the ability to come to a story in innocence and ignorance, asking the most basic "Tell me everything because I know nothing" questions. If you come in with a point of view or theory that you want your subject to confirm, you're not reporting, you're telling, and that's different.

Donna: As a Shadow Coach, one of the things I teach my students is that they have to remove all filters that they process information and thoughts and everything through, and be open to what unfolds in front of them. That is how they will best serve their clients. Just observe what's going on and see where the path or journey will go in that story. Once we think we know it all, we become stupid, because then it's about us and not them.

Ruth Ann: There is the big shift. When you ask what's the difference between the way you are now and the way you were then, it's the difference between it being about an individual personality or a collective wisdom.

Donna: As an organizational leader?

Ruth Ann: The "me versus them." I say personality, separateness, individuation, versus "All of us are smarter than any of us."

Donna: That's right.

Ruth Ann: I value the contributions of the individual, and I recognize the need for individuals to stand up as leaders right now. When the first waves of the economic crisis hit, I was profoundly affected. But I'm proud that when people phoned to ask, "How are you, *really*?" I could say, "You know me." "Oh yes, of course, you're fine." "Yes, I'm fine. Now, what is it I can do for you?" Because that's why they called. They were hoping I was fine so I would be able to offer support to *them*.

Donna: What do you think our peers have to do? What do we have to do to have global impact?

Ruth Ann: Do you know what they say? "Simple, but not easy."

Donna: Yes.

Ruth Ann: Simply tend to your own garden first. I think Thomas Leonard called it a personal foundation. I don't know what others would call it, but you should "Heal thyself."

Donna: *Self-care* was another thing that he called it.

Ruth Ann: What I'm saying is, put your oxygen mask on first, before you turn to assist others in the cabin. You can't help anyone else if you're a wreck. You can't take your ego out of the way if you haven't done your best to move toward your own healing and wholeness.

First and foremost, if you purport to coach, be coached, be coachable, and coach for free so that you learn what it's like not to be afraid to speak your truth without worrying you'll get fired. I think coaches can benefit greatly by doing some coaching for free so that it comes from the heart, the gift of coaching.

Ideally, a coach shouldn't be tap dancing to get a client to sign another contract. We should be working to help our clients learn to coach themselves, to hear our voices or their own best self-coaching voices in their heads, to help them get to where they don't need to lean on the coach for constant support.

The Harnisch Foundation's website says, "Our biggest goal in giving you a grant is to help you get to where you never have to ask us for another dime." We want to support our grantees in creating something that is self-sustaining, and that's a new model of philanthropy, which I think applies to coaching.

My hope is that everybody in the world will have a coach, and that everyone feels equipped to coach another person. I imagine a time when all of us have enough skill to say, "What could you do about that in this moment? Is there any support I could offer you right now? What do you think you need to do right this minute to change that?"

Do you know what I mean? Anybody can ask these questions. It's just like breaking out the defibrillator at the airport. These defibrillators talk! They say the words so a six-year-old can use the defibrillator correctly, effectively, and promptly to save a life. Why couldn't anybody ask the right "saving" question?

Donna: I don't think there is anything that stops us "technically" from doing it. Many are so wrapped up in themselves from a self-centeredness perspective, not a self-care perspective, that they don't pay attention to what's happening to others.

Ruth Ann: If you can't do that, why are you coaching?

Donna: That's exactly right. I've seen a lot of coaches who are so wrapped up in their own lives, worlds, and boxes that they're not paying attention.

Ruth Ann: It's that connection that allows one plus one to equal infinity. That's what coaching is about.

Donna: When I think of the next generation going into this field or many fields, and I've been interviewing quite a few in their mid- to late twenties to see where they are, many of them have huge egos, which gives them a lot of energy to go after what they want to go after. In many instances, it also gives them the impression that they are way smarter, better, more knowledgeable than they are, because they don't have that life piece yet.

Ruth Ann: Do you know what? They are smarter than they are. And they're stupider than they are. Part of our work is to help everybody at every age recognize that you are so much sharper in so many ways today than you were yesterday. Conversely, you can do less today in some ways than you could do yesterday. True wisdom is ascertaining each day, "Where am I improving? Where am I losing my faculties, abilities or strengths?" I am never at 60 going to have the body that was possible for me at 30; it's just not possible.

My eyesight is going daily, but not bad enough that I don't see the twitch that indicates Patrick wants *crème brûlée*. What I think all of us have, at all ages and abilities, is the ability to recognize in each other the current state of greatness.

Not everybody brings their A-game every day. Some days the person you're counting on to be Mr. October stumbles and the pinch hitter saves the game. Sometimes the understudy gives a brilliant performance. Each one of us brings to each day that which we have and it changes.

When I worked as a reporter, I did a story on a group called People First. Are you familiar with People First?

Donna: No, I'm not. Tell me about it.

Ruth Ann: The People First movement is the rallying cry and the militarization of the disabilities community. The message is, "Stop calling us disabled people. We're people with situations." In other words, instead of saying that the artist Chuck Close is paralyzed and wheelchair bound, or crippled, they prefer "Artist Chuck Close, who uses a wheelchair." Do you see what I mean?

Donna: I did this with cancer and long-term care patients when I first started coaching. You are not the disease; you are a person with a challenging disease.

Ruth Ann: Right. A cancer patient, I'm so and so and only one of the many things about me that's true is that I have this diagnosis.

Donna: Exactly.

Ruth Ann: Same thing with the People First movement. In some circumstances, you're the smartest one in the room and in other circumstances, you are the least able to contribute in the room. It depends on what the room requires. Anyone at any age can bring something to the conversation. The wisdom is to know how each person's contribution can best be made, heard, and valued at any given time.

Donna: It's a sharing of thoughts and ways of being. One of the conversations I had last week was with a young man who is very technologically savvy and very proud that he could do so many things simultaneously.

I asked him the question, "When do you slow down to the speed of life?" He stopped, smiled, and said, "I'm not paying attention to it at all, am I?" He told me that was the best lesson he learned that day. It's just that he doesn't have to be "on" all of the time.

Ruth Ann: I have a couple of young clients, and one of them has always been the best. He's one of a golden band of brothers, top of his class, got into his chosen profession, happens to have been made a partner while in his 20s in probably the best known firm that does what he does. He's so ambitious, it's unbelievable.

When we began coaching, I invited him to notice where he already has the kind of success that means the most to him. I told him to consider each moment of each day a success right now. To enjoy that and not be looking at the next big contest, even though he's young and filled with testosterone and needs to compete.

Donna: That is a huge gift to him, to be paying attention, and to breathe with his whole being. As coaches, I think often our greatest gift to people is to help them find that space in life, no matter what age or what they're up to, and to look at life as either a joy or through new eyes if it's not a joy.

You're a very powerful individual with a definite idea of what you like and don't like and want for yourself, what you have and don't have patience for. I really appreciate your being able to state, "This is not what I want right now." A lot of people don't do that. They're afraid of not being politically correct.

How do we teach those who will follow us how to reach out, be themselves in every sense of the word, and make a huge difference in the world?

Ruth Ann: How have others answered that?

Donna: Uh-uh. I'm not telling. I'm asking you that question.

Ruth Ann: You have the benefit of hearing this and that. I thought I'd try and cheat [she joked].

Donna: You almost caught me with that one.

I recently did a keynote in Texas with leaders of creative design firms. It was a different realm for me. I had amazing conversations with talented creatives who work with people in every kind of profession and business imaginable. Many in this group were young, up-and-coming rising stars who I continue to mentor into their (what I call) level of excellence. Whether I am speaking to creative designers or political leaders, I ask the question (or a variation of this), "How do we teach those who will follow us how to reach out, be themselves in every sense of the word in order to have an impact in the world?" I want to hear answers from all perspectives. Each answer is unique and shows me how people are approaching their contribution to the future sustainability of people, professions … the world. I want to hear Ruth Ann's answer to that.

Ruth Ann: Ask me again.

Donna: What about how you do your work? Who you are as an individual can inspire those who will follow to literally reach out through their excellence, making an impact on the world based on who they are, not what people expect them to be.

Ruth Ann: Do you remember the old Milton Bradley game of Careers?

Donna: Yes.

Ruth Ann: I used to love that game, because it let you say what "winning" meant to you. You had to set your own formula for success. It consisted of choosing a proportion of happiness, fame, and money points. You could pick different paths on the game board.

If you took, for example, a teaching path, you would not get very many money points, but you could get the most happiness points on the board from that. If you went the route of the movie star, you would get money and fame points, but you wouldn't get that many happiness points.

You had to decide before the game started what proportion of happiness, fame, and money would make you happiest, therefore successful, therefore winning the game. Then you set out on the path to acquire the correct number of points in the correct number of categories in the correct proportion.

I would say that is still what I am encouraging everyone of every age to do. Determine each day what constitutes success today. For me, does it mean love? Does it mean a one-on-one, personal relationship or service to the masses?

I think of the books that have been written by the children of the great leaders of social movements in which they said, "The cause got my parent. I didn't."

Without talking about politics *per se*, let us talk about a very popular political figure in the current imagination, the former Governor of Alaska and 2008 candidate for Vice President of the United States of America.

Donna: Yes, Sarah Palin.

Ruth Ann: When she was running for Vice President, she had a newborn with special needs, and her 17-year-old daughter was pregnant. Here's one way of looking at it: Some mothers might consider their greatest success formula consisted of happiness or love points, and they might have chosen to invest their time and energy in their own family.

There is only one person in the world who can call herself "mother" to the pregnant teen and the baby with Down syndrome and their siblings, including a son whose life is in peril at war. Only one person can say, "This is my highest calling for success."

That doesn't appear to be her choice, even though that would be the first choice of millions of other people, or the thing they might think she should do. But she feels a higher calling to serve a larger vision that may leave her own flesh and blood by the side of the road. Thus it is for every great leader.

Choices have to be made about what constitutes success for you. How many people think about the lyrics in the song, *The Cat's in the Cradle*: "When are you coming home, Dad? I don't know when, but we'll have a good time then, son. You know we'll have a good time then."

For some people, success is saying, "I can do with a smaller footprint. I can do with less money. I can do with less of everything except time with these people I love while these kids are small." Or "These kids of mine are going to have to understand that they were born to seeds of greatness. They have greatness within them and they'll never get as great as they could be if they don't see how great their genetic material can be. I'm their mom, but I have to go for everything that I can possibly make of myself, my gifts, talents and time."

I would ask you, did I sound "charge neutral" about those issues? I'm asking you. Did I sound like I valued each of those points of view exactly the same?

Donna: I can say yes, because my impression and take-away from this is your belief that people need to choose for themselves what will spark them to be their greatest. It's not about what you think is right for them. It's about what they think is right for them.

Ruth Ann: Yes. The postscript is attributed to Buddha: "Take what you want and pay for it." If you are Sarah Palin and you take what you want — a big step on an international stage — make no mistake, you pay for it at home.

I don't know what the price will be. No one knows what the price will be, but that's the price you will pay. It will be paid. You may not be aware of paying it. You may make your little baby Trig pay it, but somebody is going to pay the price of your focus being elsewhere and your greatness being achieved in an arena other than as mother to your brood. You can ask anybody, from Barbara Walters to Cesar Chavez. When you take a step on a public stage that takes you away from your family, even in the cause of great money earning or great social movement or both, the people at home are paying the price along with you.

Donna: No question.

Ruth Ann: Enrolment is in order. If you make decisions that will profoundly affect the other people to whom you have primary promises and commitments, check in with them about the level of their participation in your dream and their level of satisfaction with it.

Donna: I agree. And [they should also] own the results of what the answers are. You could ask those who you love, your family, friends for their take on where they want you to be as well, but don't hold them accountable for your misery if you go by their choices.

Ruth Ann: It's all about being the captain of your own ship and recognizing you're not alone on the sea.

Donna: When I first started my coaching career almost three decades ago, I learned the best lesson ever from my son. I was with him in the recovery room after surgery. He was bandaged and braced on 80% of his body and cracking jokes. I said to him, "What is it about you that could be so happy when you're obviously in terrible pain?" He looked at me and said, "I choose to be happy. It has nothing to do with the rest." That's Michael.

Ruth Ann: Somewhere, there's somebody like Michael showing us how to be a hero. That's what I keep saying. Dave Buck, the head of Coachville, gave a speech some time ago that was based on Thomas Leonard's notion that "confidence can be outsourced." Dave said that one of the strongest deliverables we have to offer as coaches is that our clients confidently outsource their confidence to us. People need a confident presence in their lives. Coaches can hold confidence.

I often tell my clients who don't have confidence that they can do something or meet a particular deadline, "That's OK. You don't have to. I'll hold the confidence for you. I have confidence that you can do that. I would tell you if I didn't and I'd ask you to set a more realistic goal, but I have complete confidence that you can do that. Whenever you think, 'I can't do that,' then think, 'I don't have to think I can do it. Ruth Ann will think that for me.'" It's a great source of comfort to people to know that confidence is available.

I'm big on the re-languaging, Donna. I try to use language of calm. I do not use "September 11th" as shorthand for the terrorist events of 2001. I always refer to "the terrorist events of 2001" when they must be named. Why do I do that? Because September 11th is a perfectly good day on which people were born, wed, and had parties and celebrations. People have good things happen to them every September 11th, just as they did every September 11th before that. If you make a god of the suffering of September 11th, then you rob everyone else in the world of the ability to enjoy September 11th or all the joy that it brings.

I remember when I was a kid that the adults used to not want to have a party on December 7th. Today, I don't think most young people would even think for a moment not to have a party on December 7th. They might think for a moment not to have one on September 11th. I am for bringing September 11th back into the family of a comfortable date. I don't like days that live in infamy. They're all good days. This is all an artificial construct. I don't mind referring to the terrorist event of September 11th. I don't mind referring to other things with non-threatening names.

I would prefer that they number tropical storms, rather than name them. It's not fair to all of the Katrinas of the world. Every time that name is spoken aloud, for a certain generation it will be synonymous with failure, destruction, death, hopelessness, and the worst of humanity that happened during Hurricane Katrina and its aftermath. There are too many Katrinas in the world, and none of them deserve to be tarred and feathered with that. I would like to stop loading language to create negativity. I'm also for unloading it in the overwhelming positive.

Those young people you were talking about, to them, "awesome" is average. "It's awesome!" To my generation, the Grand Canyon would be "awesome." Your new t-shirt? Not so much.

Donna: I learned a new word this week. That word is *chaordic*. Have you ever heard of it?

Ruth Ann: Sure.

Donna: That sums up my work life: chaos and order. I work with clients to help them find harmony within that. Just the concept of taking chaos and making something extraordinary out of it, which is harmony out of chaos, brings a whole new light to the work that we do.

Ruth Ann: I'm *meta* on that, because of living with that man [my husband] with his different perspective. To him, chaos is harmonious.

Donna: For example, I interviewed someone who works with the military. His ultimate goal is to find order and harmony amidst the chaos of their world. They have to do it so he and his team can make timely decisions in complex and turbulent conditions. There's a three-step process to make this happen. Step one is to explore what it would mean to be able to bring order to the chaos. [For example, a sample question might be, "What would it mean to be able to schedule in your emergencies?"] Step two is to see where order might be introduced within the chaos. [For example, "Who are your thought partners so you can get everything you need at the speed of light to move quickly?"] Step three is to do so, such that order and chaos co-exist. [For example, "How can you treat the unexpected as expected?"] When that happens, one stays centered and grounded, responsive rather than reactive, and often is energized by the juxtaposition. One is "dancing in real time." It's about generating a different way of thinking and acting.

Ruth Ann: Mine comes from the perspective of Thomas: "It's all perfect." Some see chaos and some hear harmony. What I see is what is. My husband always says, "The market's never wrong." Whatever it is, that's what it is. It's "right" because that's what it is — therefore, it is!

Donna: It's people's perceptions. One of my goals is to help people notice that their perception is their reality, but also realise that their perception can change.

Ruth Ann: Or it can be that and everybody else's, which is what I like to see. I like to see how many different facets of the diamond there are. Each one reflects light in a unique way.

Donna: What's next for Ruth Ann?

Ruth Ann: Today or in life?

Donna: In life.

Ruth Ann: I am taking the entire year, 2010, as a sabbatical. For the first time in my life, I am going to abstain from doing anything I'd call "work." This will be very difficult for me, because I've been a workaholic since I was 15 years old. In 2010, I'll turn 60, and I want to step way back so I can get some perspective. Who am I, if I am not my job? What good am I, if I'm not working to make a contribution? I intend to spend a year finding out those answers.

And I'll be curious to see if I come up with any ideas worth monetizing. J.K. Rowling had some ideas, but she also took the time to sit down and write them down, work on them, and sell them. She is rich beyond imagining, all because of what grew out of her ideas. The Google boys were tech nerds, just doing what interested them, and they came up with something that literally created billions out of nothing.

To me, it's like *Groundhog Day*. Every day is a brand new day to bring a fresh perspective to the world, to look at the glass as half full if that's what you're looking for. I always laugh about that glass half empty, half full thing. If you're thirsty, that's one thing. If somebody tips it over on your dress, that's a different thing. Right?

Donna: Exactly.

Ruth Ann: Sometimes you'd prefer for the glass to be empty. Sometimes the fuller it is, the better it's going to be for you. I strive for a constant adjustment of perspective with lightness of being. I want to be light, flexible, with eyes on the big picture, charge neutral, and willing to lead.

Donna: You're always supporting people and helping them fly. What do you need for Ruth Ann to support you in what you want to be doing?

Ruth Ann: I need a good coach, and I'm blessed to have one! It may sound like a cliché in the coaching community, but like Sy Sperling in the Hair Club for Men, he's also a member. I'm in the coach club for girls and I'm also a member.

I'm not just a coach and an observer of the coaching landscape; I also am a huge customer of coaching services. I've benefited from them. I developed my way of being through the sophisticated personal teaching of my coaches.

Donna: Is there anything you might benefit from, from the community at large?

Ruth Ann: I would ask the community at large to engage in and encourage constructive, peaceful dialogue in this world. Each of us can always be having more helpful, supportive conversations that encourage and elicit greatness in every one of us. Every one of us could use a champion, a word of encouragement, a courteous gesture, or even 30 seconds of patience from another person. Sometimes, all you need to give back to this world is a bit of personal discipline to keep your own mouth shut and don't escalate. That's what I'm looking for out there.

Donna: This has been fantastic. Thank you. I so appreciate you. I don't get to see you nearly often enough.

Ruth Ann: This may seem funny to you, but I live in such a virtual world that I honestly consider you very much a neighbor on my block. You're somebody I know. I wouldn't hesitate to come down to your house, bang on your door and borrow a cup of sugar. Do you know what I mean?

Donna: I'm ready, Ruth Ann. Any time you want to come down.

Ruth Ann: I mean that in a literal, virtual, and figurative sense. I believe that if I had a disaster and I was reaching out to my community, you're somebody whose input I would crave.

Donna: Thank you.

Ruth Ann: So even though we don't see each other in person very often, I think of you as the lovely lady who lives down the street, that we have a lot in common, and we have a cup of coffee whenever we can.

Donna: I'm going to hold you to that. I thank you from the bottom of my heart.

Ruth Ann: And I, you.

Reflections

Reflections Reflections

We have a unique capacity to change and reshape our lives. As coaches, we have a unique capacity to change others' lives. Life "lives" within every experience and conversation. Awareness can be curative. If we don't pay attention to our impact and the ramifications of what we do, we can't make the changes necessary to build a better life, a life we love. *Generative conversation* — when two or more people really listen to each other and create something new — at least brings new-found awareness and insight. From that point, we can develop people, careers, and organizations. Asking yourself, "What am I not seeing?", "What do I need to know that I don't know?", and "Who do I need to know who I don't know?" opens you to learning and to the realization that you are better *with* them, not better *than* them.

People are fascinating to watch as they evolve. I love observing it happen at so many levels. Every day can bring new bits of knowledge into our lives if we look for them. Focusing on what we expect will give us just that, over and over and over again. Approaching the same situations mindfully gives us so much more. It teaches us to pay attention to the subtleties and opens us up to looking for the unexpected. Approaching life in this way brings possibility to our worlds. I often challenge my clients to be acutely aware of everything around them, and to be ready to have a discussion about it. As a Shadow Coach who attends the same meetings as my clients, it's an opportunity for us to share information we've gathered and to see if we've picked up the same nuances. My clients love to "stump their coach," making them even more mindful of their surroundings and the underlying dynamics in the room.

I want to become redundant and not relied upon. I want to work with my clients so they can be their own observer, making sense of how the pieces in a situational and behavioural puzzle come together. Eventually, they will start to become aware of all the subtleties around them and how they too fit within that puzzle.

Ruth Ann speaks about Thomas Leonard's idea of "It's all perfect": "Some see chaos and some hear harmony." Human-based leaders recognize perfection in every situation. They seek to understand what's perfect (even when it clearly isn't), instead of looking to "fix" things. This is what creates a paradigm shift in how people learn and grow. It shapes what the conversation can look like.

Every time I recall this conversation, it brings a new level of learning for me and effects further change on how I approach my life and my work. When I teach, one of the things I listen for is when a coach tries to guide the conversation to force an outcome. One of the greatest gifts we can give our clients is to help them find a level of comfort living in the questions, rather than having the answers. This reminds me to stay charge neutral: not to have an end in mind, but to pay attention to everything that is revealed, with no judgment. I love how Ruth Ann speaks about "holding confidence" for others. I do that, but now realise I have to let my clients know it. I'm constantly learning the balance between speaking and silence, movement and stillness. This helps me and, in turn, them to slow down to the speed of life in order to make the right choices.

Now I'm wondering: What are my definitions in the context of our conversations? What do I see? How do I see things? What assumptions, expectations, and cultural tethers do I have to let go of to be charge neutral?

Awareness is the key factor in self-growth at every level. You'll often find what you look for in others and yourself. If you're open to the possibilities, you'll get more than you ever dreamed of.

> *"Be daring, be different, be impractical, be anything that will assert integrity of purpose and imaginative vision against the play-it-safers, the creatures of the commonplace, the slaves of the ordinary." – Cecil Beaton*

The human-based leader, first and foremost, cares about her people.
He creates an environment in which everyone works together towards a common goal.
She builds trust with her team.
He acts with integrity at all times and expects the team to do the same.
She has the competence to do her job and the knowledge that goes with the territory.
He sets the vision and defines the mission.
She rouses the people to achieve it.
He provides them with the tools they need to get the job done.
She takes responsibility for her actions and expects others to do the same.
He holds them accountable, fairly and equally, to achieve their tasks.
She steps out of their way and lets them perform.
He rewards them, individually and collectively, when they have accomplished their tasks.
She changes course when the environment dictates the need for change.
He communicates the results of the team's attempts, achievements, and failures.
She listens to their feedback and responds.
He mentors, develops, and coaches others.
She controls that which she can and worries not about that which she cannot.
They take care of their physical selves.
They seek to learn and develop.
They think straight. They talk straight.
They know to have fun, and they do.
They know to rest, and they do.

ED MAIER

CHAPTER 6

RON WORTON
The DNA of a Great Team

Thursday night is Chinese food night at a neighbourhood restaurant with a group of friends. In our usual animated conversation, I mentioned my desire to write this book. Brian Keller, a brilliant mediator and arbitrator, looked at me and said, "You have to call my friend Ron and interview him." I asked, "Who is he and why do you think he would be perfect for my book?" The answer was, "Just call him. Take out your notebook, write down his name, and contact him tomorrow!" I learned a long time ago to never question Brian when it comes to his recommendations ... when it comes to almost anything (unless I want to stir the pot, of course).

So I left the restaurant armed with Ron Worton's info and the intention of contacting him the next morning. The following day, I emailed Ron with a bit of background and a request to interview him. I was intrigued. I had no idea why Brian suggested him but hoped Ron would enlighten me.

All I got back was, "I'd be pleased to do the interview. I do what Brian tells me to do, just like you." We made arrangements to meet, and the rest was revealed in conversation. To say Ron is an extraordinary man is an understatement (thank you, Brian!), and I trust you will agree.

Dr. Ron Worton is a geneticist and researcher. He is the recipient of several national and international awards, including the Gairdner Foundation International Award, the Award of Distinction from the Muscular Dystrophy Association of Canada, the Centenary Medal from the Royal Society of Canada, the E. Mead Johnson Award for Research in Pediatrics, and The Canadian Society for Clinical Investigation Distinguished Scientist Award. He holds honourary degrees from the University of Manitoba and Université Catholique de Louvain (Belgium), and is an honourary Fellow of the Royal College of Physicians and Surgeons of Canada. He is a Fellow of the Royal Society of Canada, a Fellow of the Canadian College of Medical Geneticists, and a member of the Order of Canada.

His quest and drive to identify the gene responsible for Duchenne Muscular Dystrophy, a lethal disease, led to its discovery. Within a six-year period, under his watch as head of (at the time) one of the best-known centres for human genetics research in the world, a group of eight scientists discovered four important disease genes: Duchenne Muscular Dystrophy, Cystic Fibrosis, Fanconi Anemia, and Wilson's Disease.

Ron created new collaborations, encouraging his people to explore stem cell research within their existing research projects. He created the Centre for Stem Cell and Gene Therapy, a multi-disciplinary research centre whose purpose is to develop and apply the latest approaches in the study of stem cells and gene therapy, the first of its kind in Canada.

In his story, you'll see how collaboration was key in discovering the gene for Muscular Dystrophy, and how he built one of the best research teams in the world.

It is my honour and privilege to know Ron and his wonderful wife, Helen. I not only met an extraordinary man through this conversation but feel as if I've made new friends.

Come and meet Ron…

Donna: Ron, I'd just love to dive in and listen to you as you share your story with me.

Ron: I'm a scientist. I grew up in Winnipeg and went into Honours Physics at the University of Manitoba. I thought I was going to be a physicist, but decided fairly soon in the program that was not the case. I didn't like it, and even more important, it didn't like me, so I didn't do well.

I did stick it out and finished with a degree in physics. Then I wanted to do something that was related to health. To link physics to health, I went to the Cancer Foundation and sought some advice. I ended up doing a Masters degree at the Manitoba Cancer Treatment and Research Foundation, now part of Cancer Care Manitoba.

I worked on radiation physics and new technologies for detecting radiation. This is where I met Helen; she was working there. It was a good move. [Turning to his wife, Helen, who was in the room with us, he asks,] "You heard that, didn't you?"

I moved to Toronto for a PhD program in medical biophysics, a deliberate attempt to move away from physics and get involved in biology.

I read enough background information to know that the University of Toronto Medical Biophysics Department, located at the Ontario Cancer Institute, was involved in a lot of biology projects. Many of the scientists were former physicists, so they brought a physics perspective, which was good for me as it applied to biology.

I had no idea what I would be interested in working on. I was assigned to a supervisor whose laboratory, two years earlier, discovered stem cells, so I got in on the ground floor of stem cell research in 1965.

I finished a PhD in stem cell research in 1969, then spent almost three years as a research fellow at Yale. It was not a good experience. I didn't like the environment with its highly competitive nature, particularly because it was secretive.

My research supervisor didn't even want us to talk to people on other floors in the building for fear that they would steal our ideas — which was completely ludicrous. We did it anyway, but it resulted in a very tense relationship and relatively few publications. So in one sense, it was not at all a good experience. In another, I learned from that situation; I learned never to be secretive about science.

I came back to Canada to the Hospital for Sick Children (now affectionately known as "SickKids") in Toronto in 1971, and stayed 25 years less one month. At SickKids, I was in genetics, but with no formal training in genetics. In those days, many of those who went into genetics didn't have much formal training, because it didn't officially exist.

Modern genetics, which is based on analysis of DNA and chromosomes, was just beginning. That's what I wanted to get in on. When I took the job at SickKids, it was to study chromosome abnormalities in kids and babies born with congenital defects. We offered prenatal diagnostic services (that was early days of prenatal diagnosis), and did research on chromosomes.

As I said, I had virtually no experience. The only reason I was hired is that Lou Siminovitch, the department head who hired me (who also didn't have any formal genetics training, yet he was a world famous geneticist), had known me at the Ontario Cancer Institute where I did my PhD in biophysics. As part of the stem cell research group, he'd heard me speak many times. He hired me on faith, knowing full well that my experience and knowledge base in genetics was weak.

It worked out well. I took over the diagnostic chromosome lab from the Department of Pathology. When I inherited it, the lab was a year behind in reporting. The staff of eight had a strong sense of entitlement and little work ethic. That's where I learned my second lesson. After I'd been there six months, I fired the whole lab, or at least seven of the eight. I was 29 years old at the time. I didn't even ask the Department of Human Resources what to do or how to do it. I just did it, and then I went and told them it was done. They said, "You what? You can't do that!" I said, "I did. It's done. They've all signed letters of resignation which I prepared for them, and they're leaving in three months."

I hired a whole new staff. Now it was my people, people who I had chosen, people who had a strong work ethic, people who were committed to getting rid of the year-long backlog. We devised ways to do that by cutting corners, using "quick and dirty" analysis to get reports out the door and the backlog eliminated.

When you look at experiences that guide people, this was a great one. I learned that if you're going to make progress, you have to have the right people. To have the right people, you sometimes have to make tough choices. Not all scientists do that. I've seen scientists who have struggled with staff who are less than ideal, just because they don't have the courage to make the decision to let somebody go.

By the way, I learned something else from that situation. Every one of those people that were let go landed on their feet in another job.

Donna: So they were great people, but the wrong fit?

Ron: They were in the wrong place, or it didn't work for them coming together in a team, because they had developed a culture that was poisonous and a work ethic that was bad. I think being let go shocked all of them. They ended up in different places.

That taught me another valuable lesson: Don't feel too guilty about terminating someone's employment. This was confirmed many years later when I had to fire a professional PhD geneticist, who thought she was doing a terrific job when she wasn't. She was really bitter when she heard the news and remained so for weeks. However, to my surprise, a year and a half later, she came back and thanked me. She was retired and playing tennis every day. She needed that lifestyle change. That's not why I let her go, but that was the end result.

Coming back to my job at SickKids, I started there in '71, ran the diagnostic lab for many years, until about '81, and then I had a unique opportunity. Our research was going well, and I was publishing good science, but the relevance of the research to human health was not clear.

I was studying basic mechanisms of chromosome structure and function in cells, and it just wasn't clear to me, or to anyone else, how relevant that was to human health. We all realised that someday these kinds of basic research studies would provide information that would help our understanding of genetics, and maybe, eventually, our understanding of genetic disease. But that wasn't enough for me.

Between '79 and '81, I had an opportunity to switch over to a project that led to the identification of the gene that causes Muscular Dystrophy. The kind we were working on is called Duchenne Muscular Dystrophy. It was a common disease that affected approximately 1 in 3,300 males at birth. It was lethal. Most of the affected boys would die between the age of 14 and 21, and if they didn't die, they only survived because they were kept alive on a respirator.

I had never had more than a peripheral interest in the disease. In 1979, a post-doctoral fellow, a pediatrician from Belgium named Christine Verellen, came to train in my lab.

When she first came, Christine told me about a girl with Muscular Dystrophy. This piqued my interest, since girls don't usually get Duchenne Muscular Dystrophy, because it's X-linked — the defective gene is carried in the X chromosome. Did you know about that?

Donna: No, I didn't.

Ron: If girls carry the defective gene on one of their two X chromosomes, they're carriers. They don't get the disease, because they have another X chromosome that produces the protein that is required. Compare this to boys who have an X and Y chromosome. If they inherit the chromosome from their mother that carries the defective gene, then they get the disease, because they don't have a second X to compensate.

Furthermore, Christine told me that this patient in Belgium, who at that time was about 11 or 12 years old, had a re-arrangement of the chromosomes, in which part of the X chromosome had exchanged with part of chromosome 21.

We talked about this for quite a while after she arrived. We wondered if the break in the X chromosome had disrupted a gene that you normally need to make a muscle protein that prevents you from getting Muscular Dystrophy. If that gene is broken and a portion of the gene has gone over to chromosome 21 and the rest has remained on the X, then that would prevent that gene from functioning to make its protein product. That could potentially cause the disease.

However, she would have had another normal X chromosome. But I knew from my experience and reading the literature, that in girls who carry *translocations* (chromosome rearrangements) involving an X chromosome, their other normal X is usually totally inactive.

The normal X — the one that's not involved in the translocation — is inactivated in all cells. So we concluded that in Christine's Belgian patient, if the break in the X chromosome breaks through the gene on one X, and if the other X is inactive (ergo, no product being made), this could explain her Muscular Dystrophy.

Donna: What kept you going?

Ron: After these discussions with Dr. Verellen, we decided that she would work on this problem and try to prove that the normal X was inactive in all the cells in the body. She examined about 100 cells in two different tissues of the body, and 97% of the time it was the normal X that was inactive. That lent further credence to the idea that the translocation had broken through the gene. During that period, there were six other cases published: one from France, one from Britain, one from Hawaii, one from Japan and two from the U.S. All were women with Muscular Dystrophy.

Even more important, every one of them had a translocation between the X and some other chromosome, and in every case the break in the X was in the same place. So we concluded that the gene that you need to prevent Muscular Dystrophy must be located at that site on the X chromosome. When it's broken — disrupted by these translocations — it causes the disease.

After Christine went back to Belgium, having finished her term and completing her job of proving the inactivation of the normal X, I decided that I would try to use that information to identify the gene that causes the disease. What we would have to do is identify the stretch of DNA in the X chromosome that spanned across that translocation. A DNA molecule is like a very long ladder, and each gene occupies a certain number of rungs on the ladder. The challenge was to find the rung on the ladder where the X chromosome DNA broke to form the translocation. We expected that this rung would be somewhere in the gene.

So, if we could purify DNA from cells of the patient and identify a fragment of DNA that had part X chromosome and part chromosome 21 (because that's what was involved in the exchange), then that place on the X should be somewhere within the Muscular Dystrophy gene. Then we should be able to identify the rest of the gene and the product that is made from that gene. From there, we could determine the cause of the disease and, maybe, eventually a cure. It took five years, but that's what we did.

I started in '82 but the idea had been firmly implanted in '81. I went to my boss, Lou Siminovitch, and said, "Here's the idea. I think we can identify the gene that causes Muscular Dystrophy, but I need your help. I need you to hire somebody to replace me to run the diagnostic service lab, because I can't do both. I need you to give me a few months sabbatical, so I can go to other labs and learn to do this kind of stuff. I've never handled a DNA molecule in my life."

I told him we would be able to do the job in less than five years. I then wrote a grant application to get the money to do it, which I submitted to two different places. Both places funded it.

Here's another lesson learned. Dr. Siminovitch had the courage to say, "Yes, I agree this is a good project; this is what you should be doing. I'll find the money to hire somebody to replace you to run the lab." He did, with support from Aser Rothstein, the head of the SickKids Research Institute.

I took a course in a place called Cold Spring Harbor, New York, which is on Long Island. It is probably the number one research establishment in the world, run by Jim Watson, *the* Watson of "Watson and Crick" who discovered that DNA was the genetic material. The course almost killed me, because I was the oldest person in the class. We worked from 9 a.m. until 2 a.m. every day for three weeks, except for Saturday evenings, which we had off. My young colleagues in their early 20s were thriving on it; I was 41 and I was really struggling.

Following the course and a few days to recover, I went to a lab in Pennsylvania for a little while, and I learned some additional technology, particularly relating to chromosome 21. I needed to know about the structure of chromosome 21, and this was the one lab in the world that had that information, so I spent considerable time there. I collaborated with them after that, travelling back and forth to Philadelphia every month or two for the next three years.

By '86, five years from the concept and four years from when I actually started the project, we identified a piece of DNA from the patient that had part of the X chromosome and part of chromosome 21; in other words, the translocation junction.

We then showed that the DNA from this part of the X chromosome was missing in about 6% of boys with Muscular Dystrophy. We said, "OK, this DNA has to be a part of the gene. These boys with the disease are carrying deletions in the X chromosome. It's deleting part of the Muscular Dystrophy gene; therefore, they can't make the complete protein, and that's what causes the disease." We went on to identify the protein that is made by this gene, a protein which we and others named *Dystrophin*.

Because we weren't experts on the study of proteins, we collaborated with a guy named George Karpati at McGill University. Karpati was one of the world experts on using immunotechnology to localize proteins in cells. He was an expert in muscle. I went to visit him, told him what we had, and said, "You're the world's expert on identifying where proteins are in cells. If we give you the antibodies that we've prepared against this protein, would you be interested?"

Man, was he ever interested! It was like a dream come true for him! So he did that part of the project. We identified it as a membrane protein and showed that in boys with Duchenne Muscular Dystrophy, this protein was always missing in 100% of cases, an absolute one-to-one correspondence.

Looking back, I did one other thing which was important for my career development. When I made the decision to go into Muscular Dystrophy research, I wound down every other project in my lab and put total focus on this one project. By the end of four years when we discovered the gene, we had 14 people in the lab working full-time on that one project, everybody doing a different aspect of it. If we hadn't focused like that, there's no way we would have discovered the gene. In fact, we had a competitor, Lou Kunkel at Harvard University, who also discovered the gene three months before us through a different route. However, we were able to publish, within three months of his publication, with new information he didn't have.

He identified the protein and called it *Dystrophin*, but he didn't show that it was in the membrane. With George Karpati, we showed that it was in the membrane, so it was a series of Kunkel-Worton publications over a three year period that built the story together. If we hadn't focused, if we had been a year behind instead of three months behind, all the publications would have been his, and we would have been out of the picture.

That's important for my career and the careers of people in my lab who were training. More importantly, the fact that we were both publishing in unison, one after the other, meant that we were building a more complete and credible story than if either lab alone had been doing it. Any doubters of the way either of us did it were convinced by the fact that we approached it in two completely different ways and ended up with exactly the same results.

Again, another lesson learned is to *collaborate*. Find the experts who know how to do stuff, learn from them, and then apply it. In the case of my colleague at McGill, it wasn't about learning from him how to do it. It was just giving him [Karpati] the antibodies that allowed him to do it, so we could get it done in three weeks instead of three years.

I visited his lab a few times and he visited us. More importantly, the people in his lab and the people in my lab worked together, exchanged information, talked on the telephone regularly, and visited one another. By that point, it was more of collaboration between the people in our labs. George and I simply set it up and helped it get started.

Donna: Collaboration between labs — that's interesting. Tell me more about that. It must have been very powerful to create this inter-lab collaborative team.

Ron: Yes. Things get done much faster, because your learning curve is shorter. If somebody else can do the job that it would take you a year to learn how to do, then it's much better just to let somebody else do it.

Donna: Were there any periods of time within this time frame where you said, "I'm hitting my head against the wall," or, alternatively, "Nothing will stop me"?

Ron: Both. There were lots of setbacks. There were lots of times when we wished that it would go faster and tried to figure out how to do an end run around this problem or that problem. But, I don't recall a single second when we doubted the end result, because the project was so solid. We knew what we had to do. We had to find this one piece of DNA, had a sound strategy to do just that, and when we had it in our hands, we knew what we had to do with it.

I wrote my first grant application on this project in '81 and submitted it to the Medical Research Council and the Muscular Dystrophy Association of Canada. The comments were, "This project has to work!" I laid out a whole five-year plan, and they said, "The plan is absolutely sound; the project has to work! Our only doubt is whether Worton can do it. He's never done any research of this kind before." It was a legitimate concern. Of course, the Muscular Dystrophy Association was willing to take the chance, because the end result was so important for them.

Donna: Do you think it was to your benefit, having not done this before? You had no previous experience to give you doubts along the way.

Ron: Probably. I had no preconceptions. There were lots of people in the field with preconceptions about what caused the disease and who were paddling up the wrong creek. That's another important point regarding the research we were doing. There were thousands of researchers in the world, hundreds of them working full-time on Muscular Dystrophy, on ideas and approaches that couldn't possibly work. Of course, they didn't know that at the time, but once we discovered the gene, and the protein made by the gene, all of that other research came to a grinding halt. Everybody switched over to work on Dystrophin.

Donna: So the ripple effect was extraordinary.

Ron: Huge! In the early '80s up to 1986, I would go to Muscular Dystrophy research conferences and I would hear talks on every aspect — some people saying this was a membrane disease, some saying it wasn't the membrane, and some saying it was an energy problem, etc. Within two years of the Dystrophin discovery, I would go to a meeting on Muscular Dystrophy, and everybody in the meeting would be working on some aspect of Dystrophin and what it was doing.

Donna: You focused the world in many ways.

Ron: Yes. Then the inevitable happened. Once that had all been published and the research turned to the study of Dystrophin, instead of the study of the genes, it became a protein project, the study of a very large protein.

I'd already gone through a learning curve to learn how to work with DNA and chromosomes. It was another huge learning curve for me to learn how to work with proteins, isolate them, and characterize them. Of course, there were people in the world who were instantly able to do that, because they'd been trained all their lives as protein chemists. One of them was a guy named Kevin Campbell in Iowa, who had trained in Toronto just down the street from SickKids.

Donna: Unreal. That close to where you were!

Ron: I didn't know him at the time, but I got to know him well afterwards. Kevin was an expert in this area. He got antibodies from us to help recognize the protein. He quickly showed that Dystrophin in the membrane of the muscle fibre doesn't sit there in the membrane all by itself; it is actually attached to a group of proteins, seven or eight in total, depending on how you count. There's the fibre inside this whole complex of proteins and there's the membrane. Kevin and many others in the field said, "OK, there are 14 different kinds of Muscular Dystrophy. They're all genetic diseases. Why don't we look and see if this complex is missing in the kids with other forms of Muscular Dystrophy?"

The idea was that if all 14 other kinds of Muscular Dystrophy are caused by a defective gene, maybe the genes that cause those other forms are the genes that encode these proteins in the complex. If you knock out any one of those proteins in the complex, you cause the disease. It turned out to be true.

Kevin collaborated with groups, primarily in France, to show that Limb-Girdle Muscular Dystrophy, Congenital Muscular Dystrophy, and a couple of other kinds of Muscular Dystrophy are all genetic diseases caused by mutations in the genes that encode these other proteins and are part of the complex.

Not only did this research change the approach to Duchenne Muscular Dystrophy, but to every other kind of Muscular Dystrophy. In the course of the next five years, it resulted in virtually every gene causing every kind of Muscular Dystrophy being identified and characterized, not by me, but by other people.

We quickly fell behind in the protein work, because we weren't the world's experts. I was lamenting about that one time to the VP of the Muscular Dystrophy Association in the U.S.

He said, "That's the way of the world — how things work. You make your discovery, you make your contribution, but your expertise is not the right kind of expertise to take it to the next level. Somebody else has to step in and do that." I never regretted it. It would've been nicer, of course, if we'd had that kind of expertise as well as described the entire story, but at the end of the day I was part of an important story that many people contributed to.

Kevin Campbell became a close friend. Lou Kunkel, my competitor at Harvard, became a close friend. The third person who was working on the Muscular Dystrophy gene, and who also created a lot of excitement at the time but didn't identify the gene in time, was Kay Davies. Kay became the youngest professor in the history of Oxford University and also became a close friend. In fact, before the gene was discovered, about '84 or '85, the BBC had heard about all of this through the various Muscular Dystrophy Associations in Britain and the U.S. They decided to do an hour-long documentary, called *The Race for the Gene*.

They highlighted the work of Kay Davies at Oxford, Lou Kunkel at Harvard, and me at SickKids. They did it very well. They came to our labs, interviewed us, talked to our people, took pictures in the labs, showed the approach, and created really good diagrams of chromosomes.

The documentary began with the music from the movie, *Chariots of Fire*. It was the scene from the movie where they showed feet pounding on the beach. They ended up with three runners carrying three flags; British, Canadian, and American. As the race was developing, and one lab was moving ahead of the other, they had the flag of that country moving ahead of the others. It was silly but very effective.

Donna: People remember things like that.

Ron: Exactly. I hadn't even thought of telling you that story, but it does illustrate the level of interest around the world. The Muscular Dystrophy Associations were now pegging their hopes on the three of us. They knew the gene was going to be discovered in one of these three labs, just not when and where.

A lot of money was pouring into these three labs. In those days, I had no problem getting enough money to do the research. Normally, you have to write a big grant application and wait for up to ten months to see if you're going to get it.

Once we got funding from the Muscular Dystrophy Association of Canada and the Medical Research Council here, I got a call one day from the Muscular Dystrophy Association in the United States. They said, "We've heard about your project, and we want to fund it. How much do you need?"

Donna: That's awesome!

Ron: All they wanted was a two-pager. They said, "Just write me something for our files that we can justify giving you this money." That didn't continue. After that, we had to justify our progress before we got more money. That was the Muscular Dystrophy story, but there is more!

In 1985, when we were in the peak of all of this activity, the head of genetics of SickKids, Lou Siminovitch, turned 65. SickKids had a mandatory retirement policy at 65, so Lou had to retire. He went across the street and started a new research institute at Mount Sinai, because they didn't have such a retirement policy. I replaced him as the head of genetics.

From '85–'95 while we were maximally involved in this research, I was head of the department. When I took over, there was a young guy by the name of Lap-Chee Tsui who didn't have a permanent position. He was looking for somewhere to work. I had a couple of positions to offer and as he was really good, I offered him a permanent position.

He started working on the gene for Cystic Fibrosis [CF], undoubtedly the most common genetic disease in Caucasians. It has a frequency of about 1 in 2,000. Huge! CF is more than double the frequency of Muscular Dystrophy, because it affects males and females equally.

Lap-Chee started working on CF in competition with labs in Britain and in the U.S. He mapped the gene to chromosome 7 in '87, so this was between our discovery of the Duchenne Muscular Dystrophy gene in '86 and our discovery of its encoded protein in '88. In 1989, Lap-Chee's lab discovered the CF gene and the protein made by the gene, which made world headlines. He had a collaborator in the U.S. as well. It was funded by both the U.S. and Canada, and part of the funding was set up by the Howard Hughes Foundation.

In fact, when we did the press conference for that one, because it was such a big deal and the research was done in both countries, there was a big battle as to where the press conference was going to be held. We insisted it had to be done at SickKids, because most of the research was done there, and the compromise was that we get the press conference in Toronto at 9:00 in the morning. This is unusually early, but we did it then so it would be over by 10:00. A helicopter picked up Lap-Chee and his collaborators from the roof of SickKids and flew them out to Howard Hughes' private jet, which flew them to Washington, D.C. to another helicopter, which flew them to the roof of the Washington Press Building. There, they held the second press conference on the roof of the building overlooking Washington, D.C.

This tells you how important these discoveries were, how much press coverage there was, and how much importance was attached to details — even to where the press conference was being held. I didn't go on the plane with them to Washington, D.C. I stayed behind to answer questions for the local press.

So Duchenne Muscular Dystrophy came first, then CF, and then the gene for Fanconi Anemia, a disease which causes congenital defects along with anemia. That discovery was made by Manuel Buchwald, who later became the Scientific Director of the SickKids Research Institute. At about the same time, Diane Cox, who had also retrained herself to work on DNA, discovered the gene for Wilson's Disease, a disease that causes excess copper in the body, which results in all kinds of problems. She discovered that the gene is one that makes a protein that is involved in copper metabolism and clears copper from the body.

Those were four pretty important disease genes discovered in a six-year period by a group of eight scientists, all working on the same floor in the Elm Street wing of SickKids. Arguably, it established us as the best-known centre for human genetics research in the world at that time.

Donna: What enticed you to move away from all that?

Ron: My research was coming to an end. I'd done about everything I could on the Muscular Dystrophy story by '92 or '93; we were cleaning up loose ends. My term as head of genetics was coming up, and the rule was that you couldn't be head of a department for more than ten years — a good rule, by the way. I think it always encourages new blood and new ideas.

I was trying to decide whether I should go on a sabbatical and retrain to do something else, go into some other aspect of research or take on a new leadership role. I just wasn't sure what I was going to do. I got a call from a head hunter working for the Ottawa General Hospital, who said, "We're looking for a leader to start a new research institute at the hospital. Are you interested?"

Initially, I said no, because I was looking at another possibility, which was to form a genetic discovery company in Toronto. I had signed a non-disclosure agreement with some investors, stating that I would explore this to the fullest extent over a 90-day period, and during that period, I wouldn't look at any other opportunities.

I had to say no to Ottawa, but I told them that the non-disclosure agreement ended in September, and to call me back in September, if the position was still open. She did. I went for the interview. I guess they liked what they heard, and I liked what I saw.

Donna: What was the Institute?

Ron: At that time, my title was Director of Research at the Ottawa General Hospital. My mandate was to build a research institute by two routes. One was to bring together all the existing research in and related to the hospital. There was already a cancer research group. There was already a neuroscience research group working on stroke. There was already a small group of clinicians doing clinical trials. The mandate was to somehow bring all these groups under the same umbrella. In addition, the other route was to start a new research program largely of my choosing in the area of genetics.

To make this possible, they had built a new research floor of 22,000 square feet, which would house 10-12 scientists and their research groups. They had produced an endowment of $22 million. The interest would be available to me, and I estimated that would be somewhere in the neighbourhood of $1.5 million a year. I could pay a lot of scientists' salaries with that.

Donna: So you got the endowment, the research group in genetics … what was your driving force to do more and more? Was there something in the back of your mind that kept telling you, "I want to accomplish this. This is something I have to do."

Ron: By this time, I knew for certain that I wasn't going to be the one to develop the cure for Muscular Dystrophy. I had taken it to a logical point and tied up all the loose ends that I could. Thus, when I decided to move, there was both push and pull. The push was I'd finished my ten years as the head of genetics, and I had to do something else. The pull was the opportunity to carry the research to a new level through the next generation of scientists I would bring to Ottawa.

Furthermore, when the offer from the Ottawa Hospital came along, it seemed like the perfect opportunity to move to a city that I liked. Helen and I had always decided that if we left Toronto, there were only two places we would go: Ottawa or Vancouver, and I'd already turned down a job in Vancouver. So coming to Ottawa was pleasing for both of us. Helen was ready to retire from her job so the timing was right for her. The timing couldn't have been better for me, because I ended one job on June 30th — the end of my 25 years at SickKids — and I started in Ottawa on August 1st with one month of vacation in between.

That was the one month that made me short on my 25 years at SickKids.

The pull was the $22 million endowment, 22,000 square feet of research space, and an opportunity to build a research institute by pulling people together.

When asked in front of the search committee how I would do that and what my own research plans were, I said, "If I come here to develop this research institute, that's my number one priority. Everything else gets pushed to the side, including my own research, if necessary." I knew that was important. I'd seen people take over other research institutes and continue to treat their own lab as their number-one priority, then fail as an institute director.

Donna: It's because you're splitting your focus.

Ron: Yes, and not only that. If your own lab is your top priority, and a lot of the resources that you're given to develop the institute go into your own lab, you create huge resentment. I've seen that happen, too.

Donna: People look at it as self-serving.

Ron: Everything that I did was going to be for the people that I recruited and hired. It was the right decision and paid huge dividends down the road.

When I did my final interview and the president of the hospital offered me the position, we moved quickly. This was in January '96. I was on my third visit. The job was offered on a Tuesday. Jacques LaBelle, who was president of the hospital, said, "I'll fax it to you on Thursday morning," which happened. We made the decision on Thursday evening, phoned a real estate agent we'd been in contact with earlier on Friday morning, and made arrangements to come the next day on Saturday. We put in an offer on a house on Saturday, it was accepted on Sunday, and I went into SickKids on Monday morning and said, "This is what's happening." You only do stuff like that if you're convinced that it's the right thing to do.

Donna: That was fast.

If I asked you what your impact is on the world, what is the first thing that comes to mind?

Ron: Let me answer that question in two ways. First, in terms of *past* impact, there's no question the Muscular Dystrophy gene discovery had a big impact in the field of science, of Muscular Dystrophy in particular, by changing everyone's research direction and pointing the way to all these other gene discoveries.

At the end of the day, if and when we have a cure for Muscular Dystrophy (I say "when" because I think we will; it won't be a total cure, but it'll be a treatment), the path to that treatment will be traceable back to those initial discoveries, no question. That's one, in the past.

Second, in the *future*, I think the work that I did here in Ottawa was equally important, maybe even more important for future discovery, so I'd like to dwell on that for a bit.

When I started, you heard me say it was the General Hospital, and then shortly after I came, the two hospitals merged — well, actually four hospitals merged. The Grace closed, and the Riverside became a day hospital. The Civic and the General remained as the two academic centres of the hospital. The Civic had a research institute called the "Loeb Institute." I was at the General.

Prior to the merger, those hospitals were enemies. The research institutes were not quite such strong enemies, but nevertheless they were distrustful of one another. When the hospitals merged, it took two years before the foundations merged. During that two-year period, there were separate foundations raising money for the two separate sites, the Loeb Institute and the General, even though the hospitals had merged into one. We couldn't merge the research institutes until the foundations merged, because a lot of our support came from those foundations. It was very complicated.

On the other hand, it wasn't very complicated to make the decision to merge the hospitals because the government said, "Thou shalt merge," and that was it; no discussion. The merging of the foundations and establishing the conditions under which they could merge was a two-year project. The hospitals merged on April 1, 1998. The foundations merged on April 1, 2000, and the research institutes merged a year later.

When the institutes merged, they were both about the same size; each had about 50 scientists. At that time, the Loeb had already been established for 12 years, and the General had only been established for five.

The fair thing to do was to say, "This is a new institute. It's not one absorbing the other. This is a new institute based on the merger of equal partners. We're going to seek the best leader for this new institute that we can get in an international search. The two current leaders will step down. They're invited to be candidates, but they're not guaranteed the job."

The leader of the other institute by that time was Michel Chrétien, brother of the Prime Minister. Michel was not in favour of the merger; he wanted to keep the Loeb separate and fought the merger. I was in favour of it from the beginning, arguing that you can't have two different institutes in one hospital. It would never work.

We both sought the position. Despite the fact that we were both good, credible scientists and established leaders, the fact that I had been arguing for merger the whole time and he had been fighting it made the choice obvious. Once I was appointed, my first task was to integrate two institutes with quite different cultures into a new institute called The Ottawa Health Research Institute [OHRI].

The Loeb Institute had four research programs: neuroscience, developmental biology, aging, and clinical epidemiology. At the General, I had brought together a cancer research program, a neuroscience program, a vision research program and had developed a new molecular medicine program focused on Muscular Dystrophy and related disorders. Each institute had about 50 scientists and the combined budget including all the research grants and everything for the two operations was about $27 million a year. That was in 2001.

On the day of the merger, we had a single budget and reduced four programs at each site to six programs in total. For example, we had a neuroscience research program at each site and we made it into one program with one director, everybody worked together. We did the same with cancer and clinical epidemiology or clinical research. The eye institute was only on one site, so vision research remained at one site.

By this time, I'd pretty much closed my lab. I had some young people working with me when I moved. My goal by that time was to let them finish their projects, publish their papers, and move onto the next stage in their career. I didn't continue to build my lab after that.

I put most of my efforts into writing institutional proposals. Instead of writing a grant proposal to support my lab, I wrote institutional proposals to bring an infrastructure to support the institute. That's how we got our new stem cell centre.

Michel Chrétien had also written a proposal to develop a protein engineering site at the Loeb, which later was part of the OHRI. He brought in about $4.2 million and I had brought in about $8.8 million for the stem cell centre that ended up costing a lot more than that. Then I had written another proposal that brought in $2 or $3 million. Between Michel and myself, we succeeded in obtaining about $25 million to support infrastructure over that time period.

We had the foundation working for us, developing matching funds, because a lot of these federal government programs required matching funds. The foundation had raised about $18 million for us over a five-year period. In fact, they raised $40 million; $18 million was for infrastructure, and the rest was for operating expenses.

Jack Kitts had been appointed head of the hospital shortly after the merger. The foundation had gone on to its $100 million campaign. It had been agreed that $40 million of the $100 million would be for research. Again, being the director of the institute, it was up to me how that $40 million was spent.

The bottom line is that by the time I retired, we had an institute with 106 excellent scientists who were well funded, almost 300 physicians doing research (most doing it part-time), and about 30 of them were full-time clinical researchers with a small patient responsibility as well. We had about 275 trainees, graduate students, and research fellows, and about 700 support staff. Altogether, we had 1,400 people with an annual budget of about $85 million, which continues today.

My successor, Dr. Duncan Stuart, has done well. He's just pulled in $32 million in grant money to continue building on the stem cell front, now called "regenerative medicine," because stem cells regenerate tissues. He's the perfect person to replace me, because as a physician and a cardiologist, he can do some things that I couldn't do (since I'm not a physician).

He's a good, well-recognized scientist. He has a lab. He has people in his lab. He brought a young guy who runs his lab, and it's a good synergy. I think this institute is going to continue to grow, and five years from now, it's going to be over $100 million a year.

I don't think they're going to grow in the number of scientists; we had agreed that it was getting too big. However, by constantly recruiting and making sure we keep the best people (and anybody who shows weakness and fails to get grants doesn't stay), that is the recipe for success. We have no tenure and no guarantee of lifetime employment.

Donna: No tenure?

Ron: Everybody gets recruited with the understanding that they have to remain productive. They're reviewed every three years at the beginning. After six years, they can get promoted to senior scientist. Sometimes, if they're not productive enough, they're not promoted, in which case they get another three years. At the end of nine years, they may get promoted to senior scientist. If they don't, they get a year to find another job. Once they become senior scientists, they are reviewed every five years. If they fail their review again, they get a year to find another job.

Donna: Tell me more about that.

Ron: One of the things that I thought we did well (and I did it in collaboration with the scientists themselves) is we spelled out and wrote down our expectations. When you're hired as a scientist, what we expect from you in the first year, the first three years, the first five years, and in every five-year interval after is spelled out. Our expectations at each review cycle are based on the same criterion categories: the number of publications, quality of publications, amount of grant money, training of students and fellows, size of lab, or size of research enterprise if it doesn't involve a lab, etc. When we review people and say to them you're not making it, it's judged against criteria that we clearly laid out at the beginning.

A couple of people who were forced to leave were a little bitter; several others who had to leave said, "I understand why."

Donna: Excellent. Communicating that well is a feat in itself.

Ron: We weeded out about seven people after the merger. About one to two a year didn't make it and moved on to something else. That allowed us to renew and bring on new people at the same time.

Donna: So you're maintaining a level of excellence, which is the whole point.

Ron: Yes. It's important in every field of endeavour. In a company, you can measure people's value to the company by the role that they play and the number of widgets the company sells. In research it's a little more difficult, although there are things you can measure that I mentioned before.

Donna: Have you ever had somebody who, within that final year, blew you away so that you retracted that and wanted to keep them on?

Ron: One.

Donna: Only one?

Ron: Yes.

Donna: I was wondering if that was an option at all.

Ron: Yes.

Donna: If you were able to speak to the next wave coming into research who are just starting out, what would you tell them?

Ron: Good question.

It's a tough career. What's difficult is that usually people are in their early 30s by the time they get their credentials: their MDs, PhDs, or whatever. If they're physician scientists they're probably closer to 35 to 36, so you're starting late. People can be pretty good scientists for the first eight to ten years and then flounder. What do you do with people who are 45 years old? There aren't a lot of fallback positions. For physician scientists, it's better, because they can fall back on just being a physician, and they can make a lot of money. They can increase their income by failing at being a scientist. For a PhD scientist, it's much more difficult, because the number of fallback opportunities is much more limited. They can go into community college teaching or a job at a university that's not so highly dependent on research.

I let somebody go in my last year that was 55ish, maybe 54. That's too young to retire, too young to be without a job, but he wasn't making it, and we're not going to continue to pay people who aren't making it.

Donna: It takes a lot of courage to let go of somebody who is in that age group.

Ron: It's easier as you do it more often, although it never gets really easy. It's clearly for the benefit of the organization. If you don't do it, the organization is going to go down the tubes. As I mentioned earlier, people frequently land on their feet after such an experience and end up in a job that they actually like better.

Donna: So you would tell this new wave that it's a very tough career to go into?

Ron: You have to be good at it. If you're not good at it, you're not going to make it. You have to be aware of that. Think about what your options might be in that case.

Those who are really outstanding in the first ten years usually don't have a problem later. They're the ones that just have a knack for it, they work hard, and they're smart. There are other smart people who work hard who don't make it, because it requires a certain kind of insight. For example, determining the next experiment you should do when there are 12 options. If you pick wrong half the time, you're in trouble.

You have to be competitive and prepared to compete with people in other places. If you want this institute in Ottawa to be a world leader, that tells you that your competitors are world leaders, right? You're competing with Harvard, Yale, Princeton, and Caltech. Those are your competitors, not the "University of Nowhere."

Donna: What else would you tell them?

Ron: Quality is more important than quantity. Yes, we count publications. If you haven't published anything in three years, there's a problem. However, in any three-year period, I would rather see two high-quality publications in a major journal like *Nature* or *Science,* that have big impact and are getting cited by scientists around the world, than 15 papers in lesser journals that have relatively little impact. In that situation, you're churning out data, you're spinning your wheels, but you're not having an impact. In that case, why do it?

Donna: If it's a very competitive field, what is their support network, if any, while they're living it?

Ron: Their support network is their colleagues and the people around them. Most scientists choose a place to work based on the quality of the people around them, at least most of the top scientists do. Having really smart colleagues on the same floor in the same building doing similar kinds of research, as long as they're able to work together and talk to one another, is very helpful.

It goes beyond scientist 'A' talking to scientist 'B.' It's the students in scientist A's lab *talking* to the students in scientist B's lab every day over lunch, over coffee, or a beer at the end of the day. Those are the connections that are extremely valuable. When a student in lab 'A' can't figure out how to do this or that experiment, and they can talk to a student or a research fellow in lab 'B' who says, "I know how to do that. I learned how to do that last month. Here's what you need to do," bingo, there's the solution.

Being in the right environment — we talk about the quality of a research environment. We talk about a critical mass, usually considered to be six scientists, each with a lab of about ten people. We're talking 50 to 60 people to make a critical mass of active research. If you have that, then you have enough critical mass. If you have doubled that, it's better. Most really good young scientists know that, because they worked as part of their training in such labs and they've seen the benefits.

Part of my problem in coming here was recruiting. I had an empty building. I tried to recruit some top scientists. I went to three people at McGill, one at McMaster, and one at the University of Toronto, where I said, "I want you to come to Ottawa."

They said "Why would I come to Ottawa? I'm a professor at McGill. I've got tenure with a job for life at McGill. I've got a big lab with 25 people in it. I've got good grant support and I'm having fun. Why would I want to come to Ottawa when I don't know what it is you're building, what you're doing, or how it's going to succeed?"

After I talked to five people like that and got the same answer, not surprisingly, I said "OK, who are you training? Tell me about some research fellows in your labs who might like to stay in Canada. Give me the list of your best ones, and ask them to contact me, or I'll contact them." That's what I did, and I started to recruit those people. I selected eight out of maybe 80 serious applications. There were a lot more applications than that, there were ten times that many, but 80% of them were weeded out in the first pass. I recruited eight pretty good people, and they all are still there and productive.

I applied the rule that I learned from Lou Siminovitch: "Don't just recruit people who are good on paper. Listen carefully to what they have to say. Listen to what they're telling you, and look for two things: Are they forward-thinking and expressing ideas that are *avant garde*, and secondly, do you like them?" Are these the people that you would like to interact with on a daily basis? Can you have fun with these people? Can you talk with them and enjoy their company? If the answer to that is no, don't hire them.

Of the five senior scientists that I tried to recruit and failed, one of them was Michael Rudnicki. He was at McMaster at the time, and I figured I had the best chance of getting him for a couple reasons.

He grew up in Ottawa. I knew that his twin brother and his sister were here. I knew that his parents were still here. I learned later in the process that his wife grew up in Montreal, and her parents were in Montreal, and this is a whole lot closer to Montreal than McMaster. I also knew that he was having trouble with his boss at McMaster (he wasn't getting ahead, he wasn't getting the kudos and the kind of support that he needed), but it took four years to recruit him.

By the time he came he had tenure at McMaster. He had a good-sized lab with 25 people, and when he said, "I can't leave tenure and come to Ottawa and not have tenure. I need to have tenure." I said, "No, I'm sorry. We don't give tenure. If you're not confident enough in your own abilities, then you shouldn't be here."

He said, "You know what? You're right." A few days later, he made the decision to come, and part of the carrot by that time was I'd already recruited six of the eight people. I said, "You'll be the seventh, you'll be their leader. You take over that whole group, run it, and the next recruitment is yours to make."

I stepped back because I had a bigger job. The institutes were merging, and that's what happened. He and I together wrote the grant for the stem cell center that was successful. He took over the stem cell research center and is now recognized as one of the top stem cell researchers in the world.

Donna: You helped him fly as well.

Ron: He didn't do stem cell research before he came to Ottawa. So when you ask me what are the two biggest achievements, the first one was Muscular Dystrophy for a particular reason. The second one was science at Ottawa. The number of scientists at Ottawa, compared to '96 when I came here, has increased probably ten-fold. The quality has increased similarly, and the amount of money has increased way more than ten-fold.

Donna: Amazing.

Ron: It's been fun. What's important is knowing that the person who was hired to succeed me would've been my first choice, had I been on the selection committee (which I wasn't, although I was consulted). I was not on the search committee, and I had no formal role in choosing him. They did allow me the courtesy of a lengthy interview with every candidate. I was able to show them around, honestly tell them what the pluses, the minuses, and the challenges they'd face if they came here. Not only the excitement. At the end of the day I felt comfortable with their choice. In fact, when they asked me to rank the candidates, the person they chose is who I ranked the highest.

Donna: Ron, thank you. This was great!

Reflections

Reflections

Wisdom might be generated but isn't always captured, documented, and shared. Working well with teams, especially in a research environment, can make all the difference between a breakthrough and spinning one's wheels. Teams amass an incredible amount of knowledge, and, when shared with other teams, there is no telling what their collective wisdom can create. In this case, the longer it takes to develop a treatment or cure, the more it impacts human mortality. If hoarding information stalls breakthroughs, development, and solutions, is the illusion of power worth the consequences? And yes, it is an illusion of power. In truth, we have power *with* people. We are better with people.

In this virtual world, technology can connect us at the speed of light and bring people together from many parts of the globe in seconds. We should be cataloguing and banking global wisdom that can be built on, fine-tuned, and changed, when possible and as needed.

Collaboration is being able to bring together individual accomplishments and successes that create common goals and realise visions. The power of the whole is exponentially greater than each individual piece of the puzzle. Until all the pieces come together, it's hard, if not impossible, to see the complete picture. That's what being a visionary is, and that is how Ron Worton has succeeded.

We can bring extraordinarily talented people together and hope that as a team, it will be much greater than the sum of its parts. Talents and strengths are definitely factored in. However, the chemistry of the team as a whole might not be a synergistic or healthy one. As Ron says, "If you're going to make progress you have to have the right people, and to have the right people you sometimes have to make tough choices." What are the courageous conversations a human-based leader has to have? How, through helping people leave, can they support people in realizing personal and professional success so it's a "win-win" for all?

Human-based leaders know that what is most important to each person will change, depending on the day, hour, and minute. Such is the world of individuals in an intensely complex environment. If teams become distracted or seduced by the demands of others, the media, the glamour of their job, and outside recognition, then circumstances, not commitments, will define what's important for them.

Another role of a human-based leader is to connect the dots, ground the players on the team, and remind each team member of the results they intend to achieve. If teams become distracted or seduced by others' demands, those others will define what's important. Recognizing this dynamic, a defined target helps everyone realise success.

From my perspective, what this reminded me of is we are better with people, not better than others. We are always stronger when we co-create and support each others' growth, individually and organizationally. My coaching interventions are always stronger and have more impact when I co-create with my clients what our work together will look like. It's a series of checks and balances. The rhythm is dictated by how quickly my clients can learn and whether or not they integrate that learning into their everyday lives. Ron created a centre of excellence in his lab. The scientists didn't rely on tenure to keep their positions; they earned them through how well they continued to produce. As a coach, I must celebrate what my clients are doing rather than what they hope to do sometime in the future. Coaches live in the present with their clients, although we keep the future in mind as we do our work.

When I'm working with leaders, I must continually ask myself "What is true of their situation right now?" "What do we need to do?" "What's available to us to do it?" "What can I do to support leaders to continually re-invent what they're doing and how they're doing it?" Once they start answering these questions to bring clarity, focus, and direction, the sky's the limit.

> *"The only irreplaceable capital an organization possesses is the knowledge and ability of its people. The productivity of that capital depends on how effectively people share their competence with those who can use it."* – Andrew Carnegie

---

Human-based leadership is more than giving a task to subordinates.
It's about giving a task to people you value, who you want to see succeed in the
accomplishment of the task, not just for mission accomplishment, but for their growth
and development as well.
It's being as concerned with their success as you are with your own.

ELLIOTT POWELL, ASSISTANT DIRECTOR, NATIONAL BUSINESS CENTER,
U.S. DEPARTMENT OF THE INTERIOR

CHAPTER 7

J.D. MCFARLAN & THE FLiTE TEAM
The Sky's the Limit

This conversation was as a result of a journey through the ranks of leaders at Lockheed Martin. I held many conversations, and my dilemma was choosing which of them to use for this book. There was such rich content that an entire book could have been written about the leaders of Lockheed Martin.

This conversation began when I read an article about Lory Mitchell, a manager at Lockheed Martin, who decided to take a year off and live her dream — walking across the U.S. I contacted her to speak to her about this experience. It was unheard of (in my book) for a company the size of Lockheed Martin to support someone to live their dream by letting them go, and giving assurance there would be a job to return to. Lory went off to meet the "in-betweens" — people who lived in the small places in-between the large cities. She introduced me to Kay Cosper, her boss, and Kay introduced me to the Executive Vice President, Tom Burbage, with whom I spoke at length. Tom introduced me to J.D. McFarlan and the FLiTE (Future Leaders in Training Experience) Team, and, as the saying goes, the rest is history.

To think this organization, which is engineering- and military-based, operates from a human-based leadership perspective, is mind-boggling. To see how they live it every day through acceptable, published behavioural norms and defined standards of excellence, which go beyond productivity to organizational values, ethics, and work–life balance, is inspiring. To understand how, through design, purpose, and intention, they are growing the next wave of Lockheed Martin leaders, is a concrete example of a culture that supports human-based leadership at all levels.

Let me give you a bit of background. J.D. McFarlan III is currently Vice President, F-35 Test & Verification for Lockheed Martin Aeronautics Company. In this capacity, he is responsible for managing the overall flight test program and the contract specification verification for the F-35 program. This includes planning and executing testing of the F-35 at the Fort Worth, Edwards, and Patuxent River Flight Test facilities. Prior to this, he was the Vice President for F-35 Development. This responsibility included development of the Air Vehicle and Autonomic Logistics Information System. The team is responsible for the development and follow-on development for Structures, Vehicle Systems, Mission Systems, Air System Software, Lab Integration, Ground Systems, and Design Integration.

J.D. graduated from Auburn University in 1984 with a Bachelors degree in Mechanical Engineering. The same year, he joined the Fort Worth Division of Lockheed Martin's predecessor, General Dynamics, as a Propulsion Analysis engineer. J.D. received a Master of Science degree in Mechanical Engineering from the University of Texas at Arlington in 1991.

J.D. served as the F-35 Air Vehicle Development Integrated Product Team (IPT) Lead from 2007 to 2009 and the F-35 Air Vehicle Development IPT Deputy from 2004 to 2007. He previously served as Senior Manager responsible for the F-35 Propulsion IPT from 2001 to 2004. This team is responsible for the integration and optimization of the two interchangeable propulsion systems.

J.D. served as Program Manager for the F-16 Diverterless Supersonic Inlet Flight Demonstration program in 1995-1997. He managed the efforts to design, fabricate, and flight test this Joint Strike Fighter (JSF) inlet concept on the F-16. J.D. and his wife Tammy live in Fort Worth, Texas, with their two girls, Katelynn and Kirsten.

I wish you could hear his fabulous southern drawl, but in lieu of that, please join me in conversation with J.D....

J.D.:   Hi, Donna. It's great to talk to you in person instead of via email.

Donna: Yes, it's wonderful, and I appreciate your doing this. I'm getting an amazing impression of your organization.

J.D.:   Who all have you talked to other than Tom?

Donna: Besides Tom, I spoke with Kay and Lory. Tom had recommended that I use phone or email to get some impressions from the FLiTE team, which I did. I gathered some extraordinary stuff, actually. You have some very intelligent young men and women on that team.

J.D.: We do.

Donna: In addition, I've spoken with approximately 28 people for the book, and from those, I will be choosing about a dozen conversations.

J.D.: It sounds like an exciting project. How long have you been working on this?

Donna: It's been about eight months [at the time of the conversation]. Are you familiar with INSEAD?

J.D.: I am not.

Donna: It's a university in Fontainebleau, France, that is known for their global MBA program. Business, political, and country leaders, such as royalty, Presidents, and Prime Ministers are among the students who work on their business degrees. INSEAD is known as the Business School for the World©. The Global Leadership Centre runs a doctoral level program in consulting and coaching for change and works with very high-level corporate leaders.

I was invited to participate in their global conversation on leadership. During one of the side conversations, the seed of an idea for this book was planted. When I got back, I started contacting global leaders from many different areas of expertise, from genetic researchers to journalists to political leaders. Everyone has been very generous with their time and stories.

Next, I came across Lory by reading one of her quotes. I contacted her to ask if I could use it. From there, I heard about her walk across the United States and how she made the decision to go. What amazed me was how your organization supported her. This is what first intrigued me. Every person I've spoken to from Lockheed has blown me away.

I'd love to hear more about you. To start, what is your role at Lockheed?

J.D.: I'm the newly appointed Vice President of F-35 Development. This is a team primarily of engineers who develop the airplane — the Air Vehicle — as well as some of the information systems that interface with the Air Vehicle to help perform the maintenance on it. It's a newly-formed team, a combination of several teams. We're just in the middle of this reorganization and they announced my promotion last week.

Donna: Congratulations!

J.D.: Thank you. Prior to that time, I was the Director of the Air Vehicle Team, which dealt with the structure and systems in the Air Vehicle. Prior to that, I worked as the leader of our Propulsion Team. We have a fairly advanced propulsion system on the F-35, one that propels it like a conventional airplane, but allows it to take off and land vertically. That's been an area that I've worked in for ten years.

The team is Lockheed Martin, BAE Systems, and Northrop Grumman for the F-35 team. My team has engineers from all those organizations. I don't have a headcount, but I know it's 1,700-1,800 engineers for Lockheed Martin, and then around 500 for Northrop Grumman and BAE.

I'll talk about that organization, as well as the team I've been leading for a few years, to give you a little perspective of what we do. We started this program with a clean sheet of paper in October 2001. Our mandate was to develop requirements, then design an airplane and an air system that would meet them. We started going through the design and now we have airplanes that are on the flight line flying, and airplanes being built in the factory. We have orders for over 30 production airplanes, and I assume there'll be 60 airplanes by January of 2011. Then it rapidly increases to the point where we will be producing one airplane a day in and around the year 2015.

It is just amazing to see us go from a clean sheet of paper and a production line that had F-16s on it to a production line that has moved the F-16 out of the factory and put them in another facility here in Fort Worth. We replaced them with F-35s and have now started to ramp up our flight test program, so it's been quite a journey.

We started with a team of 300 folks in 2001 and ramped up to about 8,000. If people that work for all the suppliers on the program, it's well over 20,000.

Donna: If you think about the dynamics, the implications, and impact of all your decisions and everything that you do, it's quite extraordinary. Is your program the same as Tom's that spans many different countries as well?

J.D.: Tom is the Executive Vice President on the program. We have two, actually. Dan Crowley is the other Executive Vice President. Dan concentrates on running the day-to-day program. Tom concentrates on the international aspects of the program, keeping all the partner countries sold on the program and obtaining permits for their other international, foreign military sales that we'll bring on board.

That is a big job, and Tom is uniquely qualified to do that. He probably travels to Australia, Israel, and Europe as many times during a week as I travel back and forth from my home to work.

Donna: He left Ottawa the day before I spoke to him. I didn't know he was here. If I did, I would have met him here in person.

J.D.: Is that right?

Donna: Yes.

I'm looking at what you said about the clean sheet of paper. If you start a program from the ground up, you also have the possibility of growing the people who are going to work on it from the ground up.

J.D.: Absolutely.

Donna: That really is *carte blanche*. How are you shaping the people to really evolve and grow in the program?

J.D.: If I look at it historically, the first thing we did was to select the leadership structure. In a large program like this, we have vice presidents, directors, senior managers, and managers who are in our leadership structure. The managers are at the supervisory level, and each manager would be responsible for 20 to 25 individuals.

We had a structure. We did a demonstration program with our Skunk Works operation in Palmdale, so we had a structure through the organization at that time. Obviously, we used that organization to do the proposal.

We intended to grow very quickly, so we first put the infrastructure in place to add to that leadership team. We interviewed candidates, and at that time we would have five positions open. We'd interview ten individuals and select five for the different positions; it was like a big matrix. We interviewed and scored everybody as we interviewed them and decided where they would fit best.

It was up to them, the senior management, to build that team. I was selected for the propulsion job. I interviewed other folks for other jobs as well, but once I was selected, then the challenge was to ramp up. We had so much work on our plate. We really put a big emphasis on new hires from college.

We went through a period of a year where we did interviews every week, hosting engineers from all over the country to get them entered into the program and signed up. I don't exactly remember the numbers, but it went from about 300 to a couple thousand within a year, real quick. It was an exciting, growing time. I wish I'd had the knowledge back then that I have now.

From a program standpoint, Tom Burbage always has been an individual who emphasized relationships with people. We have always had a structure in the program where we emphasized getting feedback from everyone on the program and others from a personal standpoint. As I've come up through the organization, I've had an opportunity to participate and help develop some of that activity. In the last couple of years, one thing that I've been actively engaged in is the development of what we call Leaders Standard Work.

We started out with some brainstorming on how we actively engaged and empowered individuals on the team. Through that, we brainstormed about what limits people from doing their best. Is it processes, material, computers, training, the environment that they work in, relationships with their supervision, and with their leadership?

When we developed the list of ideas, many of them fell in the area of something that could be addressed by or that should be the responsibility of their direct supervisor. That emphasized the question, "What quality relationship do I have with my direct supervisor?"

We then actioned the team to go forth and generate how we want leaders to interface with their teams. We asked, "How do we want them to both operate and interface with folks in a group and on an individual level?"

The Leaders Standard Work is a guide we created, kept in three-ring binders and available electronically. It provides a checklist for a leader to use, with recommendations about what things you need to do as a leader, with emphasis on interfacing with all your employees. Here are the recommended frequencies with which you should do these types of things, structured on a daily, weekly, monthly, quarterly, or annual basis. It ranges from handling activity to engaging with your workforce. This could be one-on-one meetings with individuals, mentoring, career development, and group meetings — what we call *skip-well meetings*. If you're a director with 300 individuals, you have seven or eight senior managers reporting to you, each with 50 to 75 direct reports.

We have a skip-well meeting every month that skips a couple layers of management. It goes straight to a group of employees you don't normally interface with. You want to find out what's on their mind. That way, you get input that normally would be filtered through management. Those are things we recommend.

What we've tried to do is emphasize the tactical aspect of leadership. I think we boil that down to emphasizing one-on-one engagement with each and every one of the employees for whom you are directly responsible.

Depending on the level you are in the organization (for instance, if you're a direct supervisor with 20 individuals), our objective is that you should meet with each one of those individuals for an hour of dedicated time in your office — just with them. Let them control the meeting. Hear them out on what their challenges are.

We recommend that be done at least every two to three months so they can rotate through it. You still have to do the standard human resource performance appraisal activity, but this was supposed to be something different.

We actually created a guideline for leaders of the things you want to talk about with an individual. We mapped them out. "What have you accomplished lately?" to show interest in what they're doing. "What's your work–life balance like?" "What's your workload?" From "Are you bored?" to "I can't see straight and I don't need another thing on my plate." "What are the barriers to getting your job done?" Have a discussion about that. Is that something that you can help them with? Is it something that you have to raise up the chain to your management structure to get help on? Get feedback on your leadership style with them. Try to get the pulse of everyone. "Do you have any personal issues that I might need to be aware of that influence the type of work assigned you?"

Where does this individual want to be? Are they doing the type of work that they want to do? Could we move them around to do something that is more interesting? They've been doing the same job for a year. They're tired of it and want to change.

Just fundamental Management 101. We're getting a lot of good feedback from all the employees on the program. It's a little bit difficult to manage how well we're doing that. As you go up the leadership chain, a director should have one-on-one time with their senior managers or managers, spending that time helping them become better leaders. You can ask, "Of the 20 people on your team, what are your biggest challenges?" "What development opportunities are you providing for Suzie?

You know, I saw her in the hallway the other day, and she's tired of doing the same thing. What are you doing to help her?"

We make it a fundamental practice in the leadership of people: start with the one-on-one engagement for direct supervisor–employee and go up through the management chain. We want to make sure there's accountability, and that it is actually taking place. Like with the Leaders Standard Work, it's harder to measure and has been one of our challenges.

Again, we emphasize it, come up with new ideas, and add to the body of the Leaders Standard Work. It's been a step in the right direction. I can't say we've solved world hunger, accomplished Management 101, or have no room for improvement; but it has been an important step toward being consistent leaders. That is consistent with what we're doing at Lockheed Martin as a corporation, in that we have a program called "Full-Spectrum Leadership."

I don't know if anybody has talked to you about that program.

Donna: No, they haven't.

J.D.: It's basically a roadmap to guide all leaders to develop the skills to be the type of leader we want everyone to be. We normally measure leadership in terms of what the numbers were and how they performed at delivering results. This balances that with how we want leaders who exhibit strong leadership behaviors. We have a set of Full-Spectrum Leadership imperatives:

- Number one is shape the future;
- Number two is build effective relationships;
- Number three is energize the team;
- Number four is deliver results; and
- Number five is model personal excellence, integrity and accountability.

We have entry-level, mid-level, and executive-level guides for Full-Spectrum Leadership tailored to the level of engagement you have with customers and employees. It's consistent across the program. Bob Stevens, our CEO, has put it in place. It's really been a great program for several years.

It's a leader's standard of work that we've tried to implement with the F-35 program. It just provides a tactical aspect as a tool for each leader for things that we want leaders doing.

It is very well organized and is quite specific. It talks about building effective relationships, being socially aware of how you interact with people, and understanding how people see you.

Some other questions we ask are:

- Do you invite feedback with other people?
- Do you do self-assessment on your own behavior?
- Do you read cues from other individuals when you interface with them?
- Do you know when they're reading your body language, and you're not seeing the right things?
- If you have shortfalls in these areas, what are some tactical things that you can do to improve on that?

Donna: How do you measure results for something like this? As a Shadow Coach, I coach people in real time in complex, chaotic environments. I'm there to help them see the drivers behind their behaviours, what's driving them to do what they do, and then to implement change in real time. This is based on reality, not reported information after the fact. A lot of what I do is what you've just described.

What's amazing is people ask, "How do you measure results for that?" You can measure it in the morale of the people there. You can measure it in the retention rate. How many people want to stay in your organization? How many people do you grow within your organization? How do they look at leadership? How do they speak publicly about the organization and the people that they work with and for?

J.D.: It's funny that you mention that. It's always been one of our challenges. We do employee surveys every couple of years, and, obviously, that kind of feedback is not timely enough to see if the actions you're taking are driving the results you want.

We started with the most recent survey we had and then tailored a survey for F-35. We surveyed a large percentage of the population to get a baseline before we rolled out Leaders Standard Work. We actually did a pilot with a couple of teams of 200 to 300 people and did the pilot on JSF.

People don't like taking 40-question surveys, so we surveyed most candidates with several quick questions, such as "How often do you meet with your supervisor one-on-one?" and "What on this scale would describe your workload?" with this scale:

- I'm bored stiff.
- I could use more work.
- It's just about right.
- I really feel overwhelmed.
- I am so covered up I can't see straight and have no work–life balance.

So, three or four questions like that. We got the results and we said, "Hey, we're going to start one-on-one dialogues with every supervisor and this team of 300. We're going to go at it for a couple of months, then let them do the survey again." We did that. All those measures moved in the direction we wanted, and I think it was statistically significant. So that's one measure.

How do you measure how engaged your team is? You'd like to have a little scale sitting on everybody's desk you could see every day with "How happy are you about work?" But that is difficult.

From a leadership perspective, the 360 exercise we do gives us the opportunity to gather information from direct supervision, peers, and subordinates. I'm sure you've played with those, obviously, where you have a hundred or so questions to answer.

We also have a few ways to tactically measure the health of a team. You always get informal feedback when you're talking to people in the hallway, saying, "My team is overworked. We are just swamped, and we couldn't do any more." "How much have you been working?" "We're working 20 hours a week overtime."

Then, when you look at the specifics of that, you find out that there are team members who are working 60- and 70-hour weeks. The average overtime, though, is less than ten hours a week. Only 25% of your team is working overtime, while the other 75% are working 40 hours a week. "So, is your team really totally overwhelmed and why is that? Why is it that five percent of your team is working 60 hours a week and 95% of your team is not? Why is it not distributed better?" "That's the only expert in that area." "Well, why don't you train somebody else to pick up that load? Don't you have to do that every week?"

We try to provide those types of metrics and to encourage leaders to dig into the details of workload balance in their team. In larger organizations, I think you're always going to have people who work, live, and breathe Lockheed Martin F-35 development or production.

That's what they want to do, and they're going to work 60 hours a week all the time. But if your team needs to average 10% overtime for the next month to get the job done, and you can't pull in additional resources, then how do you get the *whole* team to work 10 hours extra a week for the next month, not five people working 90-hour weeks?

That's not necessarily a health measurement, but it is a management tool that allows you to be a little more frank about how much you are loading or overloading the team. I think leaders tend to interface with their key contributors. Key contributors are the people that they're always going to, and those folks are just overloaded.

Donna: One of my clients lives, eats, and breathes his work. He has to because of the dynamics of what he's doing. He told me that 20% of his staff does 80% of the work. He recognizes the fact that they have very short deadlines — a week, because it's military and tactical. I said to him, "How do you make sure that they don't burn out? The last thing you need is for the super achievers to all burn out collectively." His answer is to rotate in another group of very high achievers to intensely work in that environment. The others are given simpler work, as "simple" as is possible in that environment. They experience it as a break.

That way, everybody gets pumped, they're energized, and they know when it's their turn to give 1,000%. It just keeps the flow going, and the work gets done at a very quick, but effective, rate.

J.D.: Yeah, that is a key. There are so many moving parts when developing and producing the complex, fifth-generation fighter that you have to get the whole team excited about a goal. In this job, we have yearly goals, quarterly goals, and this airplane has to fly on this date. We put that out there and drive the team to that.

For example, we may have a six-month objective for that airplane. One week it's in the fuel facility doing a fuel test; the next week it's doing integrated power package runs; then it's doing engine runs and taxi tests. It's a different activity each day that produces a critical path for that period.

You have to get that team prepped and ready to respond when their system is on the critical path. A lot of the airplanes we have right now are on the pointy end of the sword and are getting ready to fly. That's a 24/7, around-the-clock operation, so you have to have fresh folks coming in.

What we've found is that when you keep an individual in the same job for a long time in that intense environment, it does a disservice to both you and that individual. Some people actually operate and thrive in that environment, like somebody who would work in an emergency room for ten years. My sister did that.

In an engineering environment, we train our individuals to be specialists in very unique areas, because it's very complicated. You kind of grow up in that environment, thinking, "I really only know how to do this one thing. That's what I'm going to do for my whole career."

We certainly have people who do that. You have seasoned specialists that are experts in the industry and that's what they've done their whole career. As I've moved up in management, I never thought (being a propulsion engineer) that I could ever lead an entire air vehicle development and know everything that goes on. I don't have to know everything that goes on.

With leaders, you have to have common leadership skills that you employ. You have to know how to ask the right questions, but you don't have to be the technical expert in everything. It's the same way with engineers. You can put them in a new environment, and if they have fundamental basic engineering skills, they can thrive in multiple environments; so we kind of shuffle people around. Even though they may be doing top-notch work at a very high level, when it's been a couple of years (and that's the peak of what you're going to get from them in that area), change them out. Put them in a different area.

Certainly, to do that it sometimes takes a little pushing them out of the nest, saying, "Hey, we're going to put you on a special assignment over here." Broaden them, and give someone else an opportunity to step in where they left off.

With that kind of emphasis on rotation of assignments, we always find it very rewarding for the performance we'd get out of the individual, as well as for them.

We probably don't do it enough, but we are emphasizing it. We have increased that and found it to be an important aspect of keeping people motivated.

Donna: It's my understanding that you're a pretty amazing person. Hey, listen; I'm just repeating what I've been told here. Why do you think Tom said that? Why did he say, "You really need to talk to J.D. He's really great."?

J.D.: That's a hard one to answer about yourself.

Donna: Uh huh. It is. But I'm still asking.

J.D.: I think I'm a little bit unique when it comes to being an engineer. They say the extrovert engineer is the engineer that looks at the other person's shoes when talking to them instead of his own shoes. Engineers typically are not highly skilled at interfacing with other people. For some reason, I have more strengths in that area than your average person who grew up as an engineer.

People tell me that I show more empathy to their challenges than your typical leader. I like to go out and see folks in their environment, sit down with them, and find out what their challenges are. I hate just sitting in a big conference room with people rotating through all day long, telling us their problems or challenges.

I certainly think my relationship with other people is one of my strengths. Where I got that from is a little bit hard to say. I grew up the son of a Midwest farmer's daughter who grew up to be a nurse, and my dad was a sales manager.

I inherited my technical desires from my grandfather who was an architect. My mother is very outgoing and probably has more acquaintances in Atlanta, Georgia, than anyone out there. She has thousands of friends.

I don't know. I have a little bit of mom's personality, so I'm a pretty emotional person — I care for people. I make it a point when someone's sick to call them, and if someone is in the hospital to try to see them. Our team is as large as it gets, so there's somebody sick every day. You have to show folks that you care personally.

I do a very simple thing every week. We have a list of all our employees and their birthdays. Anybody that has a birthday this week I send them a note and it's just amazing the feedback I get from that every week. "Thanks, J.D.! Glad you recognized it. I'm looking forward to my 43rd birthday this week. We're celebrating at the lake house."

It's very easy to do and you can get support from your administrative assistant to do that, but that seems to go a long way. It's a very simple gesture, but it's recognized. It's something not everybody gets every week. Recognizing people is key, whether it's for some personal or a job-related accomplishment.

We have programs for special recognition awards and on-the-spot awards that I insist that we consistently do. We have "Playmaker of the Week." Every week, I sit down with my HR business partners and they show me all the inputs for the week, and who should be Playmaker of the Week. We select one, and we bring that person to our staff meeting. We give them a small monetary reward, tell them what they did well, and give them an opportunity to speak to the team.

You just have to do those fundamental things, and I've tried to make that something I do consistently. Personally, my Judaeo-Christian ethics background is what I'm fundamentally rooted in. Treating people how I want to be treated, and with respect, is key to handling my relationships with people.

Donna: It's all about relationships. People take jobs because of people and they leave jobs because of people. That's the bottom line.

One of the things I implemented with one of my clients is a program called "I Caught You Doing Something Good." The staff love it, because they do it for each other, they do it for their bosses, and their bosses do it for the staff. They send out a group email, or they put a little sign up on somebody's cubicle wall, saying "I Caught You Doing Something Good." They say what it was, so it's not just random. The recognition keeps the motivation flying. It's fantastic.

J.D.: We do stuff like that. We have electronic and paper "thank you" notes. That's a good program.

We have a source of funding (like I'm sure everybody does) where you can spend the money with some type of recognition party or event off-site. We have a big airplane model — that's what we call a *poll model* — which tests the signature characteristics of the airplane. It's been a five-year activity, and hundreds of people have been involved. We had a big roll-out ceremony and invited everybody who played a role out to this facility. We ordered cakes and had photographers there to get their picture with the model.

Four of us at the vice president level gave a little talk. Mine emphasized as many names of individuals who had participated, specifically from project leaders who have led the project down to individuals who managed contracts with suppliers on them.

Everybody enjoyed that. Getting a chance to recognize people is always something that we're trying to do. Again, it ranges from individual recognition to team recognition.

One of the things, Donna, that most people would say about me personally, is that I have a sense of humor. I find it's just part of my personality. If I can get up in front of a group, I'm going to start with a joke.

In a business environment that's not very typical, but I try to make everything enjoyable. I'll tell a joke in the middle of a tense environment meeting if I want to defuse the tension that I'm feeling.

People get tense about some issue where they feel like someone is being critical of their team's performance, and that starts to wind up. I'll try to intervene to get people to feel relaxed about discussing an issue. I don't know why I try to do that; it's just part of my personality. You have to know when to use that, but I think it works well for me so people know that you have a sense of humor. People start to operate more openly when you have that.

Donna: Yes. They recognize whether or not it's authentic.

J.D.:   Truthfully, humor is a wonderful way to defuse tension and stress when used appropriately and respectfully.

You can absolutely get in trouble if it's not handled appropriately. I've had that opportunity. At home my wife says, "Now why did you say that? You hurt people's feelings." OK, I shouldn't do that.

Donna: So what's next for you?

J.D.:   This is a new position. I have my plate full here, so I'm going to concentrate on this for the foreseeable future. In fact, I have a meeting here in five minutes with my new team to kick off some planning activities. I love this program and the company I work for.

My next step: I want it to be either the next level up in the program (which is in the program office) or something where I can manage other projects within Lockheed Martin. I don't know yet, Donna.

Donna: Time will tell. Thanks a million. It was a pleasure.

J.D.:   Thank you very much for your time.

Lockheed Martin FLiTE
(Future Leaders in Training Experience) Team

As officers move into positions of greater leadership responsibility, they should expand their portfolio by using more EI [emotional intelligence] traits and fundamental leadership styles. By the time young officers have become captains, they should have achieved a technical confidence that allows them to shift gradually from focusing on themselves to focusing on others. Thus, they should consciously employ competencies associated with teamwork, which requires an ongoing awareness not only of their own growth, but also the strengths and developmental needs of their fellow workers. As officers mature in terms of self-confidence and wisdom, they should begin to focus on the traits associated with understanding others' professional and personal strengths and abilities. Developing these EI leadership competencies, especially when captains have more work to do than extra hands to do it, becomes a conscious effort — a personal development priority. Although they still seek feedback and mentoring, maturing captains find themselves mentoring others as well. – Emotional Intelligence – Implications for All United States Air Force Leaders – Lt. Col. Sharon M. Latour, USAF; Lt. Gen. Bradley C. Hosmer, USAF

Lockheed Martin FLiTE Team members have a perspective of human-based leadership that they are working towards as they move up through the ranks of the company. Their vision, perspectives, and insights are extraordinary and are indicative of why they have been selected to be a part of the FLiTE Team. Some of the team members shared their thoughts with me on human-based leadership.

Monika Mackie, Senior System Engineer

Removing the power involved in any leadership role is something that most people, me included, cannot do easily. However, I do believe that focusing on the humanity aspect allows leaders to gain a deeper and more genuine relationship with any individual. People are not just people. They are fathers, mothers, friends, soccer coaches, best friends, and members of your community. Leaders who take the time to understand the present and history that goes into what makes their employees who they are today communicate better with their team members. They instil a sense of appreciation into their team and end up with a more motivated team.

In my current position, I have been trying to focus on the task-oriented aspect of the job, and to develop the relationships I need to help me understand how to get the job done. It has involved slowing down my "state of emergency" mind set and developing genuine relationships with my team.

I learn the names of their spouses, the ages of their children, and know their personal aspirations outside of work. I've made it my mission to over-invest in people and not focus so much on the task at hand. Doing so has not only helped our team be more productive, but has brought me a sense of community.

If I were in a position of leadership at Lockheed Martin today, I would suggest that employees start a "People I Know and Things They Do" file. Write down people you met that day or even co-workers that you are beginning to know better, and jot down any personal information that they provided you. Did they tell you that their son was graduating college this upcoming weekend? Write it down and then be sure to ask them on Monday how the graduation ceremony went. Are they big into running? Take the time to mention upcoming races or ask about their training schedule. It is not a difficult task, but it provides a greater connection between you and that co-worker, and that ultimately will improve productivity on your team.

Erin Davis, JSF Propulsion, F135/F136 Engine Integration, and Julie Davis, Project Engineer

Leadership based on humanity is an ability to reach others. By reaching and connecting with people, leaders motivate employees to give of themselves. These connections should also be used to challenge the *status quo* with leaders and employees who strive for continuous growth, both personally and professionally.

A leader shows there are no boundaries or obstacles that can't be overcome when individuals freely lend their talents, recognize and embrace their shortcomings, and open themselves to learn from others. Leaders have the ability to transform individual contributors, melding them into cohesive units inspired by common goals. Those who understand the humanity behind leadership find ways to allow each person to ask more of him or herself, creating an environment of intrinsic accountability.

To evolve into a human-based leader, I'm keenly observant of others who have the talent to lead. I work to understand the ways in which leaders inspire others to overcome obstacles and rise above atmospheres awash in negativity. I strive to understand the ability to influence others in constructive ways. I observe and try to understand people's unique personalities and the linkage between successful leadership methods.

If we were in positions of leadership, we would:

- Focus on continuous personal and professional growth.
- Do evaluations that serve to recognize burnout and decreased productivity. These would motivate a "fresh breath" assignment within an individual's defined professional growth path.
- Find ways to facilitate a culture which passes down knowledge of past successes and failures. The company should embrace the lessons learned from missteps, passing these along so that history will not repeat itself.
- Recognize not only the ambitious team members, but also those who are more reserved. Individual contributions should be acknowledged regularly to energize the workforce.

Talented people are attracted to organizations in which leadership appreciates their abilities and where they are provided enough freedom and encouragement to develop professionally and solve issues affecting company performance. Talented people in general do not work well in a monotonous environment, so leadership must find ways to provide a variety of opportunities helping to nurture personal and professional growth.

Erin L Warner, Systems Engineer

Human-based leadership manifests itself through an inspired and empowered workforce. The cornerstone of human-based leadership is a person's ability to relate to others. Building effective relationships and trust takes courage, honesty, compassion, and excellent communication skills. Each leader has to find a way of inspiring and building trust, using their unique gifts and style. Tom Burbage, for example, is renowned for his incredible ability to communicate through storytelling, which has virally inspired the organization.

I believe talent is attracted to an organization largely by its culture and people. Develop the culture through seemingly small but strategic moves by the leaders to establish priorities and norms that position the company for success. In an engineering company, people could easily be viewed as secondary to the process, the design, the product, and the needs of customers. I believe that when we place proper importance on people, then inspired and empowered people will ensure that the design is innovative, the process is lean, the product is of highest quality, and the customers' needs are met. It is no small task to lead with a balance of inspiring the human spirit and operating within imposed boundaries!

Nicholas Drazic, Supervisor, F-35 Final Assembly

From my perspective, human-based leadership is the collective result of the many thousands of personal interactions that occur in the process of building our products each day. We recognize that these essential interactions occur throughout the organization highly focused on leadership development at all levels. The ultimate judge of our leadership maturity cannot be measured simply in terms of cost, quality, and schedule. It must also take into account how we have positioned ourselves for the future and what lasting relationships and synergies we have developed while executing.

I am developing into the human-based leader of the future through immersion. My career at Lockheed Martin was jumpstarted when I was placed into the Operations Leadership Development Program (OLDP). While on program, I completed four six-month rotations in the areas of operations, sourcing, and quality. Soon after completion of the OLDP, I was placed into the FLiTE Program (Future Leaders in Training Experience), a program designed by executives of the JSF program to give 0-to-5-year employees "experiences" over the span of a year. These experiences have allowed me to sit in on high-level customer meetings, present improvement ideas to executive leaders, and organize company-sponsored community service activities. These cross-functional and cross-business unit experiences prepared me to hold my first position of leadership within the company. Within my first leadership role, I have been able to use and sharpen the tools gained from my rotational and leadership experiences, while developing my leadership style. Lockheed Martin's focus on my career development has placed me in a key leadership role at the age of 24 that I would not normally get until much later in my career.

I believe the most important thing to put in place as a leader is your replacement. If we are to believe that we are truly indispensable as leaders, we are stating that the organization is greatly prone to failure. We recognize that due to Baby Boomer aging and rapid program growth, there will be a large leadership gap that many of us young leaders will be asked fill earlier in our careers. Our readiness to accept these roles will not be merely judged by our skills. It is essential for us to constantly be developing multiple leaders who can seamlessly step up to the plate.

Attracting top talent into our organization derives from several areas. We are fortunate to produce a product of childhood dreams which starts us off ahead of the curve. We must continue our focus on delivering the promise to develop leaders through education, experience, and continually perfecting programs like OLDP. We must also continue to show that we value diversity in our workforce and leverage it for success. All employees must be valued, their ideas heard, and their potential for success in the organization must only be bound by their own ambitions. I feel that if we are successful on all of these fronts, we will continue to attract and retain the best talent in the industry.

Suzy Seminara, JSF Flight Test

My current role on the F-35 program is working-level team leadership and program execution. From my perspective, human-based leadership stems from the ability to collectively maximize individual strengths to achieve organization goals, while keeping an eye on future growth and development. Good leaders are able to assess and capitalize on employee strengths, identifying areas for development and presenting development opportunities. During a recent ground test on an F-35 aircraft, we were working 12–14-hour shifts seven days a week to get the avionics software working and the aircraft back flying.

One of my co-workers was running the ground test and having a difficult time executing parallel efforts to increase efficiency and meet schedule. Recognizing this was not his strength, we shuffled the tasking and gave him a series of discrete tasks to accomplish in series. In the end, he met his goals, had a sense of accomplishment, was a part of the team's success, and we completed the ground test effort on time. I also believe in continuous learning. In my current role, I have little exposure to program cost reporting and budget management (what Lockheed Martin calls *business acumen*). I have asked my leadership for more exposure to this aspect of the program. Once I justified the need, my leadership began taking me to earned value meetings and audits.

Within the last six months, I have attended three such meetings. I don't have the terminology down yet, but these meetings have given me an appreciation for managing our budget, managing change, and guarding against scope increase. Lockheed Martin has several leadership development programs available for all levels of leadership. As a graduate of their engineering leadership development program, I highly recommend taking the opportunity and aiming high. The only limits are those you impose upon yourself.

I currently lead small teams of people on technical projects but am not part of their performance review or promotion cycle. If I were in that chain of their leadership, I would work development plans with my employees, either formal or informal — their choice. As part of my current leadership development program, I am developing something similar for myself. Studies have shown people who document goals have higher success rates than people who do not document their goals. As part of their development plan, I would set stretch goals with my employees that they could work over a fixed period of time. The purpose of the stretch goal is three-fold: to get them out of their comfort zone, to learn, and to teach others.

I believe a major contributor for attracting talent is good management. Employees tend to join and stay in an organization that cultivates trust, respect, learning, and provides the opportunity to excel. In my nine years with Lockheed Martin, I have been provided numerous challenges and learning experiences. I expect that trend to continue.

Reflections

Reflections ctions

When one considers EI [emotional intelligence] in light of these domains, it becomes obvious that the field represents a set of comprehensive, interpersonal abilities rather than hardwired native skills; as such, it can be learned. EI could well be called "affective effectiveness." The affective domain consists of mind, will, and emotions ("heart knowledge"); it contrasts with linguistic, logical, mathematical, and spatial intelligences – the cognitive domain of "head" knowledge. – Lt. Gen. Bradley C. Hosmer, U.S. Air Force

Thinking about J.D.'s leadership and the Future Leaders in Training Experience of Lockheed Martin, what came to mind was that one line that divides leaders from "wannabes" is passion. As long as you believe what you're doing is meaningful, you can always find a way to get to that next step. And if you can't visualise it as tangible and real, then you're not going to make it.

I recall a conversation I had with a leader over coffee, just before she brought me in to do some work with her and her team. She turned to me at one point and said, "You really know who you are." That comment stayed with me and I continue to use it as a barometer. I know that when I sense I'm 'off-centre,' I have to re-calibrate and re-centre. Without that I cannot be of service to anyone. I believe "knowing myself" is a defining characteristic of a masterful coach. She saw that centeredness and passion in me and wanted to feel it in her world as well. It wasn't what I did as much as what and who I was being that created the connection.

Leadership at Lockheed Martin spent a lot of time articulating behavioural norms, guiding principles, and team expectations. Since they were forming a team from scratch, they looked at how they were going to pick leaders and grow them into their excellence. They needed to find people who could fit into a job that allowed them to perform to the best of their ability and across cultures. They needed to bring teams and partner organizations together to support a human-based leadership environment.

These men and women had the knack to be able to pluck ideas from the clear blue and put them together in such a way they created a vision. In turn, they created processes to make it happen.

They spoke about it in such a way that others saw their vision of success, knew what to do and wanted to do it, thus creating a strong, committed team of players.

From that point, they began leading the team, knowing when to put their foot on the pedal and direct or back off and listen. They chose the right people with the right expertise and harnessed it in a collaborative way.

Their vision for how the organization would come together and work on a program that spanned nine countries was so powerful that it went beyond individual leaders, was embraced by all, and permeated the entire organization. Lockheed Martin's culture is based on their *Standards of Excellence*: "*Individual values and dignity, trust and respect, customer focus and engagement, work/personal life balance, and good citizenship.*"

A good leader inspires others with confidence in him or her; a great leader, like J.D., inspires others with confidence in themselves.

An individual has not started living until he can rise above
the narrow confines of his individualistic concerns
to the broader concerns of all humanity.

MARTIN LUTHER KING, JR.

CHAPTER 8

RICK KOCA
Standing Up for Kids

I met Rick Koca a few years ago at a conference in California. He spoke about his passion, StandUp For Kids, a program committed to the rescue of homeless and street kids. The first thing that struck me was "Why didn't I know any of this?" and the second was "I have to get to know this man…talk to him and find out how I could support him, even from Canada." He touched me in a deeply profound way. First, a bit of background…

Rick Koca is a retired U.S. naval officer. He joined the Navy at the age of 17 and for the next 30 years proudly wore his blue Navy uniform. During his career, he was promoted 13 times through 17 pay grades. A highly decorated naval officer, Koca was awarded the Defense Meritorious Service Medal, two Joint Service Commendation Medals, two Navy Commendation Medals, three Navy Achievement Medals, and numerous service awards and commendations. He is qualified in Submarines and as an Air Crewmember, and is entitled to wear both warfare insignias. During his 30-year career, he served in a variety of locations and positions — from the frozen harbors in Alaska to the rain forests of Panama. In Europe, he flew with the USAF as a Battle Staff Team member aboard the European Airborne Command Post. In Panama, he was the Adjutant General to the U.S. Commander-in-Chief.

In 1988, Koca was transferred to San Diego. Several months prior to his departure from the U.S. Navy, he had seen a *48 Hours* news magazine segment on homeless and street kids in Southern California. He knew what he was going to do in his free time. Within eight days of his arrival, he was training to work with kids in crisis. He also served on the San Diego Eagle Scout Board of Review.

Rick left this volunteer position in 1989 to start StandUp For Kids, a program committed to the rescue of homeless and street kids. He initially built this all-volunteer, non-profit organization exclusively with the help of his family and friends. Rick says that walking the streets and helping homeless and street kids wasn't something he was thinking about as he got ready to hang up his uniform after 30 years in the U.S. Navy.

Now, after more than 20 years of walking the streets, he can't think of a place that he would rather be. There have been many times when he just wanted to turn his back on all of it. He thought that would help relieve the pain he was seeing in the kids on the streets: the pain of his first street kid who said he was HIV positive; the first 12-year-old living in a dumpster; his first youth heroin addict; a 13-year-old prostitute; the first baby living in a cave; and his first 17-year-old who died as a result of AIDS.

There were many occasions that he would walk the streets seven nights a week. "There were so many kids who didn't trust us and wouldn't come and ask for help. How had they been so mistreated? Why would they endure terrible abuse on the streets rather than let us help them find a better place? I knew from the beginning that the problem was national in scope. Most of these kids come from troubled homes, where they were abused or neglected. It's difficult to believe that we live in a society that lets children live and die on the streets, but they are out there. They are living under bridges and are eating out of dumpsters. They are being raped."

Rick proudly stands up and says, "This isn't about money; it's about caring! What we've accomplished has no price tag. We know we've made a difference in the lives of thousands of kids. I would have paid that price for one! What we do really helps. You see kids get off the streets, and this work provides me with meaning and purpose."

StandUp For Kids has been recognized by the White House on three separate occasions, by the U.S. Justice Department, the U.S. Supreme Court, the U.S. Senate, the U.S. Congress, American Express, the Governor's Office in Arizona, the Secretary of State in Colorado, and received the JC Penney Golden Rule Award. Rick has been awarded the George Washington Honor Award for his work with homeless and street kids. He was singled out by the Midwest Center for Nonprofit Leadership as a finalist for the 2002 Edward A. Smith Award for Excellence in Nonprofit Leadership for exemplary voluntary leadership. In San Diego, he was awarded the Channel 10 Leadership Award. StandUp For Kids is listed as the first program in the book, *50 Ways to Save Our Children*. In 2006, Rick was one of its inaugural Purpose Prize Fellows, a major new initiative to invest in Americans over 60 who are leading a new age of social innovation. He was recognized again as a Purpose Prize Fellow in 2007.

Rick has three children, seven grandchildren, and a great-grandson who all live in Aurora, Colorado.

I am honoured to know him and look forward to sharing his story with you.

Come and meet Rick…

Rick: Hey, sweetness.

Donna: Hi there. Did you have a good meeting?

Rick: It was wonderful. We're all here in Atlanta. It's been so long since we've all really been together as a staff. We've been scattered here and there; now we're in Atlanta, and it's just great to have a staff to sit down and chat with on the second Tuesday of each month. I've needed a staff for so long. We're getting all our registrations done, even after a couple of hurricanes. Hurricane Ike blew the top of our building off. It was just one thing after the other. Now we're just looking for a peaceful year … hopefully.

Donna: I have this feeling that it is going to be an extraordinary year, even with the way it started.

Rick: We're in for an extraordinary year.

Donna: It's turning into a learning year for people. It's a stretch for many, but it's reminding them of what's truly important in their lives.

Rick: That makes it reality, doesn't it? I always like to stretch. It's ironic. You know, Donna, one of the things I say when people ask how things are going is, "This has just been an unbelievable year. It's been our best year ever." People who have known me for a long time say, "Rick, I don't know if you realize it but you always say that."

         I think we create the goodness that's out there or you find the goodness in everything and don't dwell on the badness or the things that upset us the most.

Donna: I sent the link to your AARP [American Association of Retired Persons] interview to my colleagues. They loved it! It's an amazing interview.

Rick: It was a nice piece I did, wasn't it? I was really pleased with it. That's for the ego-minded, but I just thought they did a great job. It was a great piece all the way around so I was really happy.

One of our volunteers, Alison, is in Los Angeles. She's been involved in leadership and doing outreach there for two years. She had her husband look at the piece (it's nine minutes long). He said to her, "Honey, I've learned more from this piece on Rick in nine minutes than you've taught me in two years."

Donna: The first time I heard you speak in California blew me away. You could see the passion in what you spoke about. You were all heart. It was a fundamental part of who you were, not only what you did. That was evident. This book is on *human-based* leadership, not *power-based* leadership. With you, Rick, it's lighting a spark in other people to continue the work that you started ... to make a difference globally.

Rick: Thank you so much. That's really kind of you to say that. Wow.

Donna: I know a lot about you but it's never enough. Every time we talk, I learn more. I'd love you to share your story from the beginning. Will you?

Rick: Let's see ... I was promoted 13 times through 17 pay grades when I was in the military. Probably less than one-tenth of one-tenth of one-tenth of 1% can say that. If you're enlisted, you can go nine pay grades; if you're an officer, you can go seven. I went from enlisted to officer with no college.

I think part of that comes from believing that whatever I do, I want to do it the best I possibly can. That means each time, you've got to put it out there. You have that one chance so you say to yourself, "What do I have to say to move people, to motivate people, to get people to commit if I don't put my whole heart and soul out there?"

I think those that do, like Richard Branson or a number of other people, inspire people. However I make a presentation, I want to stand up, walk around, look people in the eye, and convince them that there is a problem.

Now that you know there is a problem, somehow I've got to convince you this is the right organization for you to help. Sometimes, I think with Virgin Mobile, Virgin Unite, Virgin America, and all the things that they are doing ... I think Richard already has helped us convince people there is a problem. Therefore, he's cut my job in half. Now I have to convince you that you can get involved in solving the problem.

Oftentimes, charities say, "This is who we are, this is what we do. We don't ask very well." Or "We beg." I don't want to beg, because I hear too much begging, and I don't like it when people beg to me.

We all want to make a difference somehow. You can donate a hygiene product, clothes, money, or time. Whether it's time, treasure, or talent, you can give all of those things. You can make an unbelievable difference in the lives of kids who believe that no one cares about them.

Donna: Definitely. When you gather people like Richard Branson around you (which has happened), it gives it more credibility. People know he doesn't waste time on projects, charities, or helping individuals make a difference if he doesn't truly believe in it.

Rick: Being Virgin Unite's first year [supporting charities] in the United States, I think that carries with it some responsibility that StandUp For Kids has to become an even better charity. We have to do more things smartly.

I remember Al Gore's chief of staff was sitting on our national board of directors. I asked, "What kind of hoops did we have to go through so you could sit on our national board of directors?" I'm sure they wanted to make sure that we weren't going to be an embarrassment to the White House and the Vice President. He said, "You would never believe it."

What it proved to me over and over is that if you're doing the best you can do every day, that's what people will remember. Every time I stand up to talk, no matter how I feel inside, no matter what else is going on, people deserve for me to give my best.

I don't give anything less. I don't come with my second-rate piece; I stand up and give it all I've got. Sometimes it's a little embarrassing. You just don't know how people are going to take it. Sometimes I'm so overcome by emotion. I look at people and I think, "I'm not getting any feedback from you." I think the more energy I get back from people, the more I can put into it as well.

I'm certain you've been places and given presentations. Everybody sits there excited, paying attention, and they can't wait for your next words to come out. They are the ones that get the best of you. I try to give the best so that I'm going to get the best back.

Donna: That's it. It's like nourishment for your soul.

Rick: It is. I feel it. Sometimes I tell my children or close friends, "I can literally pick them up and slam them down with just a few words." It's like "shock and awe" for the military. You can do that in your presentations and I love to do that: build them back up again and then wham. So that they see the brutality of living on the streets, the brutality of what we do to homeless street kids, the brutality of what we really have to get out and accomplish or we're not going to get there. I like my shock and awe parts.

Donna: You know what I call it when I'm working with clients? *Shocking them into reality.*

Rick: You're right. That's exactly what it is and I think they appreciate that so much more. Certainly, they're going to remember it the next day and the next day. They're going to remember it when they hear homeless or street kids or something you said that comes to light again. Whereas, if you just do some slide presentation that they all have to read or you read it to them, those are just things I can't do.

Maybe I learned it early on. Of course, nothing in the Navy got me ready to do this, but I think I gave one of my first presentations to about 30 or 40 people and I gave it from the point of being a street kid. Later, I asked one of the attendees I knew, "What did you think of it?" She said, "You've got to know your audience." That's the only thing she said to me.

I thought, "OK, thank you very much." Then I thought, "Depending on whether I'm talking to high school or elementary kids or whatever, there is a different presentation for them. It can't be the same all the time."

I was giving a presentation to some church group of kids one time and I got the sense that maybe they felt they could become homeless. I wanted to assure to them that they had good parents and that's why they were in these groups, because some of the kids looked a little distressed. The high school kids and college kids, I want them to think that this could be them.

Donna: Or their best friend.

Rick: Yes. I gave a presentation to a high school group. I talked to this teacher's class every year for about four years in a row. I forget what the name of the class is, but it was about kids that got involved in the community, in peer counseling, and all those types of things. I asked them if any of them knew any kids who were homeless or street kids and about four or five kids raised their hands. I said, "Are any of you homeless?" Two of them raised their hands. It broke the teacher's heart that they couldn't have told him, but two of the kids in his class were homeless at the time.

Donna: Isn't that something!

Rick: Yes, you never know. I've met some unbelievable people who told me they were homeless. I've gotten emails from people who send me unbelievable stories about being homeless, what happened to them, who they are now. "It would shock the world to know that 20 or 30 years ago, before I was married to this famous CEO or that famous public person, I was homeless and a prostitute on the street."

Donna: I'd love to see you publish all those stories people tell you.

Rick: People ask me that all the time. "When are you going to write a book?" "When are you going to do this?" "How're you going to do…?"

I have had lots of them, but with computer crashes and all that, I don't have a lot of them anymore. I've got some from a young man who I still know and am very close with. He's not so young now. He's probably about 30, but he'd been raped by his father from the age of two-and-a-half to five.

Because he was acting out and everything, his mother finally got him to go to counseling when he was 12. I asked him, "What did the counselor say?" He said the first thing the counselor said to him was "Take off your clothes." I said, "Oh my God! What did you do then, Mike?" He said, "I spent the next four years trying not to drool on myself." Then he ended up on the streets where he was raped again. But to look at him, I mean, the way that he was raised by two imperfect parents, and just his comments…

I've published it several times in our newsletter to remind people what happens to kids on the streets. He'd been raped again on the streets. Kids on the streets are in unbelievably dangerous situations already. It's pretty damning.

Donna: Rick, what was it that told you "I should be doing this"?

Rick: I had already started StandUp For Kids in San Diego and in Denver, Colorado. In 1990, I was on my way to start the program in Virginia Beach, Virginia.

I was a mess. I questioned myself. "Who the hell did I think I was that I could just go off to Virginia and start this program?" At the time I built it, it took two months because of all the training and getting everything started myself: finding the sponsors, food, clothes, hygiene products, and the storage facility.

Now the cities have to do that themselves, so I was praying and telling the Lord, "All my life I've helped kids." I have eight brothers and sisters, and my parents weren't home. Then I helped at an orphanage for five years, little league and all that, and then I was a Scoutmaster for four and a half years.

"If this is what You want me to do, I need some help; I need some support." So this answer came to me, even though I don't believe God talks to us personally: "You're right. You have done all these things and because you have, I give you StandUp For Kids as a gift."

Therefore, in that defining moment, I knew I was doing what I was supposed to be doing and I've never looked back. I just stood up and did my thing, knowing that this was a gift.

Whether it was for seniors, cleaning homes, whatever, that's what we were going to do. The program was going to be called STAND and it stood for Super Teens Answering Needs.

Unbeknownst to me, when I got to San Diego and found all the homeless and street kids, it wasn't a program to get kids involved in; it was a program about supporting kids. The program then became StandUp For Kids.

Maybe, in some sense, we have bits and pieces about who we are and what we're supposed to do. Sometimes, people listen to it and sometimes they don't. As long as I was in the Navy, I loved the Navy. I still love the Navy. It wasn't my life but it was something I loved.

Before I retired, I knew I was going to be working with kids. I just thought it was going to be the other way around: a bunch of kids were going to be doing unbelievable, wonderful things. Certainly, high school kids and college kids are doing that within StandUp For Kids. And yes, I had a defining moment.

You just keep marching forward; you don't look back. I was just scared. I mean, I was *scared*. What was I going to do if I came back home in December, ten days before Christmas, the program had fallen apart, and they said, "We need you again"? Would I have the time, the money, or the effort to go do it again? How many times could I do that?

Donna: What was the answer?

Rick: The answer was, "You have done all of these things and because you have, I give you StandUp For Kids as a gift." So I just moved forward and never looked back.

Donna: Sometimes, we need something to give us validation that we're doing it, or confirmation that we're the right person to do it, and the ongoing energy to be able to continue with it.

Rick: That is so right. I get that feedback from kids and volunteers. It's that energy I was talking about. Just the things the kids say, too, like "If it wasn't for you I'd probably be dead." To hear Brian talk to the reporter and tell her, "I can remember nights in my squat when I would be rolled up in a ball with my thumb in my mouth. I would be crying. I could hear other kids crying and I was praying that I could go to sleep and not wake up in the morning."

It is what continues to drive me to say, "Our kids should not have to feel this. Kids should not have to know what this means. Kids should not ever have to say these words." Those things fill me up. I get filled up constantly. If you don't, then I think a lot of people simply walk away from their jobs or their projects. So I don't allow just one thing to fill me up, but lots of things. It is from the kids; it is from the volunteers; it is from the supporters and sponsors; and it is from great things like the AARP piece that filled me up when I watched it. You're dead tired after three days of filming and answering questions, but to be with kids like Angel, Christian, Michael, and the many other kids in the video, fills me up. How could it not?

Donna: What I loved about that AARP video is that you see the connection, a heart connection, between them and you.

Rick: I love that, too. Wow. People would be amazed at how close I am with some of the kids and the volunteers. When we ask kids and volunteers to be a part of StandUp For Kids, we're asking them to be a part of a family. If we create that family, then more and more kids and people will want to be a part of that, because it's more than just an organization, it's more than just a charity, and it's more than just a job — it's a commitment.

Like I said, I loved the Navy. It was my job, but I loved it. You work at that. If you've got a significant other, you work at having that great relationship. I work hard at it and the rewards are unbelievable. Everything in life isn't going to be delivered on a silver platter. Maybe none of it will be. But when you can create all that yourself, you don't need a silver platter.

Donna: Were you ever stationed in Norfolk?

Rick: I was, but in the late '60s. I was only there from 1967 to 1969 (both my boys were born at Portsmouth Naval Hospital), and I came back again for a short period of time. Norfolk was a big Navy town on the East Coast. I thought we could open some locations here, open some there, to build an actual organization, not simply have locations centered around where I happened to be located.

Donna: It was a very interesting town. Amazing how it morphed over the years. That's why I wondered if you were stationed there, and you saw how much it was needed in Norfolk.

Rick: I didn't know that beforehand, although I did get some emails from people. In fact, I got an email from a 22-year-old kid named Ted in 1991. He said he wanted to help me start a program. Here we are in 2010, and he's still there, in the same program, making an unbelievable difference in the lives of hundreds of kids.

Donna: What were the milestones? What has stayed with you the most?

Rick: They've been on different levels. Certainly, on one level, my declaration about wanting to build a national organization, because I just didn't like the idea that of the homeless, 1.3 million were street kids.

Even saying that, I don't know what that means today. Where should programs be located? How many programs are needed? I don't know. Even though we're now at 45 programs and will be at 48 this year, there's still a problem — it isn't enough. I don't know that there will ever be enough.

I don't look at it like, "Look at what I've built, look at what I've created." One milestone we reached was about six years ago in our San Diego outreach center. An artist had done some beautiful artwork in the building. He also painted all the states where we had programs and put a logo there, the state bird or the state flower, then painted in the names of the cities where we were.

The center had been closed for remodeling. When the center reopened a couple weeks later, one of the volunteers who had been in the San Diego program for six or seven years said to me, "Rick, how does it feel to stand here in this room, see all these states, all these cities and names painted, knowing you built all of that?"

I was just so overcome because I'd never looked at it like that. I was definitely moved and choked up. I couldn't even answer him. I think he felt what I was going through, but I had never looked at it as if I had created anything so fantastic.

I said, "I don't know."

I don't know how Richard Branson or Bill Gates feels when they've earned money or created all these businesses. You look at all your clients. Certainly, it's a lot different today than it was with the first one, but do you look at it any differently?

I look at it the same way every day. My mission is to help homeless and street kids. It has nothing to do with the numbers of cities I'm in, the numbers of volunteers, or anything else. It has to do with the kids.

Maybe that's why we're so successful, because we haven't lost that focus. That's what I tell a lot of people. It isn't about a whole lot of money, it's about the kids. It's never been about the money because we don't do a very good job of raising money. It's about the kids and we do that very well. We go to the streets and say, "I want to help you do what you want to do. What is that?" or "If StandUp For Kids could do one thing for you today, what would that be?"

A couple of other significant milestones were when Al Gore's chief of staff came to us, and when Virgin Mobile or Virgin Unite, Richard Branson's charity, came to the United States in 2006. They selected us as one of the charities they would interview, and then selected StandUp For Kids to launch Virgin Unite in the U.S. That was certainly an unbelievable moment for me. Again, it's one of those moments where you not only get filled up; you're just overflowing. I thought over and over, "Oh my God, oh my God, oh my God." And this year, we're going to be on *Celebrity Apprentice*!

Volunteers have done unbelievably wonderful things. Some have reached the 5-, 10-, or 15-year point. A lot of them have volunteered more than five years, and it's just unbelievable to think that they see and feel the same way I do. Maybe there's no greater accolade than people who say, "The reason I stayed is because of you."

Those are things that again fill me up, whether they come from the kids, the volunteers, the sponsors and supporters, or Richard Branson or Jewel. It was unexpected for Jewel to come up, give me a hug, and say how much she appreciated what I was doing and for how long — because she was homeless before she became famous as a singer. For her to thank me for all my hard work for homeless and street kids, those things make an even bigger difference coming from the kids, because they know exactly what it is that we're doing.

The volunteers have some greater appreciation. Sponsors and supporters love the work we're doing and know we're making an impact. They see it in the eyes of the kids, and they hear it from the kids. Unless someone else is doing what you're doing, I don't know that they will feel what you feel when you do that.

Donna: That's it. I often ask people whether or not they're paying attention to how deeply they impact people. Are you? Do you see it? Do you pay attention to it?

Rick: I certainly do. Oh my goodness, yes! I challenge myself and challenge that person as well.

One of the things that I say (and you heard me say this just a few minutes ago) is, "If StandUp For Kids could do one thing for you today, what would that be?"

I challenge our staff. "That's what we should be saying to our volunteers" and I tell our volunteers, "That's what you should be saying to kids." I also tell volunteers, "This is what you should be saying to your spouse, to your best friend, to your children: 'If there's one thing I could do for you today, what would that be?'" I think as a nation, what greater thing could we do than to just ask people, "If there's one thing I could do for you today, what would that be?" I think that helps fill you up. It might just elicit, "Oh wow! Thank you for asking."

Donna: When you're out on the streets with the kids, are they at all accountable for what they bring to the relationship? You give them so much. Do they have to give their word that they will try to do something differently? Can you give me an example of a promise that was made to you?

Rick: Yes, I have a great example. When Brian was a kid, he was a cutter, so I made Brian promise not to cut himself. One day I saw he had a cut on his arm, and I said, "You promised me you wouldn't cut yourself." And he said, "I didn't do it." That told me he was letting other people cut him now.

I think we must not just hold our kids accountable, but hold everyone accountable. I tell people, "You don't have to promise street kids, the volunteers, or the program anything. But when you do say you'll do something, you damn well have to do it."

All too often, we don't think that we have to be our word. It's so easy for us to state something and then not do it. I'm always amazed that people take their word so lightly. It's like it's not that important, but to me, it's your bond. Don't say something you're not going to do. Don't say something if you won't make it a priority to get it done when you said you'd get it done. Lots of people do this. I don't know how they succeed. I'm not about to make some promise I can't fulfil or tell some kid I'm going to do something, then not do it. That's all they've heard all their lives.

Donna: My mentor said to me a long time ago (and I've adopted this for myself), "I live my life in direct proportion to the commitments I make and keep." That is my mantra. If I can't keep my commitments, then what good is my word?

Rick: Who are you? Another question is, "What are you?" That may be more important.

Donna: *That's* the question. I think that's the best part of coaching — to help people see the impact of their word, who they are, and what they stand for. I'm wondering, are your volunteers receiving any coach training so they can coach the kids?

Rick: I don't think we are. We get the free coaching from you all; we're so fortunate. Almost everyone that I talk to who received coaching admits that they're a better person for it.

In fact, Uyoung Park, one of our co-executive directors in Detroit, had a coach. But working with her coach convinced her it was time for her to leave StandUp For Kids. Uyoung told me, "Rick, you probably don't want to hear this but…" I said, "No, it's wonderful."

A coach certainly knows who you are, where you're going, and what your dreams and wishes are. I said, "You've given me four-and-a-half years. I couldn't be happier. I'm not losing you as a friend. You're going to go on to do bigger and better things and this is the time for you." She was kind of surprised. I would love to find coaching or something for homeless and street kids. I would love to be able to sit down with someone and say, "We can help put this together."

Do you know, Donna, what's the hardest thing for a street kid, someone who's been on the street for a long time? Answering the question, "What is your goal?" Their only goal is to find something to eat today or find a safe place to sleep tonight. Every day when they wake up, that's their goal; that's their journey. Once you can get them thinking past that, then you're winning. Then they're winning and to see them win is just unbelievable.

You have to help them create a life. Homelessness is just a part of who they are. They have no family, no church, no community, no school or neighbors; no nothing. Until you can put more pieces together than just being homeless, until you can help them have other things, there's no reason for them not to be homeless.

"What would I have in common with anyone? What could I do? I'm not just homeless; I have nothing."

You start by helping them put a life together, and they will fix their homelessness. When you help anybody do anything, they become a better person because they don't feel like they're in it on their own.

I get emails from people who say, "We want to help you go feed kids." What I hear them say is they want to help me feed the pigeons. If all you're doing is feeding someone, then I think you're not doing anything. We just choose to be so much more. We want to be a part of your life. We want you to be a part of our lives. I'm going to remember who you are. I'm going to remember your name. I'm going to remember if you have any siblings. I'm going to remember where you're from. I'm going to remember all of these great things about you, and then I'm going to remind you of them and how great you are.

Donna: I have a question that you can share with your volunteers to ask the kids: "What's your intention?" It's not about what the kids' goals are. Goals are very different. Intentions equal results. Intentions go beyond just looking for food. It's intending to create a life where survival is no longer an issue. That's something to talk about.

Rick: You said, "What is your intention?"

Donna: Yes. "What is your intention for today? What is your intention for tomorrow?" They could have a discussion about what "intention" means. "What do you intend to happen that is within your control? That is within your power?"

Rick: I know what mine is. My intention is to build the largest organization in the world that helps homeless and street kids to be a part of the United Nations, and certainly to be a dynamic, international force.

Donna: Are you coming to Canada?

Rick: Yes ma'am. Absolutely! We're coming to Canada and England. But here's the biggest difficulty or dilemma I have to overcome (because we get 10 to 15 emails every week from all over the world, asking, "Would we come to this country or that country?"): All the things that are in abundance in the U.S. that we give to homeless and street children — the food, the clothes, and the hygiene products — are never going to be that abundant in a third-world country.

Donna: Right.

Rick: The biggest thing we do for them is to help them feel better about themselves. If they feel crappy about themselves, and no one can change that but them, I don't know how it's possible to change that person. Imagine that when you get up every day, you have no underwear or socks or panties to wear. All you can put on is some old filthy sweatpants or something, and you're going to beg for food. That's all each day is going to bring you.

Even if I became your friend, you still have a dilemma each day. There's no place to wash your face, no place to comb your hair, no place to brush your teeth, no place to be safe when you're sleeping. You're getting raped at different times. I mean, if I can't help you change some of what's happening, then I don't know how you change as a person. That's what we do: we effect a change in a kid. They begin to want all the things that we have as well, and work towards that. By "the things we have," I mean the family, the friends, and the church. We take our kids sailing, go to movies, make tie dyed t-shirts, have barbecues, have picnics in the park, play ball, Frisbee, and fly kites. It's all of that.

You're not a street kid when you're doing all those other things. You're not surviving on the streets. You're someone else. They want to be that someone else. As you get going and put more things in their lives, they want that social world that you have more than they want the survival world that they've been living in. Then they begin to work harder, too.

Donna: They become part of a community.

Rick: Exactly. A whole bunch of volunteers who care about them, give them hugs, and aren't afraid to tell them that they love them and care about them. This is their community. Lots of organizations call it *case management*; we call it *care management*.

Donna: I like that.

Rick: It's because we care. It's about caring about them and letting them know this is care management. If you want case management, we will find someone else. That's not what we do.

Donna: With all this time, energy, and love that you give to this organization and these kids (the homeless and the ones who are working with you), have you had to sacrifice any of your personal life?

Rick: Absolutely. Every day. I have seven grandchildren. One of the painful things for me was when I left San Diego, I was going to open up the office in Denver, Colorado. That's where my children and my grandchildren are. Then we got this free office in Houston and I decided I would go to Houston. My oldest granddaughter was 14 at the time.

She said, "Once again, Papa makes a decision for homeless and street kids over his own grandchildren." That was awfully painful. I don't want to say every day, Donna (in the sense that it's a frequent thing), but I think there are lots of things that you give up.

I don't know how many days I traveled the last few years because I haven't sat down to figure it out, but in 2007, I traveled 211 days. Most of those travel days are Wednesday, Thursday, Friday, Saturday, and Sunday. I come back Sunday, go to work Monday and Tuesday, and take off again on Wednesday. For months on end, I've never had a weekend off. I'll take a day here or a day there. I'm an amateur photographer, meaning I don't know anything, but I like to do it.

No, I think maybe all of life is a sacrifice. If you're doing what you want to do, and you're giving up some other things, it is a sacrifice to some degree. I love doing what I'm doing so much that other things — not my health, certainly — but children, grandchildren, and some other aspects of life, will suffer because you love what you do so much.

I don't think it's just me, I think it's Branson as well. I think people who really love what they're doing often overdo it. If you look at all the Hollywood movie stars, they love to make movies and they overdo it. So whatever we love to do the most, we tend to overdo it, because it just fills us up so much. We love that feeling of being filled up.

Donna: It's enticing and addictive, I know; it's hard to turn it off. There's no question. One of my colleagues at a meeting turned to me and said, "Sacrifice means making something sacred."

Rick: Wow, I love that thought.

Donna: That's exactly what you're doing, isn't it? You're making something sacred.

Rick: It's like you don't get enough of it. People ask me if I'm a workaholic. No, I'm not; I know I'm not. I love doing what I'm doing, and I want to do the best. I don't mean better than anybody else; I just want to do it the best I can. Otherwise, why would I even do it to begin with?

Donna: One of the things I heard years ago was "It seems like we don't have time to do something right the first time, but we always have time to do it over."

Rick: I don't have the time to do it again, so I better damn well do it the best I can at the time. Of course, sometimes you don't always give it your best, but I would like to think the majority of the time I'm giving it my best. No matter how bad I feel, if I'm here to do training or make a presentation, you're going to get the full load of what Rick has to offer you. It's not your fault that I feel bad today, that I'm sad today, or I'm not up to speed. I'm going to give you the best I've got.

Donna: I have a feeling I already know the answer to this, but I want to hear it from you: How are you lighting that spark that you have in others so you know this work will continue?

Rick: There are a couple of things. Sometimes people will say to me, "I can't do what you do." I say, "I don't want you to do what I do; I want you to do what you do. Be yourself, because that's certainly the thing that kids need."

I can remember in February 1991 when I started StandUp For Kids in Denver. The first person that did street outreach with me was Carol; I don't remember her last name. She had two little children at home. When the two of us did street outreach, Carol talked to and helped the kids that we met. We brought clothes and hygiene products along with us. It was cold in February in Denver, near the 16th Street Mall.

We went to a McDonald's and had hot chocolate or a hot drink of some kind. We finished several hours later, at least ten at night. We got back in the car and she just started bawling. I mean, it just all broke loose. What she was trying to tell me was, "I had no clue. I just had no idea. Oh my God!" When she calmed herself down somewhat, she said, "There is no way I could ever go back to being just a mother."

This is what happens so often, when people find out what is the truth. For example, people didn't give a damn about AIDS because it was a gay person's disease. Then, when they found out that it wasn't, lots of people jumped on the bandwagon and wanted to help the kids.

You can talk about cancer all day, but the minute you mention someone's mother or grandmother having cancer, it's a whole different story. So I talk about homeless and street kids: the number of them, how they end up on the streets, and how they don't want to be on the streets. In fact, 70% of homeless and street kids go to school. That just blows people away. 63% of all the kids on the street have attempted suicide at least once. That blows people away. These two facts tell you the kids want to go to school and how horrible it is to be on the streets. If you can just show people that none of us would choose that kind of life, you are inspiring people. Often, the inspiration is the kids as well because they see how much you believe in them.

Certainly, you have to light the spark, but if I show the need, and hopefully I do that in some way, then I proved to you there is a tremendous need. Donna, do you realize that we've been talking about this for several years? You still want to be engaged and promote the whole idea that more needs to be done. What we have to do is debunk people's belief that kids are on the street because they want to be.

Donna: Personally, I don't know anybody who is or was homeless. It's totally outside my realm of experience. I know that people often listen to others and experience life through their stories. When it becomes personal, you really can make that connection, but you go beyond that, Rick.

Rick: Randy Papetti, one of the lawyers and partners at the law firm of Lewis and Roca, LLP, in Phoenix, Arizona, told me some years ago, "I love it when you come to town and do training. The volunteers always stay in the program much longer than when we do it on our own. I think passion does have a place. People see the passion in you and they want to be a part of it."

I've seen flyers go out, saying, "Rick Koca is going to be in town, the Founder and CEO of StandUp For Kids. Come have a chance to rub elbows with the CEO!" I think, "Oh my goodness, we're making way too much about this," but I'm glad that they have that excitement, that urgency, and that need that I feel as well. Thirteen homeless kids die on the streets every day. I wake up every day and think, "We have to do more. We have to do something about this." I can understand that kids go to bed hungry or don't get an equal education. Not all kids have insurance, but no children ought to die on the streets in our country.

Absolutely none. I can wake up every day, knowing we're trying to make a difference in that.

Donna: What's next for Rick?

Rick: StandUp For Kids was 20 years old in January, 2010, and I'm going to step down as the CEO. I'll simply become the president and founder and go out to find more sponsors and support. I've spent 30 years in the Navy and 20 years in StandUp For Kids, 50 years of service. I did my thing to stand up and say, "I'm an American, I believe in what America stands for, and I did what I think Americans should do." Not everybody has to do it to the same degree. I chose this, and I'm proud that I chose this.

All my grandchildren are close to being teenagers now. One of them is getting married this year, and I just want to spend more time with them, so I'm going to move back to Denver.

I certainly want to continue, including working on some strong advocacy pieces. I was just in Washington, D.C., last week, talking with a firm that I hope will help us pick up the whole mantle and work for advocacy. What are the kinds of bills at the federal, state, and local levels we can put together so that if you abuse a child, we're going to whip the hell out of you, because that's where it all starts?

Children end up on the streets most of the time because of the abuse and everything else they experience. If we can reduce that frequency and insist on stronger and stiffer penalties, then maybe we can decrease the number of kids who run away and think that's their best option. If running to the streets is a 5 and staying at home is a 10, then I'll take the 5 beatings over the 10 beatings any day of the week.

As I mentioned, I love photography, so I want to do more of that. I published my first book of zoo pictures and gave them to my children for Christmas. They went crazy. I didn't think they would like it, but I was really surprised and amazed. I want to continue to do more of that and play with photography and pictures. That's what I've got coming up for me.

Donna: What words of wisdom from Rick (which I think people would love to hear) will move them beyond their self-centeredness?

Rick: These aren't my words of wisdom. But I've believed in this for a long time (and I think it was President Roosevelt who said it originally): "There's no limit to the good a person can do if they don't care who gets the credit."

I don't care about the credit. It can't be "Rick founded this organization. Look at this great thing." It's about all of us. People say over and over that "It takes a whole village," but it seems that the village isn't ready yet to take on that mantle of responsibility.

I think there are some people who can convince communities and villages to get involved, at least to some degree. I think that's what StandUp For Kids has been successful about, because we're all volunteers; I only pay five people to help me. Therefore, somewhere between 2,500 and 5,500 people, whatever the number is in 43 cities, are volunteers, creating communities, and saying, "In my community, kids don't have to eat out of dumpsters and sleep under bridges." There's no limit to the good a person can do if they don't care who gets the credit. Rick doesn't care.

Donna: That is a great motto. So many people just look within their own world, their day-to-day routines, and they don't see beyond that. They have the ability to have extraordinary impact on at least one person, if not more.

Rick: I know. You're right.

Donna: "What would that look like? What would that mean? What would it mean to even one person if...?" Those are the questions I ask, whether to political leaders or corporate leaders. Title doesn't matter; the will to create positive change does. "What would your life look like if you did A, B, and C? What would the other person's life look like if you did A, B, and C?"

Rick: I think that's great, too. Going back to my question, "If there's one thing I could do for you today, what would that be?" what if someone asked you that every day? The fact that you asked me is going to fill me up to some degree.

It's *you* that makes it. As an individual, we've got to quit blaming everybody else. You could wake up this morning and it could be snowing. Here's my correlation: everybody loves a beautiful rainbow. They forget that someplace it's raining.

We don't see the rain. We're looking at the rainbow. If you want a rainbow in your life, you've also got to accept the rain, and I can accept that.

Donna: Attitude is contagious.

Rick: Absolutely.

Donna: If I live my life by that perspective and I know the next person I speak to will capture and absorb some of what my attitude is, then I have to make a choice as to what that will look like. At least I need to be aware that there is an impact my attitude has, positive or negative. It's my choice, just as it's theirs, as to what to do with it.

When you speak, when you stand up and connect with people, they are absolutely mesmerized: by your passion, your attitude, your sense of what should be right or wrong, what you could do, and what one person can do if they make a choice to do it. Look what you've created. It's mind-boggling!

Rick: Thank you, Donna. I appreciate that. It's something I love to do. It doesn't matter whether it's 3 a.m. answering emails, traveling six or seven days a week, even travelling 80 days non-stop.

Donna: Oh geez, Rick.

Rick: I didn't go around the world, but it was an 80-day trip.

Donna: I am so excited about this piece!

Rick: Thank you. That's why I love you. You're one of the only ones who has stayed in touch and I very much appreciate that, Donna.

Donna: Rick, meeting someone like you is rare. One doesn't let that slip away.

Rick: Donna, thank you so much.

Donna: Thank *you* so much. Speak soon…

Reflections

Reflections Reflections

What mesmerized me when I first met Rick was how he spoke from his heart. These weren't canned words or a speech to ask for money. This was sharing the pain and reality of what he experiences every day when he goes out on the streets to connect with these kids and make their lives better. Sometimes, what he brings to their lives might seem miniscule. It might just be a conversation, but the connection has an impact on their lives in some way, forever. When he speaks, he's asking you to pay attention and do something, no matter what that might be. Human-based leaders pay attention and listen from *your* story, not only theirs.

As Rick says, "This isn't about money; it's about caring! What we've accomplished has no price tag. We know we've made the difference in the lives of thousands of kids. I would have paid that price for one! What we do really helps. You see kids get off the streets, and this work provides me with meaning and purpose."

When we speak statistics, it's about numbers. When we speak of kids, share their stories and their victories when they get off the streets, it's about humanity. When we ask someone a question and wait to really hear the answer, we're valuing their existence and showing them that we're interested. We're giving them the gift of our presence. One of my clients, Ernest Loevinsohn, captured it beautifully when he said,

> *It's really action that seals your commitment. It isn't thinking about something; it's doing something. Many people work from meaning and passion. I think it's far more of a motivator than people commonly give it credit. I think one of the lessons is how much talent there is and how important, with great work, it is to expand the scope that people have in order for them not just to demonstrate, but to exercise, their talent on a continuing basis.*
>
> *There's this huge desire to make the world a better place, whether it's the environment or helping developing countries. It's like a river, a force that will hopefully get channeled in the right direction, then actually make a difference that*

doesn't evaporate. My impression is that there are people in the next wave who could accomplish amazing things. They are achieving things earlier in their careers than they used to, and that's a good thing. You don't have to wait until you're in your 50s before you can have influence in an organization.

Keep track, not in a boastful way, but in a sober, realistic way, of what kind of impact you're having, what you're doing to achieve that impact, and focus on the prize. Then your work has meaning and you have meaning, whether or not you succeed. The key thing is not really the results. Rather, did you do everything you could to attain the results? If you're keeping track of that, then you're going to have a pretty satisfying life and, most likely, you will also get results. – Ernest Loevinsohn – Director General, Global Initiatives, Canadian International Development Agency (CIDA)

We all have limits and internal and external circumstances that have an impact on the choices we can make. When we lead by helping people maximize their potential and opportunities, while recognizing and appreciating their limits, we lead from our humanity. I continually ask myself, "How can I walk into a person's life and be so mindful of everything around me that I can quickly see the truth of 'what is' in their world?" From that point I ask, "What am I not seeing? What am I noticing that tells me I have to go deeper to see what shadows might be haunting them? How can I, in a safe and non-judgmental way, enable them to shine a light on their shadows so they're no longer as dark?" In this case, I wonder what has people turn a blind eye to the homeless they see every day? What personal roadblock would they have to remove to become involved, make a difference, and change the lives of even one person?

"What we have done for ourselves alone dies with us; what we have done for others and the world remains and is immortal." – Albert Pike

---

The encouraging thing is that every time you meet a situation,
though you may think at the time it is an impossibility
and you go through the tortures of the damned,
once you have met it and lived through it
you find that forever after you are freer than you ever were before.
If you can live through that you can live through anything.
You gain strength, courage, and confidence by every experience
in which you stop to look fear in the face. You are able to say to yourself,
"I lived through this horror. I can take the next thing that comes along."
The danger lies in refusing to face the fear, in not daring to come to grips with it.
If you fail anywhere along the line, it will take away your confidence.
You must make yourself succeed every time.
You must do the thing you think you cannot do.

ELEANOR ROOSEVELT

CHAPTER 9

TOM STERN
Shocked Into Reality

I first "met" Tom when we co-authored a blog with a group of fascinating people. It was a unique blog — we were given a book summary to read and then have a conversation about the topic, perspectives, and each others' thoughts. He intrigued me. After the blog faded away, we stayed in touch. Needless to say, when I decided to write my book, his name quickly appeared on my list. What I didn't know was where our conversation would go. And what unfolded was not at all what I expected!

Tom chose a great values-based life rather than an extravagant lifestyle. He helps others deal with their addictions to fame. His mission now is to help change the focus of corporate cultures by working with people at all levels to define success, achieve it, and enjoy the journey along the way without being obsessed by it.

Tom readjusted his goals. To keep himself grounded and truly connect with people, he counsels others twice a week. As Tom said, "The old Tom Stern saw his family as an interruption on his quest for greatness. Now I see my family as the fuel to keep me going on the quest to be of service." Now he helps others see their greatness, a hallmark of human-based leadership.

First some background about Tom…

Tom Stern is an ©Oscar® winner, business leader, author, television producer, comic strip creator, nationally-syndicated radio talk show host, and professional speaker. What better person could there be to give a talk entitled, "*Stop My Life, I Want to Get On!*"?

Tom is the great-grandson of the chairman and visionary of Sears Roebuck, philanthropist Julius Rosenwald. He is son of one of the founders of cable television and the industry's leader in the 1960s, Alfred Stern. Tom was the black sheep of the family. He was a learning-disabled and troubled youth who struggled mightily to live up to his family's expectations. After graduating from college with a BA in theatre and psychology, Tom turned to stand-up comedy in his 20s, working alongside Jay Leno and Jerry Seinfeld. He did comedy writing and development for HBO's future chairman, Chris Albrecht. Wanting a more stable lifestyle in his 30s, Tom reinvented himself and became an executive recruiter. Starting in the boiler room of a small contingency firm, Tom's rise was meteoric. Within five years, he had his own organization, and for the next eight years, he was in the top 5% of productivity in the industry. His diverse client list included McKinsey & Company, PricewaterhouseCoopers, and Universal Studios.

Unfortunately, his single-minded purpose (to prove to his extraordinarily successful predecessors that he belonged in their company) compromised Tom's family life as well as his own sense of well-being. Only after surviving a life-altering event did he awaken to a new set of priorities.

Now, exploding with passion and a desire to reach out to other success-addicted, workaholic professionals, Tom sees himself as a comedic evangelist, spreading the idea that better balance leads to greater productivity, as well as increased sanity. His nationally-syndicated comic strip, *CEO Dad*, has spawned a new book, *CEO Dad – How to Avoid Being Fired by your Family*, with a brilliant and moving forward by Stephen R. Covey. CNBC has worked with Tom as executive producer/writer to create *CEO Dad*, the animated half-hour comedy starring Martin Mull, Lisa Kudrow, and Paul Reubens, a first for any financial or business network in the history of television.

With all this activity, Tom felt it was necessary to take a vacation from his hit, nationally-syndicated radio show, *Opportunity Knocks*, on business talk radio and sponsored by Monster.com. He wanted to make sure he had enough time for his family. Now he recruits out of his home while continuing to write a column for fastcompany.com, "A Kick in the Career." He is also featured on the business page of the *Huffington Post*. Tom currently lives as a recovering CEO Dad in Woodland Hills, California, with his wife and two very junior vice presidents.

As William P. Baptiste from PricewaterhouseCoopers observed, "…few possess critical attributes of intellect, intuition, and integrity of the highest order. Tom Stern has all of these."

Come meet Tom in conversation…

Donna: Hey Tom! I am so excited you agreed to do this. A lot has happened since we first started conversing. Unlike the blog where a bunch of us discussed a central topic, this is the first time we're diving into a conversation about you. I really look forward to seeing what unfolds.

So tell me about Tom. How'd you get from "then" to "right now"?

Tom: First of all, there are two things that I prize above everything else: respect the individual and have a sense of one's identity.

Each one is reciprocal. The more you have a sense of your own identity, the easier it is to respect the individual, because you've respected yourself enough to follow your own individuality. Everything to me comes down to that. You're not going to be successful at respecting other people's individualities if you don't own your own individuality. And if you have your own identity, you're going to be less threatened by other people, and thus, less apt to want to suppress them, subjugate them, or co-opt them.

The problem for most people (I'll include myself, and sometimes it happens at a very early age) is that they lose touch with or have taken away the connection to their own identity and development. In my case, that was done primarily by my father and then (in a *reaction formation*, to use a fancy psychological term) done by my mother as a competition.

My father was a powerful CEO, a type-A personality, and overly competitive. I came into the world within a classic oedipal triangle. I had more creativity, a little more charm, maybe even a little more intellectual acuity, but I wasn't as powerful a person as my father. I had a charm over my mother that he didn't have, and I had a social dexterity that he didn't have. He was oppressive, tyrannical, and threatening to me.

As a result, that took a big piece out of me owning my identity. I became one of two things: either broken, because I had been tyrannized, or rebellious against that force of tyranny, my father. That wasn't my true identity either, because I was reacting, measuring myself, and performing against another individual, instead of connecting with who I was.

My mother saw this terrible thing happening and wasn't able to confront my father, because he was threatening to her, so she babied me. She treated me like damaged goods, but in a very loving way, and she made me underestimate myself. What she did was smother me in compliments to build up my ego, and in so doing, she created a certain degree of grandiosity. In my case, it was the perfect formula for narcissism, or the mixing of self-flagellation with too high an opinion of myself.

For me, intimacy was not put first. It was all about achievement. There was immense conflict in a high-stress environment. Children in these environments tend to develop less true organic confidence, less true sense of their own individuality, and are subsumed by the overwhelming egos of the family.

What I try to do when I'm dealing with people is listen and tune in to their individuality. For example, I'm working with someone right now whose life is clearly not in balance. I get 20 emails and 15 phone calls from them a day. I get emails at one in the morning. As far as I can tell, they don't have much of a social life. I sense that there is a great swing in one direction. I have chosen to respect their individuality at one level, while also remaining comfortable with my own identity.

I'm their boss and not their therapist. What I want to do is support them and help them be successful. Over time, maybe I can gently encourage them to have more balance. Right now, this person isn't going to be able to hear that. I realized, "OK, do I browbeat this person?" No. So part of respecting people's individuality is accepting what their limitations are, what they can and cannot hear, and what they can and cannot learn.

In terms of growing people and growing yourself, the negotiation that an individual has with themselves or with others regarding character defects is a very nuanced process that happens over time. It's about timing — and I think all growth and learning is.

You can grow and learn if you have a sense of your identity, know who you are, and can get comfortable with yourself. Then the composition of the new is less threatening, because you have a foundation from which to consider change.

I think if you're in a state of chaos or emotional disassociation, it's much more challenging to try to change or to accept new information. I think those things are key to leadership, to being a good follower, to being a good partner, and to being a good husband and father.

I have a child right now who has ADD. I had ADD and my father's reaction to it (and God bless him, I don't blame him for this as he was a control freak) was immense frustration. He asked, "Why does he keep doing this?" He was outraged that I didn't get it, instead of going, "I have to respect this individual. This individual's development, place in the world, and configuration of personality elements produces this result. They're a child. They're not planning this. This isn't a scheme, and it doesn't have a negative intention."

My father, for all his power, had a very poor emotional foundation. When he was thrown something he didn't understand or when something came at him he couldn't control, he viewed it as malevolent. He assumed it had a bad intention, because it was threatening to him.

Donna: Taking into consideration all you've shared, what lit the spark in you to move from that kind of background to where you are right now?

Tom: What happened to me was two distinct realizations and a life-altering event.

One realization was part intellectual and biological. I came to understand that there was a difference between *being driven* and *having drive*. When you have drive, you have your foot on the pedal of your own passion, and you're at the wheel. You may speed up; you may slow down; you may be quite focused; and you may have goals, but you're essentially in control of your life and your choices.

When you're driven (which actually many people aspire to and are rewarded for), you're not in the driver's seat. Someone else is driving, and you don't have control of your life.

That's what happened to me, because I was competing with my father, trying to get his approval and live up to the family name.

My second realization came from a couple of events. The first was I made a whole lot of money. I'd always thought I was making money so we could get a big fancy house. I went with my wife to Westwood, which is a ritzy neighborhood. We looked at a few homes that cost a small fortune, but I realized that if I was going to get this house, what I was really getting was a slightly larger box than the one I lived in.

I thought to myself, "So this is what it's all been for. You have killed yourself working 80 hours a week, so you could have a fancier house with a little more room so people would be impressed when they come over for parties. You completely depreciated the quality of your life for this goal of status and materialism." That made me examine this to death, until I went into a depression and thought, "That's a pyrrhic victory. It's pathetic." Then I started to examine the fact that I really wasn't running my own goals. I was living something that had been implanted in me. That was the first crack in my armor: getting the success, and then realizing I had no idea why I'd gotten it. My goals were not aligned with me, which showed me I didn't have my own identity.

That didn't make me change. It was just more depressing, confusing, and reflective of my disequilibrium. The next thing that happened was a form of shock treatment. We — my family and I — were the victims of a home invasion.

Donna: Oh, my!

Tom: It's a very dramatic story, and the moral of the story is interesting. My wife had three miscarriages, and I really wasn't there emotionally for her as much as I should've been. So, instead of changing and becoming a more emotionally intelligent and sensitive partner, I went out and bought her a big diamond ring. I knew she liked diamonds and I wanted to cheer her up with a diamond. I bought her a thing instead of giving her what she needed emotionally (although I didn't really know how to do that). It was that diamond ring, which in many ways symbolized my own emotional limitations, that attracted robbers to follow my wife.

I was in the house, and they came in through the garage. My wife was with my daughter. She didn't know what was happening and she panicked. She tried to get my daughter in the house. One of them grabbed her and began punching her in the face.

I heard screams so I came out. The first thing I saw was my five-year old walking up the steps of the garage. She thought she was in a movie, like it was play. We'd never allowed her to see violence on TV, so she didn't know what violence was. The horrible irony is that we were so protective that in two minutes, she saw more violence than most people see in a lifetime. She said, "Daddy, what's going on?"

At that moment, the other robber put a gun to my head. I just said very calmly, "What do you need?" He said, "We want the ring." I screamed at my wife, "They want the ring!" She suddenly realized what was going on, so she opened her hand, they pulled the ring off, and they ran away. I brought my wife into the home with my daughter's help. There was blood everywhere — on the walls, on the floor ... It was shocking.

The moment of epiphany happened for me in two stages. The first was as I was calling the police. I saw my five-year-old daughter ignore all the blood, ignore my wife's face because she looked gargoyle-esque, and say, "Mommy, Daddy is calling the police. Everything is going to be OK. I'll get you a towel and a glass of water." At that moment, to watch this little hero so focused on someone else and not her own fear — my heart broke, because I realized I had taken them for granted.

This little girl was so extraordinary. It was all the result of my wife's parenting. They had this connection that I wasn't part of, and I was more a witness to my family than a full participant in it.

I had this mix of pride, terror, and incredible grief. That crystallized a lot of what I had been running from. But as much as that was a shock treatment, the first thing I felt was depression over the house. That was my realization that I had been driven in the wrong direction. This was recognition, not just that I'd been driven in the wrong direction, but what I had missed out on. Now there was a sense of loss, as opposed to just depression or demoralization.

The thing that really changed everything (and there were many things) was we got through all these events. My wife had surgery and recovered, my daughter had therapy, and my wife and I got marriage counseling.

However, one night about six months later, I went to pick up my daughter at a play date. This house was on a cul-de-sac and there were no street lamps nearby, just the lights from the home. We were parked about 100 feet away. I picked my daughter up, took her to the car, put her in her car seat, and buckled her in. I shut the door and at that moment I dropped my keys.

In the one second that I bent down to pick up these keys, my daughter started crying at the top of her lungs, because for kids that age, if you disappear, it's as if you're not there.

She suddenly was terrified and alone, afraid of being attacked, so I just popped my head up. I couldn't believe that in one second she'd gone from a relatively happy child to a panic-stricken, terrified little girl.

I got in the back seat. I hugged her and calmed her down. That was when I fully understood my role as a parent: Be close to my child and make her feel safe. She was really vulnerable and that vulnerability had been intensified by trauma. I loved her, but I had to *show* my love — I had to be there for her. If I was, there would be great rewards in that for me.

The closeness that I felt at that moment, the sense of needing and purpose — all the things that that big house I was going to buy had not brought me — took me through demoralization, grief, and sense of loss to a feeling of purpose, hope, and intimacy. That was the process by which I really began to turn my life around.

Donna: What happened as a result of you making those decisions?

Tom: It took a long time. In a TV movie, it would be about three scenes and we'd be happier. In fact, it's been a process of many years. I admittedly had some behavior patterns and role models that stood in my way of having emotional intimacy. It's still a long process, and it's a road that I continue to travel. During that period, I sort of fell down, regathered myself, regirded myself, and then began walking down a different path. I've been on that path ever since.

The results are that my children and I — we have two now, we adopted one — have an immense understanding.

We have many games. We have fantasy life; we have imagination. My older daughter and I speak a made-up, nonsense language that makes us laugh. It reinforces the sense that we have our own little safe world where we can be however we want. I play a lot with my children. I educate them with my experience when it seems important. I'm dedicated. When my wife asks me to do something, I don't argue or try to get out of it (at least most of the time unless I really can't). I'm not as driven by my own agenda. I'm not always trying to be right, and for anyone who's married, you know how helpful that is!

A lot of times I let my wife vent. When I used to argue with her, everything with me was a competition. Slowly but surely over a number of years, I've become a more conventional person. I'm sure I'll look back in ten years and think I was limited, compared to where I am now. It's just a process. I have a good family life. There's a lot of shared experience. I'm at the dinner table and I don't take calls 99% of the time. I enjoy time off; I actually welcome it.

Donna: What's fascinating to me is that from all this turmoil in your life, the darkness and horrific experience, you now bring light, laughter, and humor to the world. You write extraordinarily well. I love how you write.

Tom: Humor is something I got from my mom. She really enjoyed me when I was growing up, and that's what kept me alive through all my difficulties.

I was hyperactive. I had ADD and dyslexia. I was a bed wetter. I had a lot of disabilities in this high achievement family. I was sort of the Elephant Man, but my mom kept my spirits up. I used to make her laugh, and that was sort of the thing that helped me survive. When I came out of this darkness, that's when I created *CEO Dad*. That is when I rediscovered my humor as an emotional, corrective mechanism, and I just love it. I love creating ironic puzzles.

Humor for me is a way of taking chaos and creating an alternative universe. Using irony, you can reconfigure it into an ironic puzzle and somehow it suddenly makes sense. It's actually an organizing mechanism.

Donna: Have you heard the term *chaordic*?

Tom: No.

Donna: It's when you take chaos and order and harmonize them together.

Tom: That is what comedy is. It's an organized act of sedition that is ultimately didactic. You take a point of view and you actually use satire to deliver it, but you do it using absurdity.

To me, that's what it is, but mostly it's fun. That's what I rediscovered — a sense of fun. The fun that I had lost in trying to be the best, trying to win, trying to impress. As someone said, "The ego is ultimately a dog that chases and nips at your heels, trying to devour you," and that's what happened to me.

Donna: Was there someone in your life who supported you through this evolution to where you are now?

Tom: I've never really had a mentor, and I've only become someone who could truly be educated by others in the last ten years, but there have been one or two people. Mostly, the way they mentored me was not intellectual. I've neither required nor sought intellectual mentoring. I've sought it in the arts, but comedically I was mentored by my good friend, Jerry Seinfeld. We've talked about comedy for 30 years. I've given him a lot of feedback on his writing, and he's shared his view of comedy with me.

The other mentor I've had is a spiritual mentor, sort of the father I never had. Although I loved my dad, he's a different type of man, and his whole life is community service. His wife had a stroke, and for a number of years, he's cared for her. He has many grandchildren and children, all of whom are successful, and, I think, do well. He is a very Buddha-esque man with a big belly to play the role.

He laughs a lot. Nothing seems to get him riled, and he uses very simple logic to smash any self-centeredness. He doesn't ever seem to end up in a self-centered place. He always empathizes with the other person so that diffuses his anger. He always tries to think of a higher purpose. He ends practically every conversation with people he knows with the words, "I love you." He doesn't say it to strangers or people he doesn't know well, but to anybody with whom he has an ongoing relationship.

Through example and some direct sage words, he's been a role model to me of how you can exist in the world: being really comfortable with yourself, bringing joy to other people, and, as a result, being filled with love yourself.

Donna: Do you think you impact others? Is it something you pay attention to or are mindful of? And if so, how to you see it?

Tom: I do. For some strange reason, I've chosen not to focus on that. I try. Yes, I counsel people with drug and alcohol problems, because I had one. I have almost 20 years sobriety now (I will in three months) so I work with people who are newly sober, and I counsel them. Some of them were recalcitrant cases who had gone in and out of sobriety. Nobody seemed able to reach them, and for whatever reason, I did well with these guys.

I can feel it when I speak to them. I know I'm helpful to them. I know I've contributed to that change. I try not to focus too much on it, because if I start to think about what *I* do, then I become very "I" oriented, and that's dangerous for me.

Donna: When I ask that question to political leaders (who are a large percentage of my clientele), they give me this strange look, because they are very ego-focused. I say to them, "Your impact goes well beyond your awareness and your understanding. It goes to who you are as a human being and how you interact with the world. When you pay attention to it, it's being mindful that you do have that impact and how you can give to the world in a very positive way."

Tom: The way that I do it is I focus on *intention*, rather than impact and result. The only time I focus on it is as a compass for me on when I'm doing the right thing.

If I have an idea that's well-intentioned but it never works, then I throw it out. I used to think I was being well-intentioned by giving people advice all the time. Actually, giving people advice all the time can be very patronizing, because you don't speak to them as an equal. Suddenly, you're this authority. Even though you feel you're being helpful, generous, and avuncular, in fact you're putting yourself above them. At some unconscious level, it can be perceived that way. So even though my intention at least consciously was positive, the result wasn't, and I threw it out. Now I share more of my own experience.

I know this guy who I would have told you would be headed towards bankruptcy five years ago. I tried everything to help him with his mismanagement of money and his career. He's very intelligent, so he wanted to do it his way. He's very New Age-oriented, so he only likes good, positive news. He loves to live in a happy world of bright pastel colors, which is fine, except when there's a dark cloud covering your head.

We have a difference in philosophy. I believe when you're having really bad problems, you need to square up and call them what they are. He feels that's a fear-driven approach.

Anyway, I could have predicted his bankruptcy. I used to try to stage him, advise him, intervene for him, and fund him. I gave all that up, because I have to respect his individuality and not be co-dependent. His individual path may be to be bankrupt. In fact, it may be the only way he learns. It's happening now.

His whole world is coming apart, and I don't give him advice. I have said to him a few times, "If you need a person to vent to, if you need some support, I'm certainly here for you and you can call me." I care about him, but I'm out of the "saving him" business.

Donna: It's a lot less responsibility when you take that monkey off your shoulder.

Tom: A lot of saving people is grandiose. It's a form of narcissism, and I've had to learn the cost-benefit analysis of that. A lot of my narcissism helped me be successful, emboldened me, and made me feel I was special. I stood out and I had to stand out. That was the engine and the fuel for most of my pursuits, but at a tremendous cost of isolation, exhaustion, mood swings, and rage at people who didn't seem to admire me enough.

Now I'm fuelled by "How can I help?" "What is my purpose?" "What do I contribute?" It's much less exhausting, and there are places where I cannot contribute, this friend of mine being one of them. There is no avenue or crack for me to slide through, and I totally accept that.

Donna: That is your immediate awareness of what your impact is on your one-on-one exchanges. What about your impact on people that you will never meet because of the message, your work, and how it's shared?

Tom: I have let go of that. I don't know if that's a bad thing.

First of all, I often write humor in the business community. I'm going to meet with Ed Sussman, the President of Mansueto Digital, tomorrow. I asked Ed, "Do you know about the emails that I get about my work? Most of them are idiotic." He said, "Well, unfortunately, a lot of the people that make comments are the ones with too much time on their hands." Quite frankly, in writing humor in the business community, there are so many people who are CEO Dads with no sensitivity. There are times when it's almost laughable or frustrating.

I'll write a humorous article and they'll write back, "I disagree with you because of x, y, and z." Certainly, satire has a point, but they seem to have neglected the fact that I had 35 jokes in there. It was about fun and a funny way of looking at something.

So with my writing, I really don't think too much about the impact; I just leave it to be whatever it is. Every once in a while, somebody says, "I like your writing" or "Oh my gosh, this happened because I thought about this." It's happened a few times. This guy in Burbank who was so in love with my book (he's a deputy in the city) was working huge hours. He read the book, bought 25 copies, and handed it out to everybody on his staff.

Every once in a while, you get a letter or a call and you go, "Wow, isn't that wonderful!" I don't think about it too much. The writing has been more about self-expression, throwing it out into the world. Every once in a while, the boomerang comes back with some delicious take on it, but most of the time I never see it again.

Donna: What's interesting is your focus, your reaction to the question about impact. A lot of people pay attention to their level of impact because they want that impact to be huge to feed their ego. Others look at it as how…

Tom: I did all that. Not to interrupt you, but I was that person. I was obsessed with what you thought of me. "Did you recognize that I was brilliant? Where was this connecting me, how could I be important and wealthy from it?" What I ultimately found was that it depleted what my real purpose was: To express my creativity.

Donna: A fundamental shift. The impact is no less, but the focus is not on you; it's outward. "What am I giving?"

Tom: Oh, yes. Totally. This is about *being yourself*. That all goes back again to identity. You are not looking to the world to give you your identity. I think at its deepest level that's what it is.

"Tell me who I am. Tell me I am worth something." Those are depreciated and corroded parts of the spine of an individual. If you clean that up and you align it, then you're not looking to the world to give you a chiropractic adjustment. You know who you are.

The best example I'm thinking of is Seinfeld and a guy I've known for years, Larry David, his partner. When they wrote Seinfeld, they really didn't try to make other people laugh, and when they got ratings, they didn't change the show.

In the beginning, it was not a big hit. They just kept doing the same thing, because that's what they did. Then it turned out the audience caught up to them. That's the best case scenario. Many artists do what it is they do, and they don't garner great success.

I do what I do. I do it at work. I do the same thing with my family. Sometimes, my family doesn't get me. I want them to stand up and say, "You have grown so much! You're fantastic!"

Instead, they go, "Oh, you finally became what we needed you to become. Thanks for showing up. There's no parade, and I don't think we have a trophy for you, but thanks for participating, because that's what we expected you to do."

Donna: What are your perceptions about the next generation to come and where they are in the world right now?

Tom: Oh my God, I am so bad at the socio-anthropological perspective on the world, because I live in my own little world. I work with alcoholics and addicts, so I get out of myself or connect to the community that way, but that's a particular demographic.

I would hope (and this may be wishful thinking) that the future generations will be driven by a more spiritual credo, and that they will seek out community more. I hope that the Internet, rather than a messenger or a Trojan horse that delivers even greater isolation and emotional disassociation, actually becomes what it also can be — a conduit for community, networking, and shared ideas. I'm hoping that. The only problem is that people seem to be so drawn to factions and cliques. The Internet is filled with opposing sites where people say one thing and disagree with each other. We'll always have that disagreement, that dialectic. I'd like to think that people will become a little bit more spiritual. Maybe even global warming will be a unifying element. I'd like to think that it'll be a generation that has more common ground.

Donna: I just came back from a symposium where we looked at sustainable leadership and what that means. We were talking about how it impacts not just our immediate jobs, families, and companies, but that we directly or indirectly do have impact on the world. Better people make a better world.

There's a sense of community. That's why the Internet is so popular, especially with younger generations. Those who are having a difficult time socially could still find a sense of community in some way, shape, or form through the Internet.

Tom: Yes, the only problem is that we just hope community isn't through Internet porn.

Donna: [Grinning] Yes, exactly.

Tom: I agree. I think that's a hope. The Internet is a very cerebral experience because you're stationary, and you're not connected to your body as much. I hope there are other activities that have to do with saving the planet, creating community centers, or whatever gets people out of the house and community-building face-to-face.

I wrote an article about that called "Facebook This." It's about how, in my observation, a part of the problem is that we don't have much eye contact anymore, so we can hide our emotions. We can even dissemble to the point of pretending we're someone we're not, a worst case scenario.

The other thing is that I subscribe to the theory that Freud proffered: The more we get away from working with the land and with our hands, the more neurotic we'll become as a culture and a species. The Internet is great, but I'd like to see people get out of the house, network, and do things together using all their limbs. Somehow, they'll connect in a different way.

Donna: How old are your kids now?

Tom: They are almost 12 and almost six. I have an unbelievable time with them. The amount of fun and caring I have with them is beyond belief.

It only makes me think back on my dad and how the poor guy missed out. I don't know if he really wanted it or was even prepared for it, but over-exercising one's authority in the home is an intimacy killer.

My emphasis with my kids is fun and play. Every once in a while, I will be the voice of authority when I have to be.

Donna: The way I look at it, attitude is contagious. What you give to your children is the attitude of fun loving, love, protected attention, and nourishment.

Tom: That's what I have been able to do, and I'm very grateful.

Donna: You're showing your kids what a functional, loving family unit can be.

Tom: Yes. People always speak of authority in terms of exercising it through rules and raising your voice. When people need to be authoritarian or in control, they emotionally flatten out, because they don't feel they can be self-disclosing. It's the concept of "lonely at the top."

I share my feelings when appropriate with my kids. They know what I'm afraid of. They know what hurts my feelings. If they're having a hard time, I'll share an experience where I was vulnerable, why I understand, or how I had the same problem and I dealt with it. So I'm a vulnerable person who has fears and difficulties as they do. I always try to present them in a way that is reassuring, rather than giving them the feeling that daddy is having a nervous breakdown.

I often thought of Martha Stewart. Right before she went to prison, Larry King asked her, "You won't see your daughter for six months. Do you feel sad about that?" She said, "Absolutely not," and I thought, 'Wow. Here she is, the compulsive leader, the person who never has dark feelings. She's always on top of it and so strong. What an incredible straightjacket to be living in.'

Donna: Yes. What you described is very human — being vulnerable and every aspect of who you are as a human being — and you're sharing that with your kids. It gives them permission to be human as well. That is a huge gift that you give them.

Tom: Yes. There are times with my kids when I'm aware of the impact. What I'm most aware of, though, is when they touch me.

Donna: What's next for you, Tom?

Tom: I don't think too far ahead. I'm very focused right now on providing for my family. For a long time I devalued that, because it had been so much a part of a faulty intention — to get rich and be important. I avoided it and went on this creative path. While it was great to rediscover my creativity, it was bad, because I didn't make much money. Now the balance has switched back. I'm doing my executive recruiting, and I'm now doing it in a way that has less wear and tear, and more service orientation. I'm very glad to be able to provide for my family, because God knows, we need the money.

I'm going to continue the writing. I have a book that *Inc.* Magazine wants to brand and will be taking my proposal out to publishers. It's called *Stop My Life, I Want to Get On*. It'll basically be *Inc.*'s humorous guide to balance for working parents.

Donna: Love it.

Tom: I'm really looking forward to that. It has three sections: *Our lives*, *Our inner lives*, and *Really living*.

The first section, *Our lives*, is about the world we live in, and how technology, values, and global events push us towards a certain kind of compulsive, non-stop activity.

Inner lives, the second section, are the feelings that we have that push us inside to perpetuate that which our culture promotes.

The third section is solution-oriented; in other words, *Really living*. How, in the midst of this conundrum and oppositional forces, do we find our individuality and identity, respect others' identities and individualities, and learn how to live? In this section, my personal favorite is looking at your life like a movie script that you can rewrite. This is a psychological paradigm to examine the back story — what a screen writer does before the movie starts.

They have all the characters' back stories, so you look at your history. Then you look at the unfolding of your narrative, a three-act structure, and then each day (like anyone making a movie) you have dailies. You look at the daily sheets, and then decide how to edit them. You look back at your day. If a scene didn't go well, you examine your role, and you try to rewrite it so the next time you're in that situation, you get a different outcome. It's called "rewriting the movie of your life," and it is the central driver to how I ask people to change their lives.

Donna: As a Shadow Coach, a lot of my clients tell me it's like living their day twice, except the second time it's doing it right.

Tom: To me, the ultimate movie that talks about this is *Groundhog Day*. I have a whole analysis of *Groundhog Day*, because basically he [Bill Murray] is trapped in one day. His habits and choices are fed back to him again and again, to the point where he starts to take the position of someone who's receiving that behavior rather than living it.

Then he becomes sick of himself through the redundancy of undesirable results, so he begins to try new choices, to have new desires. The movie ends with him being the center of the community, having gone from a selfish prick to a giving member of the community.

He finally discovers that this woman [Andie McDowell], who he thought he hated, was the love of his life, and learns how to get her love. Once they're a couple, they break out. He's liberated, not just from the day that he kept repeating, but from the imprisonment of his own narcissism. To me, it's literally an abstract for rewriting the movie of your life.

Donna: I love that movie. I can't tell you how many times I've seen it.

Tom: It's absolute genius. It's one of the most profound comedies ever made.

Donna: I so appreciate your time and you sharing this with me. Speak soon!

Tom: Thanks.

Reflections

Reflections ections

"We cannot tell what may happen to you in the strange medley of life. But we can decide what happens to us — how we take it, what we do with it — and that is what really counts in the end." – Joseph F. Newton

For someone who hangs out with comedians and comedy writers, writes hilarious columns and pieces himself, it would have been all too easy for Tom Stern to use comedy as a panacea for the trauma he lived through. A home invasion is a living nightmare. To think of what he and his family had lived through is inconceivable. Rather than minimize the experience or avoid the impact it had on his life, he chose to change how he lives it. He chose how he relates to those dear to him, and to help others live from a place of humanity and key personal values. He incorporates fun into his life, his writing, and his work, and doesn't mask one with the other. He believes in having fun and models it authentically.

As Leo Hindery, Jr., says, *"A great leader needs to love and respect people, and he needs to be comfortable with himself and with the world. He also needs to be able to forgive himself and others. In other words, a leader needs grace."* For some, it takes a lifetime to forgive themselves for their choices. For others, it's believing they could have done something to mitigate a crisis or trauma, even when it was totally out of their control.

Whether self-forgiveness takes a lifetime or not, it's a journey on which one learns what they're made of. It also gives those around them "permission" to forgive themselves. They can not only pick themselves up and dust themselves off to try again, but also choose a different path or lifestyle. Tom chose to be a leader, not a victim. He chose to lead from humanity, not power. He chose a great, full, and rewarding life over an extravagant lifestyle.

Years back, my mentor asked me how things were going with my son who had just undergone his twelfth (or so) surgery. I told him it was rough but that we were hanging in. He turned to me and said, "Hot dog, an opportunity!" to which I replied, "A few less hot dogs in my life would really be appreciated around now." He smiled and told me I would look back and realize that my choices in how I dealt with this would dictate where my life would go. I would learn a great deal about myself and what I was made of.

Looking back now, as I see Tom does, I believe "that which doesn't kill us makes us stronger." It doesn't mean that we won't continue to be challenged in life. The way I look at it, if I let life's challenges outweigh and diminish the joy in my life, then I'm not honouring what's already great in it. I'm giving away my personal power. For Tom, even as he reflects on what is best for him in his life, he helps others grow, align with their talents and strengths, and choose a great life, no matter what.

Social media is about sociology and psychology more than technology.
Evolution is evolution — it's happened before us and will continue after we're gone.
But, what's taking place now is much more than change for the sake of change.
The socialization of content creation, consumption, and participation
is hastening the metamorphosis that transforms everyday people
into participants of a powerful and valuable media-literate society.

In social media, influence has taken center stage.
With the spotlight perfectly fixed on the 'me' in social media,
a large shadow is now cast over the 'we' that defines the social web.
As individuals begin to realize the possibilities and benefits that surface as
a result of building connected social graphs, a very public exploration
to find the balance between influence and popularity unfolds.

BRIAN SOLIS

CHAPTER 10

BARRY LIBERT
Social Leadership

"In a world that has long since transitioned from the industrial age to the information age, we are about to see an equally profound change in business — both form and structure — from an age of command and control to one of sharing and collaborating." – Barry Libert

This conversation is all about connection and relationship, whether in person or through social media. In a world that is becoming more and more "virtual," Barry Libert honours humanity and strengthens leadership by helping people connect, collaborate, and strengthen their relationships.

Barry is the Chairman and CEO of Mzinga, the leading provider of social software, services, and analytics that improve business performance. As co-author of the critically acclaimed book, *We Are Smarter Than Me*, he highlighted the power of social technologies by using the Wiki-based contributions of more than 4,000 people to illustrate how businesses could profit from the wisdom of crowds.

Barry has been published in *Newsweek, Smart Money, Barron's, The Wall Street Journal*, and *The New York Times*, and he has appeared on CNN, CNBC, FNN, and NPR. In addition to forging Mzinga's vision and strategy, he currently serves on the Board of Directors at Innocentive, and The SEI Center for Advanced Studies in Management at The Wharton School of the University of Pennsylvania. He has written a new book published by John Wiley & Sons, *Social Nation: How to Harness the Power of Social Media to Attract Customers, Motivate Employees, and Grow your Business*. Barry is a graduate of Tufts University and holds an MBA from Columbia University. He currently lives in Boston, Massachusetts, with his wife and two sons.

As Barry says, *"People are the power behind any business."* Social networking isn't about racking up numbers to show you're connected. It's about creating and maintaining relationships. His goal is to empower and engage people in conversation so they can grow their business, learn from and support each other. He's the kind of person who brings all of who he is to a conversation. He shares generously, openly, and authentically. When we talk, it's about people, not technology. Whenever we end our conversation, I know I can't wait until the next one and the one after that.

Come and meet Barry...

Donna: I was speaking to my son, a senior policy analyst in the Canadian government. He was one of 150 up-and-coming leaders from across Canada chosen to work on an initiative for public service renewal called *Canada@150*. They were looking at how the mechanics of government must be changed to be relevant in the future. They had four in-person conferences; however, most of the work they did was through a virtual networking platform that enabled them to strengthen relationships and work across Canada and all its time zones, portfolios, and cultures. Just prior to this initiative, I asked him, "What is your impression of where education and technology are going?"

He said, "The traditional education system is failing, not because of bad teachers, low standards, or bad kids. It's because the content isn't interesting, and the environment isn't stimulating, but the rest of the world is."

The educational model has to change. It's got to be more open — such as OpenCourseWare, open source, and social networking. The physical environment is too structured and doesn't allow for individuality. He was thrilled to hear that I was going to have this conversation with you. What are your views about the current state of education?

Barry: I'm so pleased that you ask that. I have two sons. If you did an interview with either one of them, they would tell you the exact same thing you're saying.

There's nothing wrong with schools except the teachers are out of date in terms of their content. Interactions are limited to primarily in-person lectures, versus student-generated, online conversations, and they are not using today's Web 2.0 technologies. There is not enough listening by the faculty or leaders of the universities. Other than that, both schools they attend are fantastic.

Donna: It would be really nice to see them marry the in-person lectures and Web 2.0, and see how that might work. I'm hoping that since I'm writing about this in my book, public conversations with people like you will help our kids see the future in a different way. Perhaps they will be able to do something concrete to change how we work, communicate, and collaborate.

Barry: I hope you're right. I hired a young woman from Columbia University. She said, "If I come to work for you, I would become a Barry student." It's like, "Here, thanks to you, I'm getting exposure to everything all the time, good or bad." And I said, "That's correct."

Donna: It's called "life."

Barry: That's one way to look at it.

Donna: Not a "filtered life," or a life someone else designed for you, but an opportunity for you to explore and integrate life experiences as they happen. It's a different learning model.

That's the kind of coaching I do. I coach people in the context of their worlds in real time, based on reality, not perception. It's an eye-opener, both for me and those I work with. I need to understand people from the perspective of their stories, not mine. I want to see how a spark is lit by what they're doing, and to translate that spark to the next generation of up-and-coming leaders. I want to hear your story. Tell me, how did you get started?

Barry: In 1977, I went to Columbia Business School and then joined a management consulting firm. My clients used to ask, "Why would you pay a lot for a guy who knows very little about your business, someone who just graduated from business school? We'd really like to talk to our peers [leaders of other companies] to learn what the best are doing and how we can do something similar."

The question that has stuck with me is, "How can I learn from my peers to improve my performance and make better decisions?" Even today, I have friends who work at large management consulting firms, and they still say the same thing: Their clients want to talk to their peers. Large companies and their leaders are not unique:

- Kids want to talk to their peers before they talk to their parents.
- Customers want to talk to their peers before they talk to the company.

- Sick people want to talk to their peers before they talk to doctors.
- Employees want to talk to their peers before they talk to their bosses.
- People want to download music from their peers before they buy a song.

Donna: Good points.

Barry: In short, here's the only thing that's changed in the 30 years since I left McKinsey: Today's Web 2.0 technology enables everyone to talk to each other, to learn what works, and what doesn't work, from sharing their experiences online and in real time. In essence, the open source software movement has now come to business and it's called *user-generated content* — or as we call it — "the social revolution."

Donna: Tell me more.

Barry: There are examples now of how all organizations benefit from letting their constituents talk. You already gave me one: students are increasingly sharing content and insights outside the classroom to learn from each other. This occurs whether they are at the same school or not.

Another example is government. Barack Obama won the election based on citizen-generated content and his use of social media, including Facebook, Twitter, and his own website (MyBarackObama.com). By approaching his election from a social and open strategy, he ran a far more exciting campaign, managed and created by citizens, versus the more top-down, traditional approach that John McCain and Hillary Clinton took. In the end, President Obama made it personal. As a result, he raised more than $800M.

Donna: Very true. I believe it was so powerful because he made it personal. How he communicated meant something different to each person who read it. He didn't communicate in generalities or to the masses.

Barry: When you let peers do the work, they buy in. That is not new. Why companies don't get it is still amazing to me; that giving up control creates more buy-in rather than less. That's the problem for teachers. That's the problem for leaders.

That's the problem for parents. Most adults still don't fully believe that giving away control can have better results.

Donna: Why do you think it causes more trouble for teachers, for example?

Barry: Because teachers grew up in a time and age where knowledge was power. It was called the knowledge economy. Consequently, the more knowledge you had, the more power you had. Now, if I changed that paradigm and renamed our current economy the *sharing economy* or *social economy*, we would all work to help others. The more we helped each other, the more rewards we would receive. Right now, that is not the way it is.

Donna: And for leaders?

Barry: If we grew up in a social economy, then all the new, emerging ways of interacting would win. However, most leaders of today's society grew up in a *command-and-control* economy. They grew up in a time and place when people believed, and still believe, that if I sit at the top of the organization, I'm the commander-in-chief. Who wants to be commander-in-chief?

Donna: Some people do.

Barry: You bet. Every faculty member in the front of the room believes he or she is still the commander-in-chief of that classroom.

Donna: So to make a fundamental change of mindset, a paradigm shift, to change it to a more peer-based conversation and relationship, do you think the change will be subtle, or do you think it will be dramatic and revolutionary?

Barry: I think that leaders are going to learn a new skill called *followership*. It's not going to take place overnight, but social media and Web 2.0 technologies are forcing it to happen. Do I think they're going to go from *owning* to *sharing* overnight? Do I think they're going to go from inanimate to intimate? I think that's all fairly dramatic change.

Donna: And not necessarily easily accepted by the public at large, at least not right now.

Barry: It's accepted easily by the public at large. It's evident every day, based on the explosive growth in social interactions online across the world, just not by leaders yet.

Social media and open communications are being embraced by the public at large everywhere. A few examples are:

- Government by the people for the people — that's the core of democracy.
- Business by the people for the people — that's not technically democracy.
- Education by the people for the people — that's not educational democracy.

Donna: What made you get started in this social leadership realm? What got you going?

Barry: In the mid-'90s, I was working for AT&T's senior management and they said, "We'd like you to help us think about our strategy." I told them they should focus on their community — 75 million people talking to each other and six million businesses — not on their telephone poles and wires.

They thought I was crazy. They were convinced that they could own "the last mile to everyone's house." I told them that was impossible, because one day the last mile might be in space (mobile or satellite). But more importantly, I was convinced that their future resided in their community, not their infrastructure. They disagreed. So I began to realize that companies like AT&T were focused on the wrong thing — assets, not communities; products, not interactions. In short, they weren't focused on what you just said — the constituents and their content. That's the bottom line and they haven't changed since forever.

Donna: Are you doing this for governments as well?

Barry: Most of our business is focused on industry and helping leading organizations create vibrant, online communities that help them innovate. We help them measure what they hear, so that they can create the products and services their constituents want.

Donna: Measuring success is a whole other conversation. When people in another country are telling me that you're the person I need to speak to on this subject, no matter how success is measured, you know you have impact and presence globally.

Barry: Absolutely. You were asking how you would measure success in a world that's defined by purists. It's not the way the world defines it right now, by a leadership program or who commands control of it.

Donna: That's right. How do you measure it?

Barry: Businesses and government are just getting started. They need to measure how people feel (their sentiment) and then act on those feelings to ensure that people achieve their personal goals.

If you remember, there's a book by Dan Goleman about emotional intelligence and social IQ. People began to write about it and that was cool. I think the bottom line is that we're going to start measuring new capabilities and responses at work, including emotional and social skills of leaders, as well as emotional and social responses of our organizations' constituents.

If you looked at the way the world is going, we need to make sure that organizations measure the right things. Not just how much people have or purchase, but how well they are feeling and doing, emotionally and socially, at work, in society, etc.

Donna: Say more about that.

Barry: Sure. We all know we react emotionally to financial markets — their ups and downs — and we buy or sell stocks based on how we feel. The same is true in business and government. Consequently, we need to begin to measure the emotional health of a company. We'll know the strength of the company — its ability to keep and retain its employees and customers — based on the emotional well-being of that company, not just their financial capabilities.

Equally important, businesses will become more about letting their employees and customers become storytellers about their experience with the company, using social media tools like Facebook and Twitter to help win new customers and employees.

Donna: People learn and process things based on their own stories. Something has to be personal; there has to be a connection. This is why I believe peer-to-peer conversations enable that connection much more so than experts do. You might have respect, but you won't have as much buy-in, because it's more personal when it's your age group, your peer group, your community of interest, etc.

That's when *behavioral economics* become relevant. There has to be some meaning for the individual. That's the bottom line to evolve, integrate, pay attention, and learn. You're creating the environment for them to do that.

Barry: I'm trying to enable them to respond.

Donna: OK. Business-to-business?

Barry: In the business world, that's correct.

Donna: What about government?

Barry: We're just getting started there, but President Obama is surely leading the way in this new, open, and social world.

Donna: How about between governments on a global basis?

Barry: We're just getting started there as well. I think it's a good thing that President Obama did what he did. A good thing for you and me — so that we could have a foundation for this discussion.

Donna: Definitely. I had you on my list of people I wanted to talk with before your book on Obama's campaign came out.

Half of my work is done through networks and networking through my peer groups. I ask for information from people in similar areas of expertise to augment my learning and increase my knowledge base. I could not do it without technology. What you're providing is the global classroom for people to be able to fly.

Barry: I think that's exactly right. So what you're saying is that the context of learning is going to change, and I think that's right. I don't want to lead anymore in the old fashioned way; rather, I want to participate with others and facilitate their involvement. What I have learned is that the more I facilitate their interactions, the more productive they are, and the more their needs are fulfilled, and therefore, so are mine.

In short, what I have seen since the advent of social media is that people — students, parents, customers, employees, etc. — want to participate in new ways, share what they know with people they know and don't know. That's a whole new way of doing business. The more we let people participate, the better we will all do.

Donna: What keeps the fire lit within you? You've said it's difficult for you to break through into some of these new environments, so what keeps you going?

Barry: I believe that this new social and open approach to business, education, and government is "what's right" and appropriate for our age.

Donna: "What's right" … beautifully put.

It takes a great deal of insight into human nature drivers to be able to work with people in business in this new way. I'm also sure you invest a lot of emotional energy in what you're doing to keep you going.

Barry: You don't have to convince me. I give up plenty of times and then ultimately come back to it. The good news is that this year is easier than last year, and last year was easier than the previous year. Being a part of the social revolution is getting easier.

If you called me when we started, we had 500 users and nine employees. Now, Mzinga manages 15,000 communities with 300 customers, 40 million users, and nearly 180 employees. It's very different.

Donna: Congratulations! It's catching on, becoming viral and contagious.

Barry: Thank you. Maybe we can have a conversation with those you know and start similar conversations.

Donna: I certainly hope so. This book is a start. I'm sure it'll seed many conversations.

In many ways, the older wave of leadership used to look at themselves as being the best in the world. They wanted to be looked at as being the best at what they do, the most powerful, and the most visible. Now the newer leadership cadre is looking at leadership differently — being the best *for* the world, not necessarily the best *in* the world. I see groups working together as leaders much more readily than a single leader within a strongly defined hierarchy.

Not only are you changing how the conversations are happening, but the dynamics, content, and flow of them as well. The impact is a lot broader, don't you agree?

Barry: I think it's fantastic!

Donna: What would you share with the next wave of leaders who are trying to evolve into their level of excellence, into their own style of leadership as to how to move forward in their future?

Barry: That they need to act on their core instincts — that traditional and social leadership need to blend, just like the online and offline worlds. Both need to come together. User-generated content needs to blend with expert-generated insights.

Donna: I'm seeing a lot of young women and men with defeatist attitudes. They're hitting their head against the wall and they're having a very difficult time being individuals with present leadership.

There's a disconnect between the existing leadership in many organizations. People in their mid- to late 50s say, "I know. I have the experience and you don't, so be quiet and listen," a "what do *you* know?" attitude. Many of the "up-and-comings" then feel, "I've had enough. I try and try, and nobody is listening."

They don't know what to do and are struggling. How do you see them moving forward using the kind of communication style that you bring to the world?

Barry: I'm 56 years old, and I'll probably be dead before the full impact of all these changes happens. I have a lot of energy, obviously, but I think my message is, "If this is going to happen, and it may not be in my lifetime, whether it be a democracy or not, we won't accept being led in the way we're being led today."

I'm hoping President Obama will be one of the many reasons why leaders will shift. If there's anything I can do, other than to keep on speaking about this until I die, it will be to invite others to join with me.

Donna: What groups of people do you usually speak to?

Barry: Industry associations and large organizations.

Donna: Do you go to universities and do any lectures?

Barry: Yes, but not a lot … yet.

Donna: What would be the best way for you to get the message out, to get people engaged, and to light a fire inside them?

Barry: I think doing it the way you're doing it. Communicating constantly about the importance of the use of social media and Web 2.0 technologies to alter the way people communicate, teachers teach, businesses do business, governments govern, and leaders lead.

Donna: What else do you want to tell me about how you connect with people? People in the technology world are not known for being great communicators or "people" people. They're known as people who connect people through technology, but not through language or their way of being. You translate both into something very powerful. What's your secret?

Barry: I'm very emotive. There are a variety of ways I can answer your question. I believe strongly in these messages; they are personal for me.

First is to connect emotionally, in-person with individuals. Second is to use the technology that your constituents prefer. For example, some people like the phone, others like in-person meetings, and some like the Internet.

The bottom line is that all organizations have to use all mediums to let their people connect. Obviously, the fastest growing medium is the Internet.

I start with the fact that everything is personal with people, and I want to be personal about me. What's personal about me and what's personal about how I can help them is on a personal level as well.

Donna: One of the fears that a lot of people have when bringing technology into play is they'll lose that emotional, that human, connection. I'm finding myself in these conversations on a regular basis. "People don't see my body language. They don't really know where I'm coming from if they're not present in the room with me. How do we have these conversations without losing that emotional connection?"

Barry: That is correct. I think emotional connection means emotional exposure. I think my point of view has been the same forever. I've always believed that people should be able to express themselves and not get hurt in the process.

Donna: I think for some, technology provides a level of anonymity. If they're not face-to-face having the conversations, it helps them open up even more. For some who need that physical connection in a room with somebody, they have a very difficult time sharing emotions through technology. I find it fascinating to help people bridge those gaps: to be themselves, whether in person or through technology; to open up and not be afraid of a machine transmitting their thoughts and ideas. It's about creating connections.

What kind of technology are you using for peer-to-peer conversations? Is it audio? Is it through the written word? Is it video? All of the above?

Barry: It's all of them: every type of new social technology, including video, audio, tech, and mobile. You name it, we can do it all.

Donna: Do you see in the future that people will be working more and more from their homes, connected through technology to work together without sharing office space?

Barry: Absolutely. More importantly, my view is there is a way to get this done, and that includes multi-channel conversations, building whatever context or opportunity people will want to use to achieve their personal goals.

Donna: What message, ultimately, would you like to be sharing, so people really understand what you want to be doing?

Barry: I am a strong believer in the Internet as the primary medium in which all of us will increasingly share information and experiences. However, I'm also a strong believer in other channels like the phone and in-person meetings.

Donna: So no roadblocks to any kind of communication.

Barry: That's correct.

Donna: How would you suggest people become more comfortable with this kind of networking if they've never tried it before?

Barry: They've got to start by going online. They need to get involved with Facebook and Twitter. Try some of the new social technologies, just like you and I are using the phone today to connect.

Donna: Right. It seemed to be the easiest way, rather than me flying into Boston, although I would have loved that. It's a way to connect and creates an impetus for me to look for more, to want more, and to see how this connects others. That way, they can do their work better through collaboration and generative dialogue. That's what this is all about: to generate something new with a meeting of minds, correct?

Barry: Correct.

Donna: What else would you like the world to know about Barry?

Barry: I'm here to help in any way I can. As people start to transition to more open, honest, online conversations using today's Web 2.0 technologies, I'm here to build online social conversations and communities that help grow and strengthen business, government, and education.

Donna: That's great. Thanks, Barry.

Reflections

Reflections ections

"How can you squander even one more day not taking advantage of the greatest shifts of our generation? How dare you settle for less when the world has made it so easy for you to be remarkable?" – Seth Godin

I love that, "…when the world has made it so easy for you to be remarkable." Why in the world would you let anything stop you from shining?

I recently did a keynote about virtual teams. In researching about the number of tweets that happen every minute, the percentage of people on Facebook, and how many blogs are indexed globally, what became apparent was how small this world is becoming, and how social media blurs geographic borders. People want to be heard. It's no longer only publishing and recognizing data from industry experts; it's hearing and taking into consideration everyone's point of view and valuing people and their contributions.

In the not-so-distant-past, we would read articles and papers from experts and use them as gospel. Now we know what the people in the field think. We can listen to perspectives from all ranks, cultures, and industries. We know what it's really like working in the trenches from the stories we read. We connect with people through their stories and then, in turn, share ours. We no longer download information in a one-way communication style. We talk about everything.

Social media brings us a platform from which we can do research and development. We can ask questions and have them answered. We can reach out and connect with people we might never end up meeting, but who will impact our lives exponentially. We can and do create friendships.

We have access to educational institutions, networks of people, and bodies of research at the click of a mouse. I truly believe that everything we bring to the table through these growing networks will make the world a better place as we can take a stand and be heard. I believe human-based leaders will build bridges between people, then take a step back and support others to build bridges of their own. They will be comfortable letting go of the need to control the process and invite outcomes instead. These leaders bring past experience to the present and then watch how it's integrated into what has to happen to create a thriving, sustainable future.

If we think about how the use of social media has exploded in the past six or so years (which Barry illustrates so well when he speaks about people wanting to talk to their peers), what we're quickly learning is that very little is impossible. It just hasn't been discovered yet. When a few people put their heads together to create something new, it's powerful. When thousands contribute from all over the world, social media becomes a form of "global think tank," impacting people well beyond our organizations, communities, and fields of practice. However, this is changing faster than the speed of light.

I love the interaction and conversations that happen in the social media world. However, I also know I have to be discerning about what I follow and what I contribute to. Otherwise, I'll be spending all my time on the periphery and not in the midst of valuable dialogue. How can I integrate social media in my work while maintaining client confidentiality? I know I have no control over how what I share lands with people. Being mindful of what I share and the intention behind it is where stewardship lives for me. As a coach, how can I support people with the intention of doing no harm? What do I have to keep in the back of my mind with everything I write, post, and respond to?

Barry's conversation reminded me to safeguard my relationships from becoming superficial. Social media should augment my connection to others, not replace it. Leaders like Barry are making sure the human connection isn't lost in the midst of technological advancements. With this stewardship, I believe we won't have to sacrifice relationship for connectivity, and instead, bring both together as one.

All of the great leaders have had one characteristic in common:
It was the willingness to confront unequivocally
the major anxiety of their people in their time.
This, and not much else, is the essence of leadership.

JOHN KENNETH GALBRAITH

CHAPTER 11

FRANK MCKENNA
A Burning Platform

Trying to capture Frank McKenna in a brief summary is next to impossible. Frank McKenna was born in Apohaqui, New Brunswick, Canada. He was raised in his grandparents' home. They lived adjacent to his parents, because his large family could not be wholly housed in his parents' home.

He is a Canadian businessman, former politician, and diplomat. He is currently Deputy Chair of the Toronto-Dominion Bank. He is responsible for helping to build long-term business relationships that support TD's growth strategy in Canada and the United States, expanding its North American presence as one of the continent's ten largest banks.

As a politician, Frank won one of the largest electoral victories in Canadian history in the 1987 election. His provincial party in New Brunswick, the Liberal Party of Canada, won every seat in the legislature that year. His key priority throughout his term was job creation, and he was known to say that the "best social program we have is a job."

He served as Canadian Ambassador to the United States, and has been numerously identified and favoured as a potential future leader of the Liberal Party and Prime Minister of Canada. As recently as October 28, 2008, he affirmed an earlier decision of not wanting "his life to become consumed by politics." Frank said that he would not seek the leadership, stating, "Although I have been deeply moved by expressions of support for me from across the country, I have not been persuaded to change my long-standing resolve toexit public life for good.... My only regret is that I cannot honour the expectations of friends and supporters who have shown enormous loyalty to me."

He graduated from law school as a silver medalist and holds eight honourary doctorates from Canadian universities. In November 2009, he was made Officer of the Order of Canada.

Come and meet Frank…

Donna: Good morning! With everything happening in the financial world right now, are you sure this is still a good time to have this conversation?

Frank: Let's get at it. We have all hell breaking loose in the banking community today, but there's no time that'll be better.

Donna: I wanted to start by asking you, "What got you started?" I know the political world is not easy, that's for sure. And I recognize the banking world isn't either, especially in the middle of an economic crisis. What is it that keeps you going?

Frank: I think everybody in their life needs a burning platform and that burning platform can come about in different ways. It can be a combination of financial need and ambition. In the case of successful entrepreneurs, they often come from limited means and have a desire to move up the ladder. In other cases, they would have ambition instilled in them as part of their upbringing and socialization when they were young.

In my case, it's probably a combination of both. I came from a poor family, so I had a strong desire to try to do better financially. I was raised by a grandmother who was very ambitious and set high expectations for me. I think that combination resulted in having an ambition to move up the ladder, whether it was in education, business, or whatever.

Politics was a natural corollary to that. It was another way to succeed, achieve, and try to do better. In my case, the transition from business to politics that I was involved in wasn't very easy, because I had enjoyed my other life so much. I felt, at the time I made the move, that the province was in dire shape, and all of us had to stand up and be counted. I was in a good position to do that, so I did.

Donna: Did you ever turn around and say, "What am I doing this for?"

Frank: Yes. I think everybody who has gone into public life feels that way. The amount of scrutiny and stress is very high, and the amount of gratitude is very low. So, at times, you often question why you're doing what you're doing.

Donna: Did you have an ongoing mentor while you were working in the political world? That's often very difficult for somebody who was at your level in politics.

Frank: No, I didn't, although it would have been a very nice thing to have.

Donna: It's interesting how people look back and say that they didn't think they did, and then remember someone who did influence them in some way. What was your journey like?

Frank: I've never had much chance to reflect on it because I've always been on the journey.

Everybody is different. I don't want to reflect on people who are different from me, but in my case, I've never ever had rear-view mirrors on. It's just been straight ahead: one door leads to another, one at a time. I've never really turned around to survey the journey or thought about it at all.

It's always just been straight ahead. I've never taken any great sense of pride of accomplishment in past achievements or been too overly apoplectic about failures.

Donna: Do you have any idea how many people told me that you were the first person they thought of for me to contact for this book? From very young political leaders of the future to people who are working in government right now. It's fabulous. I'm just wondering, do you realise how strong your impact is and has been?

Frank: Not really. Not to be falsely modest, but I've always thought that I was pretty ordinary and have never had the confidence to feel otherwise. I don't feel that way even today. I have never felt that way about myself, so I guess I've never really thought about what other people might be thinking.

Donna: One's circle of influence goes well beyond their understanding. You included, obviously.

Frank: Thank you for saying that. That is a very nice thing for me to hear today.

Donna: Last year, I coached a very young man who decided to run for the Liberal Party in Saskatchewan. We met before he left to do his Masters degree at the Kennedy School of Public Policy. I told him about the book I was writing. As an up-and-coming political leader, I wanted his opinion as to who he thought would be perfect to have a conversation with for this book. He said, "Frank McKenna." My son was here at the time. He works in government as well and said, "Yes, absolutely."

You have impacted people of all ages, in many areas, not only political. I'm glad I could share that with you. These are comments and opinions one doesn't often get a chance to hear.

Frank: I appreciate it. Thank you.

Donna: So, what do you think the next wave of leadership needs to pay attention to?

Frank: I think people have to get out in front of the public. Canadians, I think, are becoming increasingly restless and impatient. They know we have a great country, but they don't see it achieving really great things. I think we have to show more ambition for our country than we're showing.

We also have to be prepared, not only to accept a role on the national stage, but on the international stage, as well. Right now, Canada is kind of an oasis of peace and tranquility in a world that either politically or economically is imploding.

We have the experience to share and we have the leadership to provide. I think the next generation of leaders needs to step up their game from just being average Canadian leaders to punching above their weight and taking on a role in the world.

Donna: I know it's possible; anything is possible. Sometimes I don't think the word "impossible" should be in our vocabulary. I'm looking at the present leadership in government. How much do you think they're paying attention to those who will follow them, so there can be this kind of change?

Frank: It's a hard question to ask today, because we're in the middle of an environment of "pending election," and people in an election can have a different kind of horizon. I don't know the answer to that.

I've found that our governments, both liberal and conservative, in the last 20 years or more, have been of modest ambition. It's worked reasonably well politically, but I think the time has come to be more ambitious than that.

Truthfully, I don't see it happening. I am just making the argument that I think Canadians are ready to go further than we've gone before.

Donna: I'm looking at this group of young, rising stars who worked on the Canada@150 Initiative, I'm wondering about how they have such great expectations and about how the results of this initiative will be implemented or at the very least, paid attention to. I hope that they won't be disappointed. It's an extraordinary Initiative that, if used wisely, could create radical improvement in how government works.

Frank: Yes. Young people still have all of that passion, energy, enthusiasm, and idealism that's necessary for change. Maybe if we have enough young people who get excited and impassioned about things, they'll push the rest of us along. Usually, dramatic change comes from the minds and the hearts of younger people.

Donna: Are you in any way working with students or teaching in any capacity to pass along some of your insights?

Frank: Yes, I have. I participated with a group of young people in New Brunswick who are doing exactly this, developing their leadership skills.

I've also been mentoring some business leaders. I wouldn't call it a mentorship, exactly, but I do have a lot of friends at the premier level or in the federal political apparatchik who I consult with on a regular basis. In fact, I had your Premier in this morning for breakfast here at the bank. We had a very good chat, and then he did a public address here. I do that sort of thing a lot. I speak a lot with the political leadership across the country. I don't know if I'd call it a mentoring role, but it's certainly a collaboration role of some kind.

Donna: What words of wisdom would you pass on to them? Often, I think it's difficult to be a human-based leader in politics, although not impossible. In business as well, people want to work with leaders who will help them evolve into their level of excellence and who offer some definite ideas of how to get there.

What would you recommend for those just going into business or politics right now, when times are more than difficult?

Frank: I've probably never been a student of textbook leadership, so I guess my contribution tends to be dusting off old bromides and anecdotes from what I've observed in my normal everyday life. There are all kinds of texts written about leadership, but, quite frankly, I haven't read them nor would I necessarily recommend them.

What I usually tell young people or anybody who aspires to be a leader is this: The only limitation on your achievements is going to be your own ambition. If you're ambitious and persistent enough, you can do anything. Just never give up. John

Diefenbaker, I recall, ran in the Federal Election five times, I believe, before he ever won. Sometimes you just have to have that attitude of "I'm not going to give up."

Anyone I have ever met who was a successful entrepreneur has run from door to door, had them slammed in their face, and had that "stick-to-it-iveness" that means they'll never give up; that they can overcome. I think that's an even more important element than skill.

Skills are necessary to move to even higher levels. You have to have either interpersonal skills and/or, hopefully, strong technical, business, or government skills, or a broad-based knowledge. You really do need to have that human quality of persistence and ambition, and I find that goes an awfully long way. I've got great faith in those people who just never give up.

Other things are common to leaders. You need to have respect for other people. You need to transcend partisanship, whether it's business or political. I find that most remarkable leaders are not purely partisan in their hearts. They tend to see the good in other people and in other ideas. I think you need to transcend partisanship, and you need to set the bar high for your associates.

Don't let people get away easily. If you set the bar high for yourself, then set it high for other people. You'd be surprised at how many people will strive to get over that bar.

Be generous with praise for achievement. There's nothing that motivates people more than being recognized and praised for the accomplishments they've achieved. I think people will walk through machine-gun fire for leaders who have rewarded them with praise for genuine accomplishments.

Those are all things which I don't think are very original ideas, but it's amazing how dramatic the impact can be if you can introduce them into the workplace.

Donna: What do you think are the attributes that contribute most to your success?

Frank: I think persistence is part of it. I ended up getting out of school with high marks. I was at law school and had scholarships all the way through, but I never felt like it was because I was so smart. It's just that I worked hard at it. I made sure that I was going to make every effort possible to achieve that kind of success.

Getting elected was the same way. I just out-worked opponents. I'd love to think that it was some kind of raw talent, but I've never thought that. It was just working harder than other people.

I don't mean to be vain about this, but I think that I've possessed, almost from birth, a passion for what I'm doing. When you feel passionate about what you're doing, you make other people feel passionate as well. Passion is a very powerful tool for leaders, because as a population, all of us want to feel hope, feel good about ourselves, and we want to feel like we're moving towards somewhere positive. Passionate leaders bring that out in us and make us feel good about what we're doing, so I think passion is awfully important as well.

Donna: If you defined success for yourself, not how others see you, what would that be?

Frank: Having three terrific kids and seven beautiful grandchildren who are the highlight of my life.

Donna: Beautiful. Are they all out east?

Frank: No. I have one son out east, one in the centre, and one out west.

Donna: So they're all over the place.

Frank: Yes.

Donna: After you finish your work here (and some people will never retire because they just love what they're doing), what's next for you?

Frank: I love everything physical, so for me exercise is play. I was out this weekend biking. I'll be golfing tomorrow. Every day, I get some kind of exercise, and I enjoy that.

In terms of what I intend to do going forward, I'll continue to be involved in corporate and political Canada. I think I'll be increasingly involved in international aid in some form or other. I've always thought about it academically and theoretically, but I've been involved a little bit more in recent months. I've come to feel a great deal of satisfaction about that involvement, so I believe that will fill part of my life going forward.

Donna: I'm going to wrap this up, because I know you're pressed for time. You have set records when it comes to being elected in your province. I would think you are aware of some of the impact that you have had, and that you continue to have. How might you use some of that impact in an extremely positive way to reach out further than your immediate circle?

Frank: That's a good question. I don't know if it's impact, but certainly taking advantage of my longevity. At the bank, I speak to literally thousands of employees across the bank throughout the year and thousands, maybe even tens of thousands, of clients and customers. I speak to thousands of members of the general public in other ways across the country. I also speak out frequently on national and international issues in various forums, so I'm hoping that I can continue to have some impact on that.

I would like, in a small way, to continue to be part of the national dialogue on the future of Canada. I have strong feelings about that. I have very strong feelings about our own region of Atlantic Canada, and I tend to have a lot of input with various decision-making bodies in that region. I believe those are all areas where I could have my best impact.

Donna: Thank you so much.

Frank: Listen, good luck. It's a good day to be calling, because when the world is falling in, it's nice to have some distraction.

Donna: Thanks.

Reflections

Reflections Reflections ections

I have always been struck by a sense of wonder whenever I listen to Frank McKenna. His stance for Canada, the Canadian people, justice, and human rights across cultures, countries, economies, and political systems is indicative of his human-based leadership. It would be all too easy for him to go back into politics, as his following remains loyal and strong. He chose instead to make a difference behind the political scenes, to remain involved, active, and to be an advocate for what he believes in.

He wants to see our country create a learning culture among all Canadians, not just pockets of them. He reminds Canadians and people of other countries not to sell Canada short. We have presence and prominence on the world stage. At the same time, he urges Canadians to never become complacent and to maintain their focus on what's truly important within Canada and the world as a whole. He challenges respectfully, leads honourably, and reminds us all to look deep within our psyche to rekindle our energy and passion for what's right. In this day and age, with the advent of social networks, we have the ability to remind political powers what we want to stand for as a global community. He tells us to stand up and be counted.

When I work with political and government leaders, we know choices are rarely black and white, right or wrong. It's not easy to live by personal values in the public realm. To be able to do both, leading from humanity and transparency, is about living your words, not just speaking them.

These human-based leaders accept complete responsibility for everything they think, say, feel, and do. They are not afraid of making mistakes or of taking reasonable risks. They are life-long students, always ready to learn, recognizing that growth takes sustained effort. Through that, they own and celebrate successes and failures alike, as both are instrumental to growth. For them, anything else would be mere existence, and not genuinely living life. Each risk taken allows them to invent their futures and, by example, gives others permission to invent their futures as well.

I recall a saying that goes something like "If you've never failed, you've never lived." Life equals risk. Without stretching beyond that which is safe and comfortable, we won't know success. Reflecting on how willing I am to take risks, both personally and professionally, I realise it's more difficult for me to risk in my personal life. Professionally, once I let go of fears and worries about what will unfold in my business, I am overflowing with abundance and opportunities. When I am so focused on what isn't working and try to force an outcome, things just don't happen the same way. In business, if something doesn't work, I can change, tweak, and reinvent until it clicks. When I risk personally, it's by opening my heart, and the rewards are immeasurable. However, when things don't work out as intended, I can't just fix it. It's about my healing, learning, and then risking yet again. Bringing both together, leading from head and heart brings a whole other dimension. A large part of my work is helping others to live their dreams and to have no regrets, to risk and reap the rewards of what unfolds for them and those they lead.

> *"Leadership must be based on goodwill. Goodwill does not mean posturing and, least of all, pandering to the mob. It means obvious and wholehearted commitment to helping followers. We are tired of leaders we fear, tired of leaders we love, and tired of leaders who let us take liberties with them. What we need for leaders are men of the heart who are so helpful that they, in effect, do away with the need of their jobs. But leaders like that are never out of a job, never out of followers. Strange as it sounds, great leaders gain authority by giving it away."* – Admiral James B. Stockdale

Frank McKenna is such a leader, one who lights a fire under those he leads. There is a reason why he won every seat in the legislature.

---

*Leaders establish the vision for the future and set the strategy
for getting there; they cause change.
They motivate and inspire others to go in the right direction
and they, along with everyone else, sacrifice to get there.*

JOHN KOTTER

CHAPTER 12

ROBERT ZITZ
Courageous Leadership

Robert S. Zitz is currently the Deputy Associate Director for the United States Secret Service, a senior government official with almost 30 years of intelligence community and Homeland Security experience. He is widely known and respected by the most senior leaders in U.S. Intelligence. A visionary with the knowledge, passion, and leadership qualities needed for transformation, Robert has been at the forefront of many of the changes in military and civilian intelligence during the last two decades. He began his career as a civilian intelligence analyst and rose through to senior executive service. He has held leadership positions in Army Intelligence, the Central Intelligence Agency (CIA), the National Geospatial-Intelligence Agency(NGA) , the National Security Agency (NSA), the Department of Homeland Security (DHS), and the Secret Service.

Robert's honours and awards include appointment as the first Deputy Under Secretary in DHS, recipient of the DCI National Intelligence Medal, the NIMA Distinguished Service Medal, the U.S. Army Superior Civilian Service Medal, and the Thomas Knowlton Military Intelligence 'Hero' Award.

His colleagues say, "Rob is the exemplar of leadership, exuding, first and foremost, professional courtesy to all employees regardless of person, authority, or position. Rob is a person to watch, to learn from, to work with, and, if you cannot see the path, simply follow him. In my *Can Do* book, Rob gets it." – Marion Georgieff, Deputy Chief Information Officer, U.S. Secret Service

"Rob Zitz embodies leadership values we hold dear: integrity, courage, and loyalty. To stand in his presence brings revelation when he begins to quietly speak. His words, which become his deeds, create the indelible image of a great person with whom it is a privilege to serve." – John Ives, Vice President, A-T Solutions

I'd say, "that says it all," but our conversation brings out so much more.

Come and meet Rob…

Donna: Ready to dive in?

Rob: Yes, but before we do that, I want you to know that I'm a huge believer in the idea of executive coaching. No matter how talented a person is, it is important to have a coach who can help see where one might have gaps in understanding and provide ideas for improvement. I've been using an executive coach on and off over the last 10 to15 years, so I just want you to know that I think that's an important capability that you bring to people.

Donna: Thanks. I really appreciate hearing that. I think the best part of my work, whether corporate, political, or in government, is to help them see talents and strengths they're not paying attention to. Rather than fill in the gaps, I help them remove roadblocks and figure things out that aren't working. We also look at what's working amazingly well, competencies they aren't using or using enough of, and talents they might not be consciously aware of. In the latter case, I call it "revealing the client to him or herself," so they can start purposefully using their talents to evolve and strengthen their leadership.

My clients are extraordinary individuals who are constantly open to learning and growing. This shows the strength of character they have to be open to the coaching process. It takes courage to dive in with a coach, but it's great to have a "partner in crime," excuse the pun. So tell me, what was the driving force that got *you* to where you are?

Rob: I'm an Army brat. My father was an Army artillery officer. I'm also a product of a family of three boys. We moved around quite a bit, as any Army family would do, and we spent a lot of time overseas. We settled back in the Northern Virginia area. I went to high school in Fredericksburg, Virginia. I went off to college at the University of Arizona and also George Mason University.

I was always interested in the military, world affairs, and politics. I'm also very interested in journalism, so I ended up with a major in political science and a minor in journalism.

Journalism is about information gathering, assimilating facts, trying to synthesize meaning, and then putting it all into context. I can liken journalism to the intelligence community's jobs of collection, analysis, and dissemination of information. So getting into the intelligence community enabled me to do all the things I am interested in.

As far as the driving force that inspired me, I give all the credit (or blame) to my mother. My parents got divorced when I was 12, and my mother took on the lion's share of the responsibility for raising three sons. My mother went to work at Marine Corps Headquarters. With only a high school diploma, she rose through the ranks to a very senior civilian position. She told us, "Anything is possible. You just have to put your mind to it, and you can achieve it." She really shaped my brothers and me to do what we believe in.

I graduated from college in 1979 and went to work as an intelligence operations specialist with Army Intelligence. At the tender age of 22, I was supporting the new Army counter-terrorism unit, Delta Force. I learned a lot while working with Delta. I learned there are young men and women around the world who, as we're speaking, are putting their lives on the line to protect our families and ourselves.

There I was, just out of college, supporting these young commandos. I was getting to know what they did and how they did it. It seared into me that this is not about a job; it's not just a career; it's not a salary; it's not about being in at 8:00 a.m. and leaving by 5:00 p.m. What intelligence is about is giving the people who take action the information they need in time and of a sufficient quality to make smart decisions.

Donna: Was there something you could put your finger on that created a fire in you? Some shaping event?

Rob: The September 11th attack was clearly the seminal event, much like Pearl Harbor was for another generation. But for me, 9/11 didn't create the fire, it merely accelerated things. I already felt a sense of urgency about the threat to our nation; 9/11 sharpened everyone's focus on the threat.

I had worked with Delta Force and other counter-terrorism activities before they became the imperative of the national security arena. Most people weren't thinking about or talking about terrorism as a grave threat to the United States in the late 1970s or 1980s.

Still, people who studied it understood that it was a growing storm. The 9/11 attacks showed everyone how vulnerable we are. For agents of change, it made us feel the need to accelerate the transformation of our processes and capabilities.

Donna: Just a quick question. Somebody that I'm working with who's one of the heads of the Afghanistan Task Force was saying that when it comes to tasking jobs, 15% of his staff does 80% of the work. He has to make sure he rotates people in and out on a regular basis so he doesn't burn them out. Is that applicable there as well?

Rob: Unless you're in a really unusual circumstance or organization that is populated exclusively by extraordinary achievers, you are going to have a bell curve of performers. What happens all too often, and we have to guard against this, is gravitating only to people who have your own perspective, passion, and commitment. The risk is always going to these hard-chargers who "get it" because you will burn them out, not get opposing or different perspectives, and not develop other members of your subordinate staff.

Every good leader has to temper their own expectations about how quickly they can achieve their goals. It is true that sometimes you have a timeline that you have no ability to influence. It's got to be done by a certain time so you've just got to make it happen. But often you have more time. A good leader should think about how they can develop the entire staff and improve everyone's skills. This is easier said than done, and I will admit it can be frustrating and easy to just keep piling the work on the 15%, the so-called "workhorses."

Donna: When it comes to you (and I assume you're in that 15%), how do you guard against burning out?

Rob: I try to make "finding balance" not just a platitude. I really try to have downtime. When I go home at night, I try to turn off my mind about work unless there's something that's in a crisis mode. I work out, do things together with my wife, spend time with my children (all in their 20s now), read, and try to learn things unrelated to my professional life.

One of my former bosses used to say, "Don't worry about your job while you're gone because nobody else wants to do it. It'll still be here on Monday." I take vacations. I go away. I try to do more than just one day off at a time. I try to get away for a week or even two weeks and to get some perspective on things.

Donna: That's good. What was your transition of thinking about what you wanted to do? People dream about things, but few actually go out and do them.

Rob: The key event that told me, "Wow! You've got to do this and make things better for people!" happened in late 1983, while supporting the Army special operations forces who liberated Granada and rescued many Americans.

It was an event that was seared into my mind and soul. It's indelible. You cannot experience something like that — and I wasn't even in Granada. I wasn't pulling the trigger, and I didn't have bullets whizzing by me. But knowing that people that I and many others were supporting were on the ground, many of them wounded, and some killed — you can't live through something like that and say, "Hey, this is just a job." You can't ever think that way.

I know it changed me. Throughout military history, when you ask a solider what they are fighting for, they invariably answer "for my buddies." You're in a firefight, and what you want to do is ensure your buddies get out alive — and that you get out alive. That's the imperative right there, right then. Then you can scale up from that, all the way up to the national imperative, national security, and national survival. It's about taking care of that person right next to you. It's really about human needs and human survival.

At the risk of sounding like I am wrapping myself in the flag, supporting the young men and women who are on the front line of defense for America is what motivates me. These are our military forces, our law enforcement, our emergency personnel. Helping them is what keeps me going, even in the face of bureaucratic and political roadblocks.

Thinking about improving the front line's lives and their capabilities is what steels me when others around me cut and run, or when I get a "not only no, but hell no" for a response from decision makers on change initiatives.

I try to be fearless in terms of what I try to accomplish. Not reckless. I get my facts in order and try to ensure what I am proposing will measurably improve things. I'm not in harm's way. What harm could come to me and my career if my proposal is shot down? I might be embarrassed. I might not get a bonus at a certain level. I might not get the title that I'm looking for in that next job. That is nothing compared to really being shot at and really being in harm's way.

Donna: It sounds as if it's a no-brainer, that it wasn't a conscious thought. It's just your "Rob DNA" turning around and saying, "OK, I'm diving into this, regardless."

Rob: Yes. Again, other people might say I'm reckless. They might be surprised to hear I don't do an analysis on the implications for me, personally, when I am proposing a change initiative.

I don't care about that part of it. What I care about is getting our front line what they need in time to make a difference for them. If I run into a roadblock or resistance, I don't take "No" for an answer. I start thinking, "OK, it didn't work the first time. That approach didn't work. Back up. Re-assess. How do I go after it?" My friends call it the "R Factor." They say, "When Rob meets resistance and reluctance, he counters with relentlessness."

Donna: What was the journey like getting there? What attributes contributed most to your success along the way?

Rob: What's it like? If you associate two words with my name, they are "Change Agent." What's the journey been like these last 30 years? It's been exciting. It's been rewarding. I have to admit it's been professionally and personally rewarding for me, because I have had some success. In addition to being exciting and rewarding, it's challenging. It's been really hard. Being a change agent — and I talk to young change agents all the time — the life of a change agent is one in which you've got to accept the fact you're not in this for personal glory. If you are, you will be sorely disappointed.

You're also not in this for immediate satisfaction or gratification. You're not in this because two or three months or a year from now, you're going to be standing on a platform and all the big guns, the elephants, are going to be saying, "Joe Blow here was the chief architect responsible for this and it led to that." You get the acclaim, the glory, and the accolades.

The reality for a change agent is different. The reality is if it's worth changing, it's probably something relatively significant that you're trying to accomplish. It's going to take time and energy. There are probably going to be many people resisting the change.

What I have found happens is that you get the boulder moving up the hill. Then two, five, or even ten years later, the things that you got moving and got people thinking differently about will finally come to fruition. By the time they come to fruition, you've moved on to two, three, or four jobs beyond that and nobody says, "Oh yes. It was Joe Blow who started that." It's whoever is in the position at the time that the ribbon is cut, the deal is struck, and they're the ones who are getting the accolades. I always tell people following me as change agents, "If you're in this for some kind of instant gratification or getting that pat on the back, forget it. This isn't the job for you."

Instead, the satisfaction we get as change agents is knowing that over a career, you've made things better for a lot of different people and organizations, and knowing important changes are "forever" changes.

Donna: That speaks to your level of impact. It goes well beyond your understanding, knowledge, and immediate view. However, it is extraordinarily strong and powerful when you don't pay attention to it in the moment.

Rob: It's like chaos theory, where one change can ripple around the world and change all sorts of things in ways that you hadn't even imagined. Hopefully, they're positive changes.

Donna: What are the lessons learned?

Rob: One of the lessons of a successful change agent is you've got to be good at visioning. You've got to be able to foresee the future and understand what the possibilities are. Visioning involves understanding the strategic changes that will irrevocably change your customers' operating environment. These changes include threats, geopolitical shifts, economic trends, health issues, climate change, etc.

The second lesson I have learned is the importance of knowing the customers' mission. You've got to understand the mission focus of your customers, of your users, of your clients. The best way to do that is to live, breathe, eat, and work in their space.

I've known many officials over the years who sit back and pontificate in an ivory tower about what needs to be done to support their customers. Yet, they have rarely gone "down range" or into the real world of their customers. You've got to get up close and personal with your customers — understand what they're doing, what they're up against, and how their needs are changing. Otherwise, you're going to be totally disconnected with what they need.

Donna: Yes, because then it becomes about you, and not about them. Then you're not serving them.

Rob: That's exactly right.

The next lesson is to carefully strategize about how to get a change initiative underway. Often, when things change, officials' resources shift from A to B. Unfortunately, too many officials tie their own personal and professional egos to the traditional trappings of power and authority: number of staff, amount of money controlled, etc. Significant change proposals invariably change this power alignment. This perceived (or real) shift of authority can quickly lead to resistance.

People also resist change for the right reasons, such as a lack of vision for the future, lack of clarity about what needs to be done, or an ill-conceived change proposal. In these cases, smart people resist, because they realize if we are wrong about the changes proposed, we won't be operating effectively right now or in the future.

The lesson is to be smart enough to understand and acknowledge that these dynamics exist, and to plan your approach with the dynamics in mind. I have found three attributes that can help a leader effect change in both favorable and unfavorable environments.

I call them the "Be Ps": Be Persuasive, Be Persistent, and Be Patient.

Change agents, by nature, recognize that the sooner we change, the better off we'll be, so it's hard to be patient. The older I get and the longer I've been in this business, I have learned that the "Be Patient" lesson is essential.

Sometimes, if you're pushing against that wall or you're banging your head into a wall, and it feels like you're not making any impression at all (that is, no change is occurring), then go look on the other side of the wall — you will clearly see small cracks in that seemingly immovable object. The lesson learned is it may not be obvious that things are changing, but they are.

Donna: I call it "slowing down to the speed of conscious thought."

Rob: Yes, patience and delaying the pace of change can be fine as long as it does not end up killing your customers. If the need is so great and there's a true imperative, you've got to work your way around that wall or even right through it with a brute force approach.

Another lesson learned is to get out of your comfort zone and to understand the issues from all the different angles and all the different players' perspectives. Don't let yourself spend all your time in one stovepipe, one agency, one organization, or one discipline. You've got to understand it from different levels.

I think that one of the most important changes in the intelligence community is the new requirement for our employees to move between different agencies, or they will not be permitted to become senior executives. This dictum will, over time, change the way the intelligence community views itself. It will lead to a culture that more readily adopts change. My own boss, Vice Admiral Robert Murrett,

Director of the National Geospatial-Intelligence Agency [NGA], deserves a lot of credit. He has put almost 25% of his agency's employees out in his customers' workspaces.

Getting outside your comfort zone is especially important for a change agent. If you've just grown up in your own little stovepipe, and you're trying to convince people to do something radically different, they say, correctly, "How would you know? You've never been out there. You've never done that."

Donna: Yes. And you know what? If you do it, people admire you, are watching you, and are being influenced by observing how you're doing your work and where you're going within your work. Then it's easier for you to mentor and inspire the next generation as they evolve.

Rob: Every month I am the last speaker in the end of our week-long New Employee Orientation Course. I have a two-hour block of time to speak passionately to our newest employees about all of the changes underway and the importance of feeling it in your gut. We want them to share a sense of urgency. The new employees look at me and think, "Here's a guy who's actually done the change agent things and he's relatively successful. Maybe I can take a risk, step out, and try to do some of that, too."

Donna: Bingo.

Rob: You asked, "Is there a difference between being the best in the world or being the best for the world?"

Donna: Some people actually can bring both together.

Rob: I think humility, being humble, has got to go hand-in-hand with the things we're talking about here. If you start feeling like you know better than anybody else, you've already lost it. You can never know what everybody else knows. I'm not the best in the world at what I do, and I don't think I'm best for the world at what I do. What am I? I am compelled to do my best.

I'm just like everybody else. I get tired. I get cranky. I feel sick sometimes, and sometimes my biorhythms are just off. But, by the time I get in the car and drive into work, I'm telling myself, "I'm going to do my very best. I'm going to do the best I possibly can today to try to make things better."

Better for whom? Better for the people I'm working with. Better for the people I'm trying to support. Better for the country. Better for my kids or better for the nation. I'm just trying to make things better every day. God knows, I'm not perfect at any of this stuff. You just have to accept that but keep trying to do the best you can.

Donna: That's it. I ask that question because I want to see where people consider themselves in relation to that question. Everything we do has implications and ramifications upon ramifications, right? We do our best in the realm of what we know and what we can figure out. We don't necessarily know what will be. It's all a matter of taking a more global perspective outside our own stories. I think if we do that, what we're doing is being stewards. That's where I'm going with this.

Rob: You've got to own the challenge. You've got to own the problem, and you've got to own what you yourself can contribute to try to make things better. That is what you can be best at.

Donna: How are you impacting other people? Are you trying to help grow other people?

Rob: I do feel that I'm doing those things. I think I can do more. I'm always trying to do more coaching and mentoring of the next generation. Sometimes, I'll do so much that my friends, my peers, and my family will say, "Come on, why are you doing that? You don't need to do that."

For example, I talk to college students at local community colleges to try to get them a helping hand getting into the intelligence, Homeland Security, and federal law enforcement communities. I try to inspire these young kids to join us in my profession. At the end of it, I say, "Here's my personal email, my cell phone number, my work number, and my email at work. Let me try to help you with getting your foot in the door in different agencies. They send me their resumes, and I edit and tweak them to give them a better shot. I connect the most promising ones with associates in the agencies so they can network.

I'm always trying to do that. At any given time I am working with 15 to 20 different people who are looking for a start in the field. I'm also regularly involved in assisting people move from one agency to another to help them grow in their career.

I spend 25-30% of my time at this point in my career focused on mentoring, growing, and shepherding people. Part of that is recruiting people to come into my line of work.

I'm a "futures" guy. My job is about change and where we're going. It's about people changes, process changes, and technology changes. I ran Research and Development at NGA, but I also know that technology is not the only thing. It's also about having people with the right skills, the right attitude, and the right sense of urgency.

The lasting impact that a senior leader can have is to help recruit and develop the next generation of people who "get it," who understand that this can't be the way we've done things for the last 50 years. It's got to be very different as we move forward into the future.

Donna: What's next for you? What haven't you played at yet?

Rob: I'm talking now to the leadership of the intelligence community to see how I can continue to contribute. I expect to work on transformation, meaning helping to connect the dots inside the Intelligence community, the military community, the Homeland Security community, and law enforcement community. I expect I will continue to be in a position to help integrate and share information up, down, back and forth, and sideways.

What can I do now in my remaining years as a government employee to inspire new people, new employees, and to help them stay focused on what really matters? What can I do to make things better so that we can hopefully preclude another attack on the United States, but if, God forbid, another one happens, to recover from it as quickly as we possibly can? That's what I'm thinking about over these next few years.

Donna: What haven't we covered that you'd like to add? What words of wisdom would you want to share?

Rob: I talk to many new young talented people every month in the New Employee Orientation Course. I tell them, "Know that you can challenge the conventional wisdom and survive to make a difference." I also tell them, "If you can imagine the future, you can achieve it." Be willing to imagine it, be willing to have people giggle a little bit about it or think that's a little bit zany. Be willing to accept criticism for your attempt to change things.

We all have a very human need for a pat on the back, for approval, to be nurtured, for positive feedback. I tell people, "Be willing to set that aside in exchange for knowing that you can make a real difference in the long-term and make things better for everybody." Taking the path of least resistance will get you titles, promotions, and bonuses. But sometimes, taking the harder path is the right thing to do. You will find no matter how hard it is, there are other like-minded people out there. Sometimes, they may not be as visible as you've chosen to make yourself, but they are there. You'll come to know them if you have decided to be an agent of change.

Periodically, you all need to get together. You need to talk to each other, kind of buck each other up, and say, "What you're talking about isn't crazy. It is real, it's important, and it's powerful. I agree with what you're trying to do, and I feel the same way as you."

Finally, it's all about your client, your customer, or your user. The words of wisdom I would give anybody in any field are these: "Make the time to go into the environment." Whether it's on the loading dock or out in Afghanistan where people are firing rockets at you, get into the footprint of your client, customer, or user. Understand what it is they're trying to do and what they're up against.

This is particularly true the further up you go in ranks to as a leader. A leader's time is often controlled by the calendar. All too often, leaders end up bouncing from meeting to meeting to meeting. You don't even have time for any introspection or reflection on what it all means and what you're trying to do.

What I have found is you've got to force the time to get out there. In the Army, they would say, "Smell the cordite." It's amazing how it changes your perspective on how important something is or isn't when you're out there seeing how people are trying to do something, when their lives are on the line.

It doesn't have to be a combat situation. It could be a ride-along with a police officer. It could be going with a first responder. It could be going with a firefighter, watching them running up the stairs when everybody else is running down and out. To me, that energizes me. It reinvigorates me. It focuses me and it reminds me what this is all about.

Donna: This is wonderful. Is there anything else you'd like to share?

Rob: Executive coaches have helped me apply my strengths in ways I had not considered and against areas I had not previously succeeded. I applaud your profession and sincerely thank you for all that you do.

Reflections

Late September, en route to a meeting in Boston, I showed up early to the airport. I anticipated lines at security, and wanted some quiet time to write as I waited for the plane. As a Nexus card holder, pre-clearing customs is usually done very quickly, as I hand in my card to the customs agent and make my way to the gate. Well, that day was my lucky day. The agent turned to me and said, "You've won the lottery!" I looked at him, puzzled, so he continued, "Every so often, we do a check for Nexus holders. It's random, and today you've been the one chosen. It's like a lottery." So off I went into the back area, waiting to be interviewed. I watched people come and go, most of whom didn't have the appropriate paperwork to enter the U.S. I was fascinated by the people and agents in this area, a place I'd never been in before.

When it was my turn, I entered a small office. The agent explained to me why they do this random search (which I commend and heartily agree with) and asked me why I was going to the U.S., what kind of work I did, and so on. When I told him I was an Executive and Political Leadership Coach, he asked for clarification. I thought this was the perfect opportunity to share what I did in a way that had meaning for him.

I told him I work with people in complex environments and help my clients think differently more than "do differently." I then asked him, "Since 9/11, hasn't your work changed? Hasn't your perspective and thinking changed? Your pressures and concerns?" He looked up at me and said, "How much time do we have before your plane takes off?" We talked as long as we could before I had to leave.

When we go through Customs, all we want is to get through as quickly as possible and be on our merry way. We don't want lines; we don't want to be interrogated. We want to just go. From his perspective, every time he stamps a passport and lets someone into his country, something in the back of his mind lingers as to whether or not he let a good guy in or a terrorist. His remark, "Everything has changed since 9/11" stuck with me. We might want ease, but I know I'm grateful to this man for watching my back and my well-being.

How am I watching my clients' backs? Like Ruth Ann said earlier, how can I "hold confidence" for my clients so they know I believe in them? Holding confidence comes from a belief in who they are, their potential, and what has been revealed to me as I Shadow Coach them. What emerges through our work illustrates what they're capable of. It's not blind faith. I wouldn't be serving my clients if I told them, "You can do it. I have confidence that you can, even if you don't yet see it in yourself," with nothing to back it up. I need to share applicable, specific situations when I observed them that illustrate where they shone. In doing this, it goes beyond telling them "I believe in you" to showing them what it's based on. How do I maintain that charge-neutral stance between honesty and non-judgment, truth and perception, fact and assumption? One of my clients said, "You only see the good in people," to which I replied, "I don't only see good. I see all sides of my clients and accept them for all of who they are." We can celebrate weaknesses while we strengthen talents. Because of that acceptance, I can hold the space and confidence for my clients to confront their shadows and still shine. I can do that for myself as well.

Thinking of Rob, this feeling must be multiplied exponentially. Everything he does is about watching someone's back, connecting the right people in the crucial conversations to keep people safe. It takes a huge amount of humility and confidence to park one's ego, have faith in the processes that are in place to protect the county and its people, and think of the people themselves. He leads from humanity, not fear.

This is what human-based leaders do. They watch your back, help you think bigger, see broader, and see who and what you can be. It's not about them; it's about everything and everyone. They're change agents, as they challenge status quo and help you see possibility beyond roadblocks, even in intensely complex environments.

> "Few men are willing to brave the disapproval of their fellows, the censure of their colleagues, the wrath of their society. Moral courage is a rarer commodity than bravery in battle or great intelligence. Yet it is the one essential, vital quality for those who seek to change a world which yields most painfully to change." – Robert F. Kennedy

Rob knows that as a change agent, he does have to brave the possible disapproval of his peers and is willing to do this for the sake of the greater good.

To Sum It Up

The human-based leader thinks first of the greater good, from multiple perspectives of the people around them, with empathy and compassion, but still with the focus on leading others toward shared goals. These leaders can be more directive or participative, more team-oriented or working primarily through a network of individual relationships. It is not the leadership style that defines human-based leadership. And human-based leadership is not to the exclusion of being results-driven. It is just that whether the priority is on achieving results or building relationships or the means to achieve goals, the human-based leader lives and works with the value, dignity, and potential of people as their primary focus.
– Lewis R. Stern, PhD

Under the surface, where the key dynamics of a personality lie, is the person who builds pieces of our world as we know it; one who dreams and translates that dream into a vision we can all wrap our heads around. These leaders are risk takers, because going after their dreams is their only possibility. Their energy and passion feed a bottomless spring that never dries up. With each person who comes on board and wants to "live their dream, too," that passion continues to feed the human spirit.

We are socialized by narratives and live a story. Every day, a new page is written as life unfolds through design and circumstance. Some stories are as old and familiar as time itself, becoming an integral part of our lives. From early camp days when we'd sit by a roaring bonfire, share stories, personal anecdotes, horror stories, or stories we created in broken telephone games, they all played a vital role in our lives.

Stories and narratives have a way of reaching beyond models and concepts to what's real. Everyone can relate to a story. Not everyone has as easy a time understanding conceptual material. Through our stories, shared memories, and others' experiences with us, people can "see" us. They're three-dimensional snapshots of who we are and who we say we've become.

In sharing these stories with you, I hope you've gotten more than just a glimpse of the superficial — a title, award, role, or responsibility — and are able to see these extraordinary people who make a difference by virtue of who they are, as much as what they are doing or have done.

Is there a connection between these leaders? I believe so. The common thread that weaves from one story to another is about valuing people, *human-based* leadership, and a desire to make this world a little bit better and the people within it stronger, happier, more successful, and fulfilled.

I meet amazing people. Each one knows something I don't know about life. I approach them through their humanity, not their title. I honour those who give of themselves, despite how busy they are and regardless of their status.

As coaches, we bear witness to our clients' lives. In the scheme of things, with all the people we come across in our lives, what does any one life mean? When I Shadow Coach, I promise to bear witness to everything: the great things, the challenges, the mundane everyday routine, the successes and failures, their lives as a whole. They know I hold confidence for them. I'm noticing, I'm acknowledging. I'm focusing on them, seeing all of who they are. I'm taking a stand for them and partnering with them to support and design what success looks like so I can help them get there. This is one of the few times in anyone's life where they have a non-judgmental supporter whose total focus is on them. I am their witness, their advocate. Then they move forward, design, and realise a life they love.

David Zach, an insightful futurist I have the pleasure of knowing, said, "Progress is the ability to choose between change and tradition. In this frenetic age, people have to pause and think more deeply and differently about that which they've been thinking. They need to think about and revisit what has been sitting on their back burners. What are the implications of the implications of the implications? You can't know, but at least you can explore the possibilities. You can consider there's more than one pathway into the future."

There are so many possibilities available to us right now. The world is fast becoming an even playing field when it comes to gathering knowledge. Just as Laurier spoke about wanting to teach that which isn't factual, sharing wisdom is priceless. How it's shared is ageless. Leaders who impart their wisdom give guidance rather than direction. They see and distinguish context, relevance, and impact. They see where we might fly or fail. They help us see what they see, so we can make choices that work for us.

Leaders have a responsibility to create an environment in which everyone has the possibility to work to the utmost of their capability, discover their potential to do more, and shine in the process. Great human-based leaders marry a passion for what they do with compassion for those with whom they do it. When we're lucky enough to be touched by them, our passion and our spirit are sparked by the encounter.

In this fast-paced world, we have to "dance in real time." However, we also have to remember to slow dance once in a while and reflect on life, the choices we make, and how they impact the world — one person at a time.

How we dream is what gives our lives value.
How we choose to live is what determines
whether our dreams have value.
I believe we each carry a dream of a life
we were born to realise that shows up through desire.
And I believe that we all have the ability to realise
our personal and professional dreams
if we commit ourselves to not settling for
anything less than what we really want.
It is when we move toward our passions
that we experience our own greatness,
and it is then that an incredible contribution to ourselves
and the world is made by being who we truly are.

DONNA KARLIN

About the Author

Donna Karlin is internationally recognized as a pioneer in the field of leadership coaching and is known for her specialized practice of Shadow Coaching®. Through her company, A Better Perspective®, Donna has worked with a diverse range of clients from global political, government, corporate and business leaders to medical professionals and creative designers. Donna has spent close to 30 years helping leaders figure out how to bridge the gap between where they are and where they want to be.

Early in her coaching career, Donna realized she was coaching clients' perceptions, not necessarily their reality. The seed of the Shadow Coaching® methodology was planted in the waiting room of a surgeon where her clients revealed their fears, their realities, and their truths. Now, almost three decades later, you will see Donna coach on the run with her clients through the halls of corporate headquarters, government departments, and agencies and political offices. She coaches extraordinary people to become even better than they ever thought possible.

In response to widely expressed interest to her highly successful and innovative approach to coaching, she established the School of Shadow Coaching®, a coach training program recognized and accredited by the International Coach Federation. It was designed to meet the current needs being expressed by the community of graduate coaches in support of integration and evolution of their graduate learning.

Donna is a member of the Advisory Council of The International Academy of Behavioral Medicine, Counseling and Psychology (IABMCP), Past President and current Dean of the International Consortium for Coaching in Organizations, Communications Advisor and coach for Brussels, Belgium-based firm INSPIRIT International Communications, and a SupporTED Coach, a member of the team that coaches the TED Fellows.

Her work has been written up in *Fast Company* Magazine, *The National Post* (Financial Post), *The Globe and Mail*, The *New York Times* Business Section, *The Boston Globe*, and *Personal Success Magazine*. She is an avid blogger; her blog Perspectives™ is subscribed to by readers from 144 countries and territories. She also is a leadership expert for *Fast Company*, a Platinum Author for Evan Carmichael, Motivation and Strategies for Entrepreneurs, and a contributor to *IJCO The International Journal of Coaching in Organizations*™.

Donna has been certified by the IABMCP as a Diplomate in Professional Coaching, and was certified in Organizational Psychology with a focus in Executive Coaching by the Professional School of Psychology.

She is based in Ottawa, Canada, and coaches, lectures, and presents keynotes in many parts of the world.

References
and Resources

Chapter 1 – John Spence
- Quote from "Breakthrough Ideas for Tomorrow's Business Agenda," *Harvard Business Review*, 2003 (April)
- Quote from Alfred Taubman, American real estate developer and philanthropist from Bloomfield Hills, Michigan (personal communication)
- Making the complex … awesomely simple – John Spence: www.johnspence.com
- CliffsNotes was created by Cliff Hillegass in 1958: www.cliffsnotes.com
- *Fast Company*: www.fastcompany.com

Chapter 2 – Ron Kitchens
- Quote given by Denis Kingsley, Assistant Deputy Minister, Department of Foreign Affairs and International Trade, Government of Canada (personal communication)
- *Fast Company* online: www.fastcompany.com
- Stephen R. Covey quote from LeadingThoughts: www.leadershipnow.com/leadershipquotes.html
- Southwest Michigan First: The Kalamazoo Region's Economic Catalyst: www.southwestmichiganfirst.com
- *Good To Great: Why Some Companies Make The Leap … and Others Don't* by Jim Collins. New York: Harper Business (2001)

Chapter 3 – Joe Saltzman
- Norman Lear quote from Great-Quotes.com: www.great-quotes.com
- The Jester & Pharley Phund: www.thejester.org
- USC Annenberg School for Communication & Journalism – The Image of the Journalist in Popular Culture Project: www.ijpc.org

Chapter 4 – Laurier LaPierre

- Frank Smith quote from LeadingThoughts:
- www.leadershipnow.com/leadershipquotes.html
- Quote from Denise Amyot, President and CEO, Canada Science and Technology Museum Corporation (personal communication)
- Wangari Maathai quote from LeadingThoughts: www.leadershipnow.com/leadershipquotes.html
- Facts about Nunavut, the largest and newest federal territory of Canada:
- www.gov.nu.ca/en/
- *This Hour Has Seven Days*: www.museum.tv/eotvsection.php?entrycode=thishourhas
- The Order of Canada: http://en.wikipedia.org/wiki/Order_of_Canada

Chapter 5 – Ruth Ann Harnisch

- Marianne Williamson quote from Brainy Quote: www.brainyquote.com
- "Cat's in the Cradle" is a 1974 folk rock song by Harry Chapin, Elektra Records
- Cecil Beaton quote from LeadingThoughts: www.leadershipnow.com/leadershipquotes.html
- The Harnisch Foundation: www.thehf.org
- *The Dip: A Little Book That Teaches You When to Quit (and When to Stick)* by Seth Godin. New York: Portfolio (2007)
- Thomas Leonard, known as 'The Grandfather of coaching': www.thomasleonard.com/bio.html

Chapter 6 – Ron Worton

- Quote from Ed Maier, Leadership Coach and Business Advisor, Frisco, Texas (personal communication)
- Andrew Carnegie quote from LeadingThoughts: www.leadershipnow.com/leadershipquotes.html
- Muscular Dystrophy: http://en.wikipedia.org/wiki/Duchenne_muscular_dystrophy
- Cystic Fibrosis: http://en.wikipedia.org/wiki/Cystic_fibrosis
- Fanconi Anemia: http://en.wikipedia.org/wiki/Fanconi_anemia
- Wilson's Disease: http://en.wikipedia.org/wiki/Wilson's_disease

Chapter 7 – J.D. McFarlan

- Quote from Elliott Powell, Assistant Director, National Business Center, U.S. Department of the Interior, Washington, D.C. (personal communication)
- Lt. Col. Sharon M. Latour, USAF, and Lt. Gen. Bradley C. Hosmer, USAF (Retired), quotes from "Emotional Intelligence – Implications for All United States Air Force Leaders." *Air & Space Power Journal*, 2002 (Winter)
- Lockheed Martin Aeronautics Company: www.lockheedmartin.com/aeronautics/
- F-35 Joint Strike Fighter: www.lockheedmartin.com/products/f35/
- INSEAD Global Leadership Centre: www.insead.edu/facultyresearch/centres/iglc/index.cfm

Chapter 8 – Rick Koca

- Martin Luther King, Jr., quote from goodreads: www.goodreads.com
- Albert Pike quote from LeadingThoughts: www.leadershipnow.com/leadershipquotes.html
- Quote from Ernest Loevinsohn, Director General, Global Initiatives, Canadian International Development Agency (personal communication)
- StandUp For Kids: www.standupforkids.org
- "My Generation: Homeless Not Helpless," Rick Koca video on AARP: www.aarp.org/personal-growth/life-stories/info-06-2010/homeless-not-helpless.html

Chapter 9 – Tom Stern

- Eleanor Roosevelt quote from *You Learn By Living*. Philadelphia, PA: The Westminster Press (1960)
- Joseph F. Newton quote from LeadingThoughts:
- www.leadershipnow.com/leadershipquotes.html
- Tom Stern Central: www.tomsterncentral.com
- *Huffington Post*: www.huffingtonpost.com/thomas-stern

Chapter 10 – Barry Libert

- Brian Solis quotes from @BrianSolis: www.briansolis.com
- Seth Godin quote from *Small Is the New Big: and 193 Other Riffs, Rants, and Remarkable Business Ideas*. New York: Penguin Group (2006)
- Barry Libert: www.bdlibert.com
- Innocentive: www2.innocentive.com
- Mzinga: www.mzinga.com
- Canada@150: www.policyresearch.gc.ca/doclib/can150_rp-eng.pdf

Chapter 11 – Frank McKenna

- John Kenneth Galbraith quote from LeadingThoughts: www.leadershipnow.com/leadershipquotes.html
- Admiral James B. Stockdale quote from LeadingThoughts: www.leadershipnow.com/leadershipquotes.html

Chapter 12 – Robert Zitz

- John Kotter quote from Brainy Quote: www.brainyquote.com
- Robert F. Kennedy quote from 1966 Speech: www.quotationspage.com

To Sum It Up

- Quote from Lewis R. Stern, PhD, executive and leadership coach, and consulting psychologist, Lexington, Massachusetts (personal communication)
- Quote from David Zach, futurist, lecturer and speaker, Milwaukee, Wisconsin (personal communication)

Index